The Collective Unconscious in the Age of Neuroscience

The Collective Unconscious in the Age of Neuroscience brings the connection between C. G. Jung's theory of a collective unconscious, neuroscience, and personal experiences of severe mental illness to life. Hallie B. Durchslag uses narrative analysis to examine four autobiographical accounts of mental illness, including her own, and illuminate the interplay between psychic material and human physiology that Jung intuited to exist.

Durchslag's unique study considers the links between expressions of the collective unconscious, such as myth, fairy tales, folk tales, and 'big dreams', and the experiences of those diagnosed with severe mental illnesses, such as schizophrenia and bipolar I disorder. The author's personal narrative account of a psychotic episode is at its heart, bringing both an intimate foundation and exceptional insight to the book. With reference to neuroscientific and genetic research throughout, *The Collective Unconscious in the Age of Neuroscience* highlights gaps in depth psychological notions of etiology and treatment, highlights patterns of collective material in the qualitative experience of these genetic and biological disorders, and explores how the efficacy of pharmacological treatment sheds light on Jung's theoretical model.

The Collective Unconscious in the Age of Neuroscience will be essential reading for academics and students of Jungian and post-Jungian studies, consciousness, neuroscience and mental health. It will also provide unique insight for analytical psychologists interested in severe mental illness and the collective unconscious.

Hallie Beth Durchslag, Ph.D., is a Jungian-oriented psychodynamic psychotherapist who has presented both in the United States and abroad on severe mental illnesses and their connection to Jung's theory of a transpersonal collective unconscious. She is based in Ohio, USA, where she teaches, writes, and maintains a private practice.

The Collective Unconscious in the Age of Neuroscience

Severe Mental Illness and Jung in the 21st Century

Hallie B. Durchslag

LONDON AND NEW YORK

First published 2021
by Routledge
2 Park Square, Milton Park, Abingdon, Oxon OX14 4RN

and by Routledge
52 Vanderbilt Avenue, New York, NY 10017

Routledge is an imprint of the Taylor & Francis Group, an informa business

© 2021 Hallie B. Durchslag

The right of Hallie B. Durchslag to be identified as author of this work has been asserted by her in accordance with sections 77 and 78 of the Copyright, Designs and Patents Act 1988.

All rights reserved. No part of this book may be reprinted or reproduced or utilised in any form or by any electronic, mechanical, or other means, now known or hereafter invented, including photocopying and recording, or in any information storage or retrieval system, without permission in writing from the publishers.

Trademark notice: Product or corporate names may be trademarks or registered trademarks, and are used only for identification and explanation without intent to infringe.

British Library Cataloguing-in-Publication Data
A catalogue record for this book is available from the British Library

Library of Congress Cataloging-in-Publication Data
A catalog record has been requested for this book

ISBN: 978-1-138-05734-0 (hbk)
ISBN: 978-1-138-05736-4 (pbk)
ISBN: 978-1-315-16490-8 (ebk)

Typeset in Times New Roman
by Taylor & Francis Books

Contents

	List of illustrations	vi
	preface	viii
1	Introduction	1
2	Methodology	13
3	The importance of diagnostic distinctions	24
4	Thematic alignment in psychosis	48
5	The personal narrative of psychosis	62
6	The brain and pharmaceutical actions	76
7	Radiating outward and the collective unconscious	97
8	From the transpersonal to the suprapersonal: Individuation and the unavoidable dilemma	121
9	Reeling in the net and readying it to be recast: Conclusions and future research	137
	Index	150

Illustrations

Figure

9.1 Chemical compound of Lamictal — 138

Tables

3.1 Psychotic delusions by type (APA, 2013) — 41
4.1 Perry's (2005) delusional categories and definitions — 54
4.2 Political or religious constellations of hero archetype in delusions of 12 psychotic patients — 55
5.1 Coding of delusional content in personal narrative — 64
5.2 Replication of Perry's (2005) delusional categories in autobiographical selections — 65
6.1 Medications at time of discharge — 86
8.1 Behavioral manifestation of manic symptoms (APA, 2013) — 129

"I do not know for what reason the universe has come into being, and shall never know. Therefore I must drop this question as a scientific or intellectual problem. But if an idea about it is offered to me—in dreams or in mythic traditions—I ought to take note of it. I even ought to build up a conception on the basis of such hints, even though it will forever remain a hypothesis which I know cannot be proved."

C. G. Jung (1989), *Memories, Dreams, Reflections*

Preface

In introducing a proposed English translation of the Eranos Conferences, Jung (1939/2015) wrote:

> No work of serious research can be done in our days without equally serious specialization. The enormous extension of knowledge exceeds the capacity of a single brain, which alone might [not] be able to form a synthesis of the innumerable parts contributed by every department. Even the greatest genius, equipped with a fabulous power of memory, would be forced to remain an incompetent dilettante in quite a few important respects .... But as it is well-nigh impossible to establish a careful comparison of all the detail and knowledge, one should seek a platform of an idea which is common to several forms of knowledge. It would then be possible to gather the various contributions round a central problem. (p. 83)

I openly own that I am merely a dilettante in many respects. However, I offer what I believe to be a solid piece of work that offers renewed access to Jung's bedrock *a priori* construct of a collective unconscious. As was true for Jung, this illusive proposition has lines to complex scientific fields and philosophical traditions, not to mention a debate of time immemorial about the human relationship to the world—be it spirit, matter, or the uniquely created human mind. I am stuck with this dilemma and with my own intellectual constraints, but believe in the contribution to the field. I ask the reader for consideration.

References

Jung, G. G. (1989). *Memories, dreams, reflections*. (R. Winston & C. Winston, Trans.). New York, NY: Vintage Books..

Jung, C. G. (1939/2015). American Eranos volume: Introduction. *Spring: A Journal of Archetype and Culture, 92*. (Spring), 83–85.

Chapter 1

Introduction

Opening the door

I had a dream shortly before deciding to write this book. In the dream, I have fallen asleep in a lounge chair on a thin sliver of beach, which the dreamscape has placed in my current suburban neighborhood in front of my home. I wake up from the nap groggy and disoriented. I see I have dropped a magazine off of my lap while dozing. I reach down to pick up the magazine, still groggy, and see that it is my own face on the cover. I am surprised. As I get more oriented, I look out at my surroundings. My eye is immediately drawn to a huge, three-story banner on the brick wall of the school across the street from my home. Four heavy black letters are printed on the white banner: DSMV.

Many people familiar with the mental health industry will recognize these letters as the abbreviation for the *Diagnostic and Statistical Manual of Mental Disorders*. The V relates to the fifth edition of the work, which came out in 2013. I found this dream to be a fitting commentary on what is at stake for me in sharing this book: much of the argument I will pose in the pages to follow is based on my own experience with what is classified as a severe mental illness. My personal story is consistently present in the chapters to follow. The dream seems to represent the simple truth that my "face is on the cover" and that it will be boldly "advertised" in a huge banner across the academic world (as represented by the location of the banner, which is a school). Starting with this dream does two things early. First, it rips off the Band-Aid of disclosure that I suffer from a severe mental illness; and second, it brings the reader into what will often be an intimate, first-person approach to providing what is at the same time data from a rigorous and free-standing piece of research. The lens moves from the personal—experiences of my own and the accounts of others—and out into the world of theory and postulation at a broad and impersonal level. The goal of this book is to highlight a human physiological thread to Jung's construct of a collective unconscious through an exploration of severe mental illness and advances in its treatment. There are several implications for this venture, the most primary of which is to reaffirm Carl Jung's organizing principle of a collective unconscious and to open new doors of exploration into Jung's later work on a unifying principle between psychic material and the material world.

Defining severe mental illness

The term *severe mental illness* (SMI) can be difficult to define, but definitions always include psychosis as a primary criterion (Ruggeri, Leese, Thornicroft, Bisoffi, & Tansella, 2000). Additional defining markers include duration of illness and levels of impairment (National Institute of Mental Health, 1987; Parabiaghi, Bonetto, Ruggeri, Lasalvia, & Leese, 2006). Psychosis is a primary means of differentiating these illnesses from other mental disorders. (Ruggeri et al., 2000). Stahl (2013) defined psychosis as follows:

> Psychosis is a syndrome—that is, a mixture of symptoms—that can be associated with many different psychiatric disorders, but is not a specific disorder itself in diagnostic schemes such as the DSM or ICD. At a minimum, psychosis means delusions and hallucinations .... Therefore, psychosis can be considered to be a set of symptoms in which a person's mental capacity, affective response, and capacity to recognize reality, communicate, and relate to others is impaired. (p. 79)

The psychotic syndrome is always a part of certain illnesses, including schizophrenia and illnesses in the schizophrenia spectrum; substance-induced psychosis; delusional disorder; and brief psychotic disorder (APA, 2013; Stahl 2013). Psychosis is often present, though not always, in certain medical and cognitive disorders (e.g., Alzheimer's, Huntington's, head trauma, epilepsy), within manic episodes of bipolar I disorder, and in some severe depressions (APA, 2013; Stahl, 2013).

Schizophrenia and manic depression have been recognized by the medical community as chronic and severe illnesses since the late nineteenth century (APA, 2000; Farquhar et al., 2007; Goodwin & Jamison, 2007; Marneros & Angst, 2000a). The dyadic relationship of mania to melancholia, and the cyclical pattern of the illness, were marked for the first time in the mid-nineteenth century by French psychiatrists working at Hospital La Salpêtrière in Paris. The most influential landmark in the historical legacy of these illnesses came in 1899, when Emil Kraeplin codified the distinction into two categories: *manic depressive insanity* and *dementia praecox* (Farquhar et al., 2007; Goodwin & Jamison, 2007; Marneros & Angst, 2000b). Obviously, the names have changed with time, but the legacy of this codification and separation between the two continue to influence medical practices today. The prevalence of schizophrenia is currently estimated to be 0.3 percent to 0.7 percent of the adult population; while what is now labeled bipolar I disorder is estimated to affect 0.0 percent to 0.6 percent of the population (APA, 2013). There is evidence that this is a relatively consistent incidence rate across South America, North America, the South Pacific region, and Europe (Goodwin & Jamison, 2007). However, differentiation between these two severe mental illnesses is often difficult and sometimes arbitrary. Culture, socioeconomic status, and biological similarities between the two disorders all contribute to this difficulty. From a cultural lens, socioeconomic status and race often play a role in the clinician's inclination to diagnose one illness versus another (APA, 2013; McIntosh et al., 2009; Sanchez-Morla et al., 2008). From a scientific standpoint, current research suggests that bipolar I disorder has more genetic similarities to schizophrenia than to other illnesses defined in its current category as a mood disorder (Goodwin & Jamison, 2007; McIntosh et al., 2009; Sanchez-Morla et al., 2008). Furthermore, certain types of psychoactive drugs, namely atypical antipsychotics, are effective in treating both illnesses. Overall, genetic and neuroscientific research is leading to questions about whether the initial splitting of these psychotic disorders, beginning with Kraeplin and the *dichotomous disease model*, may be too rigid (O'Donovan, Craddock, & Owen, 2009; Stahl, 2013).

I am a part of the estimated 0.6 percent of the population with bipolar I disorder. Currently, the World Health Organization has ranked bipolar I disorder as one of the top ten disabling disorders across the globe (Goodwin & Jamison, 2007; Thase, 2005). This is a lethal disease with severe familial and societal costs (Steinkuller & Rheineck, 2009). In general, lower wages, higher unemployment, work absenteeism and disability, reliance on worker's compensation, general difficulty with interpersonal relationships, and higher rates of divorce are just some of the additional burdens in the lives of people experiencing the effects of the disease (APA, 2013; Leahy, 2007; Steinkuller & Rheineck, 2009). Seifuddin et al. (2013) cited estimates that bipolar disorder "costs the United States $78.6 billion dollars annually in direct and indirect costs" (p. 1). Of those who suffer from this form of the disease, 15 percent die of suicide, a rate 60 times higher than the rate of suicide in the general population (APA, 2000; Leahy, 2007).

Jung and severe mental illness

The collective unconscious

The roots of analytical psychology are inextricably bound to the unique character of severe mental illness. Jung's work with schizophrenic patients led him to conclude that Freud's theory of an unconscious was too limited. Jung's definitive shift away from Freudian psychoanalysis reflected his conviction in the presence of an additional layer of unconscious material that transcended personal history. Herein lies the initial glimpse of an *a priori collective unconscious*. Jung (1917/1966) did not deny the credence of Freud's theory: that of a personal unconscious containing memories and private fantasies repressed due to individual development, familial experience, and socialization. But patterns of psychotic material led Jung to posit that the personal unconscious actually "rests upon a deeper layer, which does not derive from personal experience and is not a personal acquisition but is inborn" (Jung, 1934/1968, p. 3 [*CW* 9, part I, para. 3]). Jung wrote:

> This part of the unconscious is not individual but universal; in contrast to the personal psyche, it has contents and modes of behavior that are more or less the same everywhere and in all individuals. It is, in other words, identical in all men and thus constitutes a common psychic substrate of a suprapersonal nature which is present in every one of us. (Jung, 1934/1968, pp. 3–4 [*CW* 9, part I, para. 3])

Insights from his schizophrenic patients led Jung, at various times, to describe the collective unconscious as "a second psychic system of a collective, universal, and impersonal nature which is identical in all individuals" (Jung, 1936/1968, p. 43 [*CW* 9i, para. 90]); and as "the matrix of all conscious psychic occurrences ... compris[ing] in itself the psychic life of our ancestors right back to the earliest beginnings" (Jung, 1929/1969, p. 112 [*CW* 8, para. 230]). These definitions highlight that the collective unconscious (a) was considered as an entity that existed without reference to individuals; (b) existed as a common thread throughout the evolution and history of races and cultures; and (c) influenced and organized individual conscious activity. Describing it from another angle, Jung (1931/1969) wrote:

> The collective unconscious—so far as we can say anything about it at all—appears to consist of mythological motifs or primordial images, for which reason the myths of all nations are its real exponents. In fact, the whole of mythology could be taken as a sort of projection of the collective unconscious. (p. 152 [*CW* 8, para. 325])

These conclusions were rooted in a 6-year period during which he studied mythology, comparative history, religion, and rituals from non-Western cultures. His work with severe mental illness was so instrumental, Jung stated the title of his definitive work, *Symbols of Transformation* (1911), was "misleading, for the book represents the analysis of prodromal schizophrenic condition" (Jung, 1953, p. vi).

Challenges to this construction rest broadly in two points. First, there is a challenge to the assumption that knowledge of mythic material was not a part of the individual's scope of conscious knowledge. The second challenge rests in inconsistencies in Jung's definition and model of how "myth-forming structural elements," the archetypes, come to be transmitted.

Archetypes

At its root, archetype is defined as the vehicle by which the unconscious becomes known. Jung was exploring the organizing patterns, themselves, as well as the mechanism by which these organizing patterns came to influence conscious behavior. Jung defined archetypes as the "formal factors responsible for the organization of unconscious psychic processes: they are 'patterns of behavior'" (Jung, 1952/1969, p. 436 [*CW* 8, para. 841]). Jung (1989) wrote:

> We know that something unknown, alien, does come our way, just as we know that we do not ourselves *make* a dream or an inspiration, but that it somehow arises on its own accord. What does happen to us in this manner can be said to emanate from mana, from a daimon, a god, or the unconscious. (Jung, 1989, p. 336)

Jung's construct of archetype begins with a desire to understand how this transcendent and alien spiritual material comes to be known. The emanating source—mana, or a daimon, even a god construct—either resides in, or is a synonym for—some type of collective unconscious.

Jaffé (1971) traced Jung's first use of the term *archetype* to 1919, when he shifted from the term *primordial image*. Unfortunately, over the next 40 years of his writing, there are inconsistencies that are difficult to reconcile. Jung's collected works do exhibit important changes in language, and the changes in language can dramatically alter the points he is trying to convey. Part of the lack of clarity rests in Jung's own omissions:

> Jung omitted to compare his early formulations with the later ones, and he did not always delimit the meaning of a concept he used from the meaning other writers had assigned to it. He was no systematiser, and it cannot escape the attentive reader of his work that the application of concepts and terminology is not always carried through consistently, that occasional contradictions and obscurities arise. (Jaffé, 1971, p. 27)

However, Jaffé (1971) argued that a certain amount of inconsistency is unavoidable when exploring the unconscious:

> Though the psyche can be captured in any number of concepts and images it can never be wholly grasped. When the collective unconscious is at work, the conceptual statements of the psychologist are valid as definite truths only within certain limits. Beyond those limits he often has to make do with approximations and paradoxes. (p. 28)

When looser circumambulations are accepted as the general necessity when making postulations about material that is by very definition unconscious,

Jung's shifting and sometimes contradictory language models the multifaceted exploration necessary. Jaffé (1971) wrote: "The laws and connections he discovered in this way are remarkably consistent throughout his work. The occasional lack of uniform terminology, of clear formulation or precision, is not indeed cancelled out by this, but it nevertheless loses its importance in principle" (p. 28).

The use of the term *law* above is again minimally problematic when tempered with the following: "The 'ultimate' conclusions of science are always the last but one. The science of tomorrow will modify them, complete them, reformulate them or arrive at new insights. Even the meaning of the concepts change" (p. 27). Jung (1947/1969) wrote:

> This question, regarding the nature of the unconscious, brings with it the extraordinary intellectual difficulties with which the psychology of the unconscious confronts us. Such difficulties must inevitably arise when the mind launches forth boldly into the unknown and invisible .... It is not a question of his *asserting* anything, but of constructing a *model* which opens up a promising and useful field of inquiry. A model does not assert that something *is* so, it simply illustrates a particular mode of observation. (p. 184 [*CW* 8, para. 381])

Therefore, multiple ways of describing the unconscious can be seen as an attempt at looking at the un-seeable from as many lenses and angles as possible, not for the benefit of the reader, necessarily, but because of Jung's own working and re-working of the material.

The challenge of inconsistencies

With this in mind, the structure of this book asks the learned reader to live with a broad, sweeping, and largely undifferentiated definition of archetype. Otherwise, the debate will collapse in on itself, and leave a global picture impossible. It is the penultimate difficulty with seeing the forest through the trees. There is a need to return to the roots of why initial constructs of a collective unconscious and archetype were necessary. Jung did not create the theoretical models first; the terminology arose to describe a type of a prior patterning of psychic material. There was a need to imagine a container for such material, and also a need to imagine a potential vehicle for its manifestation into a person's scope of experience.

Jung's use of terminology remains a source of constant consternation in the study of his legacy. The question is how something suprapersonal becomes intrapsychic. Can notions of a collective unconscious even be supported in the age of neurological advances in how the brain receives and processes information? Moods and emotional impressions are coming ever closer to being linked to brain function and brain function alone. There is less and less need of an exploration of psychic content from this perspective, especially the complex strings of transpersonal imagery and stories that seem to manifest across cultures, time, and location. Many consider such a notion implausible, and these constructs increasingly are criticized due to recent developments in neuroscience. Tresan (1996) stated the issue succinctly:

> A subject of ongoing debate is whether the clinical practice of depth psychology will or should continue to exist .... It is my belief that a body of clinical theory that is in frank variance with how the brain works will not survive as a mainstream modality. (p. 399)

This book offers evidence that neuroscientific advances can also be a springboard toward reaffirming them.

Research: background and methodology

Initial research questions

The goal of this particular work is to use the method of narrative analysis to add empirical support for collective material, as well as to offer evidence of physiological connection through the temporal connection between medical intervention and its manifestation. This research links chemical disruptions in the human body to the manifestation of archetypal patterns in the collective unconscious. The fulcrum of this line of exploration rests in the chemical actions of the pharmaceutical, *lamotrigine*, one of three primary mood stabilizers used to treat bipolar I disorder. It is a snapshot in time—primarily between July and September 2006—which captures a temporal relationship: between the presence or absence of this mood stabilizer and collective material.

The driving force for my choice of research topic was to build a relationship between neurochemical activity on one hand, and psychic material affirming Jung's notion of a collective unconscious on the other. My own experience with bipolar I disorder—the relationship between my medical treatment and my fall into and rise out of this collective realm—offered marks and remnants of evidence that left me unable to ignore this crossroad. At the time, I was especially interested in two things: First, in bringing the medical community into the fold of analytical psychology, so it could see the value of deeper exploration into Jung's work as imperative to understanding the experience of psychotic patients with schizophrenia or bipolar I disorder; and second, to add the exploration of severe mental illnesses from a medical lens into the dialogue for depth psychologists, a lens which is glaringly missing from discussion. However, my attempt to build this bridge between medical and Jungian paradigms was more complex than initially expected.

At first, it seemed to me a clear split between two sides based in large part due to the differing types of acceptable research. In general, quantitative experiments are considered the gold standard for medical research. In contrast, depth psychology has its roots in qualitative research methods such as case history and naturalistic observation. So my goal was to lay the quantitative data on severe mental illness side-by-side with qualitative data on the expression of archetypal material in psychotic episodes, thereby enriching both fields. Additional complexity arose when it became clear that the validity of qualitative data at the heart of Jung's theory of the collective unconscious was being questioned from within the field of analytical psychology itself. The debate rests in whether Jung's theory of a collective unconscious can remain plausible in light of quantitative research on the human brain and how it functions. This concern has created a shift in the developmental school of analytical psychology toward a rejection of the collective unconscious and a move back toward Freud's model of a solely personal unconscious.[1] It is unfortunate that research on the unique biological manifestation of severe mental illnesses has been conspicuously absent in this debate. And so the primary aims of the research decidedly shifted toward a concern over a debate within my own field.

Narrative analysis

This book extrapolates on empirical, qualitative data gathered through the method of narrative analysis (Durchslag, 2015, 2016). Narrative analysis is a multidisciplinary research approach widely utilized in the human sciences. It shares hermeneutic roots in Western philosophy, beginning with Aristotelian connections between action and narration. Later, it became central in issues of temporality, thematic ordering, meaning-making, and construction of self explored by existential and rational philosophers such as Weber, Heidegger, and Ricœur.

There are four narratives explored for the purpose of this research. One is my own, the construction of which is explored in more detail in Chapter 2. Exposure to Jungian psychology, beginning in 2004, led me to reexamine my position on medication management for the first time. I began to believe that medication was a means of skirting a commitment to real psychological growth, and that I was cheating my own development. In April 2006, I chose to discontinue my medication. That decision is the crossroad that led to my research over the past six years. The initial choice to discontinue medication became an unintended experiment conducted in my own life. The other three narratives are autobiographical works by Anton T. Boisen (1936), Morag Coate (1965), and John Custance (1951, 1954). Both Custance (a pen name) and Coate were natives of England; Boisen was American.

The need for first-hand narrative material is becoming increasingly recognized. In the natural sciences, new approaches to consciousness studies have increased the value placed on first-hand narrative (Varela & Shear, 1999); and the importance of the phenomenological bracketed [I] is increasingly recognized in the field of quantum physics due to the interactive nature of observer on the observed (Capra & Luisi, 2014).

Impressions and extrapolations

Several things become apparent on analysis of autobiographical narratives in the project. First, the bulk of the impressions regarding these symptomatic times are steeped in a connection to a suprapersonal force—a connection to numinous experiences of god and a remove from a time-bound frame of reference. Second, there is a split between how first-hand narratives describe the psychotic experiences on the one hand, and how depth psychologists have chosen to categorize them on the other. Are these connections due to intrapsychic reorganization and change, as depth psychology suggests, or are these insights into a larger, archetypal realm? This book suggests the latter.

Structure of the book

Chapter 2 focuses on the methodological choice of narrative analysis, as well as the decision to use my own autobiographical material. Chapter 3 addresses the importance of differentiating severe mental illness, like that of schizophrenia and bipolar I disorder, from other types of mental disorders. It highlights the gap between depth psychological notions of etiology and treatment of these specific illnesses, and highlights important medical advances that need to be considered. The next two chapters explicate and code the autobiographical narratives studied for the project.

Chapter 4 codes thematic material from the four autobiographical accounts—Boisen's (1936), Coate's (1965), Custance's (1951, 1954)—in order to highlight the manifestation of material that aligns with the utility of Jung's terminology. The narratives reinforce the existence of an *a priori* repository that matches Jung's notion of a collective unconscious. Chapter 5 looks more specifically at my own narrative. A fulcrum of the book is the temporal relationship between collective patterns in my psychosis and the rise and fall of my pharmaceutical treatment. Chapter 6 looks in increasing detail at the ways in which pharmacological treatments for severe mental illness function.

The final chapters of the book move into an analysis of the ramifications for Jung's later work, including moves into a notion of a psychoid archetype, the relationship between mind and matter, and the more modern permutations of the collective unconscious that followed. This has important implications for ideas of individuation, which assumes a connection to a transpersonal entity, although this is being left behind in many post-Jungian circles. Yet it is essential to the imagination regarding a collective unconscious. The debate over such constructs seems to have left much of Jung's later musings behind, most especially in his collaborative work with Marie-Louise Von Franz (Le Mouël, 2018; Von Franz, 1974, 1992).

Moving forward

My own experience with such things has been difficult for me to fathom, and even more difficult to put into form for this work. And, in the end, this is not a treatise on any one subject of Jung's sweeping constructs. This research does not pose any answers, only deeper questions that must be explored in due diligence to constructs so hotly debated. It would seem to me that Jung caught a glimpse of something that transcended his profession and his lifetime. He found empirical evidence enough to become rooted in its significance, and he moved forward as ploddingly and methodically as he could. In spite of all of the criticism, the most criticism might be that he tried to do so without his elemental personal experience laid bare. I apparently have fewer qualms to do so. In fact, it seems as though I might be on the side of current trend. The natural sciences seem enamored of first-hand, qualitative experience, as if it has not existed in a parallel universe all along. While the human sciences move ever closer to training themselves to follow the rigorous experimental designs of quantitative, variable-based research practices; so the natural sciences are longing for a subjective lens into the scientific mysteries yet to be solved.

Note

1 Initial research was conducted for my dissertation to meet requirements for a PhD in Clinical Psychology with an Emphasis in Depth Psychology at Pacifica Graduate Institute in Carpinteria, CA (2015). A subsequent article was published in *Psychological Perspectives, 59*(1) (Durchslag, 2016), which built on a paper presented at the 4th Joint conference of the International Association of Analytical Psychology and the International Association of Jungian Studies at Yale University, New Haven, CT (2015). Aspects of this research were most recently presented at the Center for Psychoanalytic Studies, University of Essex conference on Holism: Possibilities and Problems. Colchester, UK (2017).

References

American Psychiatric Association (APA). (2000). *Diagnostic and statistical manual of mental disorders* (4th ed., text revision). Arlington, VA: American Psychiatric Association.
American Psychiatric Association (APA). (2013). *Diagnostic and statistical manual of mental disorders* (5th ed.). Washington, DC: American Psychiatric Publishing.
Boisen, A. T. (1936). *The exploration of the inner world: A study of mental disorder and religious experience*. Philadelphia: University of Pennsylvania Press.
Capra, F., & Luisi, P. L. (2014). *The systems view of life: A unifying vision*. New York, NY: Cambridge University Press.
Coate, M. (1965). *Beyond all reason*. Philadelphia, PA: J. B. Lippincott.
Custance, J. (1951). *Wisdom, madness and folly: The philosophy of a lunatic*. London: Victor Gollancz.
Custance, J. (1954). *Adventure into the unconscious*. London: Christopher Johnson.

Durchslag, H. B. (2015). A narrative analysis of bipolar psychosis: An empirical relationship between neurochemistry and the collective unconscious. (Doctoral Dissertation). Retrieved from Proquest https://search.proquest.com/docview/1668380821.
Durchslag, H. B. (2016). Severe mental illness: A bridge between neurochemistry and the collective unconscious. *Psychological Perspectives*, 59(1), pp. 30–45. doi:10.1080/00332925.2016.1134210.
Farquhar, J., Le Noury, J., Tschinkel, M., Harris, R., Kurien, R., & Healy, D. (2007). The incidence and prevalence of manic-melancholic syndromes in North West Wales: 1875–2005. *Acta Psychiatra Scandinavica*, 115 (suppl. 433), 37–43.
Goodwin, F. K., & Jamison, K. R. (2007). *Manic-depressive illness: Bipolar disorders and recurrent depression*. New York, NY: Oxford University Press.
Jaffé, A. (1971). *The myth of meaning: Jung and the expansion of consciousness*. (R. F. C. Hull, Trans.). New York, NY: Penguin Books.
Jung, C. G. (1917/1966). On the psychology of the unconscious. In H. Read, M. Fordham, G. Adler, & W. McGuire (Eds.), *The collected works of C. G. Jung* (R. F. C. Hull, Trans.) (2nd ed., Vol. 7, pp. 9–171). Princeton, NJ: Princeton University Press.
Jung, C. G. (1929/1969). The significance of constitution and heredity in psychology. In H. Read, M. Fordham, G. Adler, & W. McGuire (Eds.), *The collected works of C. G. Jung* (R. F. C. Hull, Trans.) (2nd ed., Vol. 8, pp. 107–113). Princeton, NJ: Princeton University Press.
Jung, C. G. (1931/1969). The structure of the psyche. In H. Read, M. Fordham, G. Adler, & W. McGuire (Eds.), *The collected works of C. G. Jung* (R. F. C. Hull, Trans.) (2nd ed., Vol. 8, pp. 139–158). Princeton, NJ: Princeton University Press.
Jung, C. G. (1934/1968). Archetypes of the collective unconscious. In H. Read, M. Fordham, G. Adler, & W. McGuire (Eds.), *The collected works of C. G. Jung* (R. F. C. Hull, Trans.) (2nd ed., Vol. 9, part I, pp. 3–41). Princeton, NJ: Princeton University Press.
Jung, C. G. (1936/1968). The concept of the collective unconscious. In H. Read, M. Fordham, G. Adler, & W. McGuire (Eds.), *The collected works of C. G. Jung* (R. F. C. Hull, Trans.) (2nd ed., Vol. 9, part I, pp. 42–53). Princeton, NJ: Princeton University Press.
Jung, C. G. (1947/1969). On the nature of psyche. In H. Read, M. Fordham, G. Adler, & W. McGuire (Eds.), *The collected works of C. G. Jung* (R. F. C. Hull, Trans.) (2nd ed., Vol. 8, pp. 159–234). Princeton, NJ: Princeton University Press.
Jung, C. G. (1952/1969). Synchronicity: An acausal connecting principle. In H. Read, M. Fordham, G. Adler, & W. McGuire (Eds.), *The collected works of C. G. Jung* (R. F. C. Hull, Trans.) (2nd ed., Vol. 8, pp. 419–519). Princeton, NJ: Princeton University Press.
Jung, C. G. (1953). Foreword. In J. W. Perry, *The self in psychotic process: Its symbolization in schizophrenia* (pp. v–viii). Berkeley, CA: University of California Press.
Jung, C. G. (1989). *Memories, dreams, reflections* (R. Winston & C. Winston, Trans.). New York, NY: Vintage Books.
Leahy, R. L. (2007). Bipolar disorder: Causes, contexts, and treatments. *Journal of Clinical Psychology: In Session*, 63(5), 417–424. doi:10.1002/jclp.20360.
Le Mouël, C. (2018). Jung's axioms: An introduction to Jung's "Note on Number." *Psychological Perspectives*, 61(4), 414–430. doi:10.1080/00332925.2018.1536504.
Marneros, A., & Angst, J. (Eds.). (2000a). *Bipolar disorders: 100 years after manic depressive insanity*. Boston, MA: Kluwer Academic.

Marneros, A., & Angst, J. (2000b). Bipolar disorders: Roots and evolution. In A. Maneros & J. Angst (Eds.), *Bipolar disorders: 100 years after manic depressive insanity.* Boston, MA: Kluwer Academic Publishers.

McIntosh, T. W., Moorhead, J., McKirdy, J., Hall, J., Sussman, J. E. D., Stanfield, A. C., Harris, J. M., Johnstone, E. C., & Lawrie, S. M. (2009). Prefrontal gyral folding and its cognitive correlates in bipolar disorder and schizophrenia. *Acta Psychiatrica Scandinavica*, 119, 192–198.

National Institute of Mental Health. (1987). *Towards a model for a comprehensive community-based mental health system.* Washington, DC: National Institute of Mental Health.

O'Donovan, M. C., Craddock, N. J., & Owen, M. J. (2009). Genetics of psychosis; insights from views across the genome. *Human Genetics*, 126, 3–12. doi:10.1007/s00439-009-0703-0.

Parabiaghi, A., Bonetto, C., Ruggeri, M., Lasalvia, A., & Leese, M. (2006). Severe and persistent mental illness: A useful definition for prioritizing community-based mental health service interventions. *Social Psychiatry and Psychiatric Epidemiology*, 41(6), 457–463.

Ruggeri, M., Leese, M., Thornicroft, G., Bisoffi, G., & Tansella, M. (2000, August). Definition and prevalence of severe and persistent mental illness. *The British Journal of Psychiatry: The Journal of Mental Science*, 177, 149–155.

Sanchez-Morla, E. M., Garcia-Jiminez, M. A., Barabash, A., Martinez-Vizcaino, J., Mena, J., Cabranes-Diaz, J. A., Baca-Baldomero, E., & Santos, J. L. (2008). P50 sensory gating deficit is a common marker of vulnerability to bipolar disorder and schizophrenia. *Acta Psychiatrica Scandinavica*, 117, 313–318. doi:10.1111/j.1600-0447.2007.01141.x.

Seifuddin, F., Pirooznia, M., Judy, J. T., Goes, F. S., Potash, J. B., & Zandi, P. P. (2013). Systematic review of genome-wide gene expression studies of bipolar disorder. *BMC Psychiatry*, 13, 1–19. Retrieved from http://www.medscape.com/viewarticle/811759.

Stahl, S. M. (2013). *Stahl's essential psychopharmacology: Neuroscientific basis and practical applications.* New York, NY: Cambridge University Press.

Steinkuller, A., & Rheineck, J. E. (2009). A review of evidence-based therapeutic interventions for bipolar disorder. *Journal of Mental Health Counseling*, 31(4), 338–350.

Thase, M. E. (2005). Bipolar depression: Issues in diagnosis and treatment. *Harvard Review of Psychiatry*, 13, 257–271. doi:10.1080/10673220500326425.

Tresan, D. (1996). Jungian metapsychology and neurobiological theory. *Journal of Analytical Psychology*, 41(3), 399–436.

Varela, F., & Shear, J. (Eds.). (1999). *The view from within: First-person approaches to the study of consciousness.* Thorverton, UK: Imprint Academic.

Von Franz, M. (1974). *Number and time: Reflections leading toward a unification of depth psychology and physics.* (A. Dykes, Trans.). Evanston, IL: Northwestern University Press.

Von Franz, M. (1992). *Psyche and matter.* Boston, MA: Shambhala.

Chapter 2

Methodology

Methodological choices

In October 2010, the day before departing for an intensive weekend seminar in the second year of my doctoral program at Pacifica Graduate Institute, I had a dream. In the dream, I am tasked with creating a display of fish for my boss. I go to the pet store and purchase two plastic bagfuls of small fish, filled to capacity. One of the bags breaks and spills in the parking lot. I begin to wonder if one bag might not be enough for the display, so I leave without replacing it. The dream's scene shifts. I am ready to create the display for my boss. But as I look at the display with the still empty fishbowl, I wonder if perhaps a single, larger fish might be more impactful. The scene shifts one more time, to a basement apartment, where my brother is preparing some fish in the kitchen. It is a commonplace fish, nothing special. My brother asks me to slice the fillet. He tells me how to do it, but I am skeptical of my knife skills and the ability to deal with the fish's flaky texture. But the fish slices cleanly and uniformly into glistening medallions. I am surprised how meaty and beautiful this fish has become. I share this dream because I can reflect back on this October weekend and mark it as a turning point in how I would approach the research I present in this book, which had its beginnings in my doctoral dissertation.

The above dream highlights some methodological choices I made. I chose not to explore multiple schools of thought from a distance (symbolized by the schools of fish). Instead, I would delve into an analysis of my personal experience (the single fish). And in spite of being a relatively average specimen (the commonplace fish), when examined carefully (slicing the fish), the results were surprisingly special. Unfortunately, the dream might also suggest I am "putting myself on a platter"—to be sliced, diced, and eaten. Placing my own experience so firmly into the research might lead to being "cooked." First, severe mental illnesses are highly stigmatized, and this surely leaves me vulnerable. And, in general, because any academic work needs to be critically analyzed and challenged, it could be a very personal endeavor: I am the data in many respects.

Methodology and procedures

Method as path

Research methodologies are based in the epistemological root of the term, *method*, which in Greek translates as "*path*" (Giorgi, 1970). Therefore, methodology refers to "the logos of method" (Coppin & Nelson, 2005, p. 89), or the explication of the thought process behind the path the researcher chooses to follow. Coppin and Nelson (2005) defined methodology as the "level of *moves*," meaning "the actual operations—the turns, starts, and stops, the gathering and arrangement of ideas, words, and concepts—that one makes" (p. 90). Romanyshyn (2007) echoed this definition:

> A method is a way into one's work. It is a way of going to work on one's work, the making of a path that one follows into one's work. When one designs a method, one is mapping out the journey that one will take from that place of not knowing one's topic to that place of coming to know it. (p. 215)

In human science research design, methodology is created according to the subject being studied. This differentiates the process from natural science, quantitative experimental design where a subject cannot be studied if it does not first fit into the "moves" of the natural scientific method. However, because qualitative moves are not as universally constructed as they are in quantitative research design, it is imperative for the qualitative researcher to construct a rigorous path, meaning one that can be examined and re-examined by any critical reader of the work (Giorgi, 1970). Methodological rigor and transparency are the keys to the same issues of validity and reliability addressed in the scientific method. Polkinghorne (1988) explained:

> The general concept of "validity" has been redefined by natural science. It has become confused by the narrowing of the concept to refer to tests or measuring instruments. In [qualitative] research, "valid" retains its ordinary meaning of well-grounded and supportable. (p. 175).

This research project utilized narrative analysis as a way into the subject matter and as a framework from which the reader can review the material and the conclusions.

Narrative analysis

Narrative analysis, which rests within hermeneutic traditions, is a well-established mode of inquiry in the human sciences (Coppin & Nelson, 2005; Polkinghorne, 1988; Riessman, 1993). The umbrella of the human sciences encompasses diverse but related fields of study, including psychology, history, sociology, and anthropology (Giorgi, 1970). The human sciences tradition recognizes the importance of positivism and experimental design as a kind of knowledge, but holds the underlying philosophical assumption that a full understanding of human experience cannot be understood entirely through the reductive process of quantitative research. Instead, there must be a qualitative amplification of the context within which the human experience is imbedded, including the specific personal, cultural, and historical lenses from which it is being researched (Giorgi, 1970).

Anthropologists and sociologists began using narrative inquiry in the first half of the twentieth century to capture experiences of marginalized populations, such as Native Americans, immigrants, and juvenile delinquents (Chase, 2003). In the latter half of the century, spurred by the Civil Rights Movement, narrative inquiry was recognized as a way of understanding the social construction of identity. Narrative methods provided a structure by which to examine African-American slave narrative and oral histories; the feminist movement understood personal narrative as primary documents for feminist research. Sociolinguists became interested in narrative analysis because of the ability to analyze structural components of the narrative itself, and to explore how that structure commented on broader cultural contexts (Chase, 2003). There are also strong connections between narrative inquiry and the field of education research, especially Dewey's triad of experience, which includes continuity, situation, and the nature of experience (Clandinin & Connelly, 2000).

Although there are several permutations of narrative methodology depending on the field and subject of study (Polkinghorne, 1988; Clandinin & Connelly, 2000; Riessman, 1993; Creswell, 2007), in general all have five distinctive features (Chase, 2003). First, narrative is a retroactive form of meaning-making. It describes the "who, what, where, when, and how" aspects of experience, and the "why" of its importance. Second, narrative analysis is not only a retroactive form of meaning-making, it is also an active process that explains, describes, informs, and defends experience. In essence, narrative not only recounts experience, but creates a more complex and meaningful layering of that experience. Third, this active meaning-making process has personal and collective implications. At the personal level, narrative expression of an experience (or group of experiences with particular themes in common) helps the teller to make sense of experience in new ways (Chase, 2003; Polkinghorne, 1988). At the collective level, each narrative has a "social character": a structure that is indicative of different cultural and societal structures, patterns, and experiences (Chase, 2003; Polkinghorne, 1988). The fourth distinctive feature of narrative inquiry (Chase, 2003) is related to the collective and social character of the account, because all meaning-making is either enabled or constrained by circumstance, be it personal or cultural. Finally, narrative analysis acknowledges that researchers are active participants in the process. The narrative is always a co-creation between narrator and researcher, and the narrative is always influenced by the intended audience.

Narrative analysis and the hermeneutic tradition

The five features described above are recognizable as qualities of a larger hermeneutic tradition. The image of a hermeneutic circle (Packer & Addison, 1989) expresses the ongoing attention to the dialectic of researcher and research, from the outset of the project; through the research, itself; as well as in the final interpretation. This process begins again each time an interpretation is made, thereby creating a circle by which the research is taken up again, this time with the new perspective, and so on. Packer and Addison (1989) explained:

> Any final construction that would be a resting point for scientific inquiry represents an illusion that must be resisted .... So although hermeneutic inquiry proceeds from a starting place, a self-consciously interpretive approach to scientific investigation does not seek to come to an end at some final resting place, but works instead to keep discussion open and alive, to keep inquiry under way. (p. 35)

Rennie (2007) and Craig (2007) argued that all qualitative methods are hermeneutic, and that hermeneutics could be considered a "meta-methodology" in the field. Therefore, although speaking specifically about narrative construction, we are generally speaking of the hermeneutic tradition.

The nature of narrative construction necessarily excludes perspectives that disrupt cohesion, thereby concretizing a unique perspective created by the dialectic of the researcher and the research. Clandinin and Connelly (2000) highlighted:

> To understand what narrative inquirers do as they write field texts, it is important to be aware not only that selectivity takes place but also that foregrounding one or another aspect may make other aspects less visible or even invisible. Field texts, in an important sense, also say much about what is not said and not noticed. (p. 93)

Echoing the concept of the dialectic between researcher and research, Cushman (1995) wrote: "Thus, research is unavoidably a process of tracking between the part and the whole, between the researcher's context and the object's context, between the familiar and the unknown. This is the hermeneutic circle, and it is basic to the research process" (p. 22). Cushman added dimensionality to the hermeneutic circle through the image of a three-dimensional sphere. The horizon is the limited scope of vision where the known and the unknown meet and is the meeting point between what is seen and what is not seen. Cushman described this horizon as "both liberating, because it makes room for certain possibilities, and limiting, because it closes off others" (p. 24). The hermeneutic tradition addresses issues of validity by providing transparency both for what is included and what is left out of the final narrative analysis. In summary, this research project utilized the hermeneutic tradition of narrative analysis to engage in a retroactive form of meaning-making regarding my personal experience with bipolar psychosis and the relationship between that experience, Jungian psychology, and medical models of severe mental illness. This meaning-making process is reflective of the hermeneutic circle which, on the one hand, opens new fields of inquiry while, on the other, eclipses others.

Data collection and the path into the work

Initial review of the literature

This research project explored how the efficacy of pharmacological treatment might shed light on Jung's theoretical model of a collective unconscious. The first review of the literature included attention to Jung's work on the collective unconscious and archetype, a broad primer in medical models of severe mental illness, and a review of post-Jungian literature on the subject of severe mental illness. This included John Weir Perry's (1953, 1999, 2005) work on thematic content in psychotic delusions. I did not decide to use my own autobiographical experience until it became apparent that the key to the research lay in constructing a plausible relationship between medication and psychosis, which only seemed possible through clear data supporting such a relationship. At that point, my intention became focused on keeping my own recollections as free from inadvertent cross-pollination of content as possible.

Personal narrative

My narrative contribution was constructed through stream of consciousness writing. First, I gathered and organized emails from the time I began my medication titration (April 2006) through my release from the hospital in September 2006. Second, I scanned journals and daily planners from around this same time period. Third, I gathered psychiatric notes and medical records from my own psychiatrist, as well as from the three different hospitals to which I was either admitted or sent to the emergency room. The goal was to create a frame of reference related to time and place. This skeleton allowed a means of containing and organizing a stream of consciousness with temporality and order, one of the goals of narrative construction (Polkinghorne, 1988).

Other autobiographical accounts and the addition of personal field text

Once my own experience had been written, I reviewed two works by Custance (1951, 1954), and works by Boisen (1936) and Coate (1965). Both Custance (a pen name) and Coate were natives of England; Boisen was American.[1] As I read through their own accounts, I was struck by how much and how often my own exploration in personal journals and creative writing efforts aligned with theirs. I expanded thematic content in their work with field texts of my own that were not a part of the narrative created for the purposes of this research but aligned with and supported these accounts.

Second review of the literature

Once I had the narratives organized and ready for data analysis, I returned to a review of the literature. This time, I approached the medical research with greater specificity and attention to genetics, neurotransmitters, and the action of particular psychopharmacological drugs. Initial reviews of post-Jungian discourse focused specifically on references to severe mental illness. The second review expanded into debates around notions of the collective unconscious and archetype.

Data analysis

The chapters that follow present case material according to their alignment with Jung's and Perry's work on categorizing archetypal material. Finding answers to the "who, what, why, where, how" questions is an implicit part of narrative analysis, and the purpose of the method is to sort and order information into a cohesive explanatory form (Polkinghorne, 1988). Polkinghorne (1988) wrote: "A narrative explanation draws the gathered past facts together into a whole account in which the significance of the facts in relation to the outcome to be explained is made clear" (p. 175). He compared the process to detective work, which involves pulling together disparate stories to make a cohesive whole:

> Data collection results in a collection of stories. The goal of analysis is to uncover the common themes or plots in the data. Analysis is carried out using hermeneutic techniques for noting underlying patterns across examples of stories. ... The analysis of narrative data does not follow an algorithmic outline, but moves between the original data and the emerging description of the pattern (the hermeneutic circle). (Polkinghorne, 1988, p. 177)

Keeping in mind the cautions related to narrative construction and the concretization of a single perspective in an effort to create cohesion, data analysis supported the efforts to build a relationship between common themes in delusional content and psychopharmacological treatment. This research project analyzed data in relation to scene, temporality, and the importance of the experience (own and others) in order to inform the reader of meaningful implications for people suffering with severe mental illnesses and of the continued relevance of Jung's work in today's landscape of neuroscientific research.

Researcher reflexivity

Bias

All hermeneutic inquiry must acknowledge limits of perspective related to personal and cultural constraints, as well as the restraint necessary whenever conscious meaning-making is imposed on unconscious processes. I have been transparent for the reader regarding my personal agenda and biases, and how these have potentially influenced the results. This is explored in greater detail below. The sample of narratives is also a Western perspective. Additional narrative contributions span 85 years, and include both male and female perspectives, but both cultures—American and British—share commonalities and are clearly limited in scope in relation to multiculturalism.

The wounded researcher

I was both the researcher and the researched in this project. This made the task of researcher reflexivity an ongoing priority. I have already noted that at least a part of my interest in this research is that it offered a means of exploring my disillusionment with analytical psychology. The desire to heal the disillusionment through research follows Romanyshyn's (2007) definition of the wounded researcher:

> The wounded researcher is a complex witness who, by attending not only to conscious but also the unconscious subjective factors in his or her research, seeks to transform a wound into a work. The work comes through the wounding ... but without letting the work become merely a confession about the wound. The wounding is a way of being present, and what this presence requires from a truly objective researcher is the sustained commitment and the capacity to open that wound for inspection so that the work it addresses can be differentiated from it. Such work is a complex affair. (p. 111)

This excerpt highlights the importance for the wounded researcher to separate one's self from the wound in order to allow the work to unfold in an organic way that may or may not hold with the researcher's initial intent. Several methodological tools from Romanyshyn's (2007) alchemical hermeneutic process were used during this research, including attendance to my own dreams, and invitations to the ancestors through the use of transference dialogues. However, there was not adequate attention to regularity and methodological rigor to include this work as a piece of the narrative analysis.

My intention in the research was to build common ground between Jungian psychology and medical models of severe mental illness, but as a wounded researcher I am also required to allow the work its own agenda. Romanyshyn (2007) wrote:

> Research also always has its moments of falling apart, moments when the work falls out of the hands of the researcher, when the work seems to resist the conscious intentions of the researcher and begins to twist and turn in another way. Such moments are crucial to an approach to research that would keep soul in mind because they signal a shift from what the researcher wants from the work to what the work wants from the researcher. (p. 48)

I entered the work as a defender of my particular belief in the subject matter, but I was also willing to be defeated. Romanyshyn (2007) described this type of defeat as a mourning process for the ego-based research agenda. He used the image of dismemberment, of a tearing apart of a researcher's intent, in service of the research. But it is only through this dismemberment that the true voice of the research is, as Romanyshyn constructed the word, *re*-membered:

> Through the process of dismemberment, the researcher's initial complex relation to the work is transformed. The complex wound becomes a work and in this transformation the researcher finally becomes a witness and spokesperson, not for himself or herself, but for what has been left unspoken, unsaid, neglected, marginalized, or otherwise forgotten. The work is no longer about the researcher. It is about the weight of history in the work that has been waiting for its voice. (Romanyshyn, 2007, p. 76)

An example of the agenda of the work rising outside of my ego intention was the additional difficulties with internal challenges to Jung's work within the field of analytical psychology.

Ego defeat

As will become apparent in the chapters that follow, I have opened myself to the potential for a great deal of scrutiny and judgment by choosing this research topic and method. The implications for my personal and professional life really cannot be known. I only hope the reader will understand that the construction of my personal narrative and its use for the purpose of this research had nothing to do with ego. In fact, I feel my ego has always been forced to look back helplessly at what has transpired in my own personal history. It feels as though it has to do with a complete eclipse of ego. Laying the experience bare for the purposes of this research feels like an additional layer of helplessness, but was the only way I saw to strengthen a relationship between psychopharmacology and the collective unconscious. That said, I believe I have accomplished the difficult task Romanyshyn (2007) set for the wounded researcher. This work is not merely a confessional about the wound; it opens a wound for objective inspection. I would have much preferred to leave myself out of this entirely, but the work demanded otherwise.

The embrace of qualitative research in the natural sciences

Currently, there is a trend in the natural sciences to include qualitative research methodology and contributions from the human sciences perspectives. Referenced in Chapter 1, the interaction of subject on object in quantum theory and consciousness studies is increasing cross-pollination. For example, Capra and Luisi (2014) highlighted the need for subjective experience to be a part of any truly scientific understanding of the physical sciences: "In addition to complexity theory, scientists will need to accept another new paradigm: the recognition that the analysis of lived experience—that is, of subjective phenomena has to be an integral part of any science of consciousness" (p. 261). Quantum mechanics and emergence theories have forced a scientific reconsideration of the bracketed phenomenological [I], as the observer's effect on the phenomena being observed is now a position scientifically studied in the arena of quantitative inquiry. Capra and Luisi highlighted: "While we have come to realize that the subjective dimension is always implicit in the practice of science, in general it is not the explicit focus" (p. 262). They continued: "In a science of consciousness, by contrast, some of the very data to be examined are subjective inner experiences. To collect and analyze these data systematically requires a disciplined examination of 'first-person,' subjective experience" (p. 262). The acknowledgement of the value of qualitative inquiry in the hard sciences offers a much-needed bridge.

Ethical considerations

The stories of my illness are unavoidably interwoven with family, friends, and other professionals, including those I worked with in a professional capacity, and those I worked with as a patient or client. Confidentiality has been maintained according to best practices on presenting case material as defined by the American Psychological Association. Ethical standards 4.06 and 4.07 for disclosing confidential information for didactic and other purposes allow for a choice between obtaining consent and disguising material (Behnke, 2005). Disguise has been deemed sufficient for the potentially confidential information included in the research.

A hermeneutic homage

Moving forward, I would like to honor the provisional nature of knowledge, science, and theory. In fine depth psychological fashion, Nancy Moules (2002) paid tribute to the communication of the known to the unknown through the energy of Hermes:

> Truth is a living event; it is changing, not stagnant, and is expansive and full of possibilities. The truth is what allows the conversation to go on, recognizing that understanding is not a solo undertaking for it always occurs with others. Truth is not a judgment about worth; it is always being worked out and one truth is not intended to reprimand all the others, but to show the eventfulness of a topic. It occurs in keeping something open, in not thinking that something is known, for when we think we already know, we stop paying attention to what comes to meet us. (p. 11)

Something without voice being left behind often screams a little the first time to be heard. If, in the coming pages, there is a tone of critique, it is only a plea to reorient and revisit views of classical Jungian tenets of analytical psychology before they become lost or discarded in a shuffle of seemingly scientific advance.

Note

1 Custance's work has been anthologized in the medical literature (Goodwin & Jamison, 2007) related to manic depression. An academic mentor in the field of psychology (Harry T. Hunt) also suggested his work is particularly pertinent, as well as that of the two other authors whose experiences are included in the body of the research.

References

Behnke, S. (2005, April). Disclosing confidential information in consultations and for didactic purposes: Ethical standards 4.06 and 4.07. *Monitor on psychology: A publication of the American Psychological Association*, 36(4). Retrieved from http://www.apa.org/monitor/apr05/ethics.aspx.

Boisen, A. T. (1936). *The exploration of the inner world: A study of mental disorder and religious experience*. Philadelphia, PA: University of Pennsylvania Press.

Capra, F., & Luisi, P. L. (2014). *The systems view of life: A unifying vision*. New York, NY: Cambridge University Press.

Chase, S. E. (2003). Learning to listen: Narrative principles in qualitative research methods course. In R. Josselson, A. Lieblich, & D. P. McAdams (Eds.), *Up close and personal: The teaching and learning of narrative research* (pp. 79–100). Washington, DC: American Psychological Association.

Clandinin, D. J., & Connelly, F. M. (2000). *Narrative inquiry: Experience and story in qualitative research*. San Francisco, CA: Jossey-Bass.

Coate, M. (1965). *Beyond all reason*. Philadelphia, PA: J. B. Lippincott.

Coppin, J., & Nelson, E. (2005). *The art of inquiry: A depth psychological perspective*. Putnam, CT: Spring Publications.

Craig, E. (2007). Hermeneutic inquiry in depth psychology. *The Humanistic Psychologist*, 35(4), 307–321.

Creswell, J. W. (2007). *Qualitative inquiry & research design: Choosing among five approaches*. Thousand Oaks, CA: Sage Publications.

Cushman, P. (1995). *Constructing the self, constructing America: A cultural history of psychotherapy*. United States: Da Capo Press.

Custance, J. (1951). *Wisdom, madness and folly: The philosophy of a lunatic*. London: Victor Gollancz.

Custance, J. (1954). *Adventure into the unconscious*. London: Christopher Johnson.

Giorgi, A. (1970). *Psychology as a human science: A phenomenologically based approach*. Oxford: Harper & Row.

Goodwin, F. K., & Jamison, K. R. (2007). *Manic-depressive illness: Bipolar disorders and recurrent depression*. New York, NY: Oxford University Press.

Moules, N. J. (2002). Hermeneutic inquiry: Paying heed to history and Hermes An Ancestral, Substantive, and Methodological Tale. *International Journal of Qualitative Methods*, 1(3), 1–21. doi:10.1177/160940690200100301.

Packer, M. J., & Addison, R. B. (Eds.). (1989). *Entering the circle: Hermeneutic investigation in psychology*. Albany: State University of New York Press.

Perry, J. W. (1953). *The self in psychotic process: Its symbolization in schizophrenia*. Berkeley, CA: University of California Press.

Perry, J. W. (1999). *Trials of the visionary mind: Spiritual emergency and the renewal process*. Albany, NY: State University of New York.

Perry, J. W. (2005). *The far side of madness* (2nd ed.). Putnam, CT: Spring Publications.

Polkinghorne, D. (1988). *Narrative knowing and the human sciences*. Albany: State University of New York Press.

Rennie, D. L. (2007). Methodical hermeneutics and humanistic psychology. *The Humanist Psychologist*, 35(1), 1–14.

Riessman, C. K. (1993). *Narrative analysis*. Newbury Park, CA: Sage.

Romanyshyn, R. D. (2007). *The wounded researcher: Research with soul in mind*. New Orleans, LA: Spring Journal Books.

Chapter 3

The importance of diagnostic distinctions

Overview

The goal of this chapter is to highlight fissures between depth psychological and medical models of understanding and treating psychoses belonging specifically within the subset associated with severe mental illnesses. These are shorthand labels meant as a frame of reference. The summary label of *medical model* refers to a dominant paradigm of understanding the etiology of severe mental illnesses as physiological in nature, and of treating these illnesses with psychopharmaceuticals. The moniker of *depth psychology* refers to an umbrella psychological notion that an unconscious repository of unprocessed information and content can radically affect the surface of human activity and feeling. Modern notions of depth psychology arose from the ground-breaking ideas and practice of Sigmund Freud's classical psychoanalytic theories and of Carl Jung's departure into analytical psychology. Interest in this reciprocity predates the work of Freud and Jung, most notably in the French legacy of exploration at Salpêtrière in the mid-nineteenth century (cross-pollination with Jean Martin Charcot would influence Freud's own approach) (Ellenberger, 1970; Hunt, 1994). While on the one hand, the medical model has ignored nuances related to psychotic content and personal psychological experience, depth psychology has ignored nuances in types of psychotic manifestation.

Overall, the label of mental illness, itself, is a problematic one. The medical model is a disease model in a classical sense: something must be cured, made to disappear, often by rooting it and cutting it out as a foreign object. But depth psychological notions are of a *dis*-ease (Romanyshyn, 1989): a generally less than optimum level of psychological function that causes some type of friction in one's way of being in the world. Any notion of psychosis within the field of depth psychology presupposes a clinically and developmentally relevant fissure in the ability to integrate one field of experience with another. The label of *severe mental illness*, then, only becomes a descriptor of a continuum in this fissure. Psychosis is a severe degree of this type of disorganization. In the medical model it is a different nomenclature, altogether. It is no wonder that psychosis is treated differently between the two.

For example, *DSM-5* (APA, 2013) can be seen as the primary compendium of etiology and treatment of mental illness within the medical model. The definition of psychosis used is based in five nosological markers, including the presence or absence of delusions or hallucinations, and patterns of disorganized speech or motor behavior. Depth psychology utilizes many of these same markers, but it is the exploration of each that becomes meaningful in the unique experience of the individual. A move into content offers a depth of understanding and growth potential. The medical model uses psychosis as a phenomenological tool that becomes a piece of a larger diagnostic puzzle, one that is based in onset, duration, and chronicity. Psychotic disorders range from those that are drug-induced, to brain trauma, to dementia, or to those that are central to this particular study: schizophrenia and bipolar I disorder. In depth psychology, psychosis is meaningful, in and of itself. It is seen as an invitation "to engage more fully with the individual as a way of making sense of those symptoms within the context of the experience in which they arose" (Charles, 2017, p. 58); and as a meaningful inroad to "intrapsychic and intersubjective complexities" (Mills, 2017, p. 81). Medical models of psychosis have very little interest in this type of reciprocity because they have very little interest in the unconscious.

In the medical model, treatment is mostly chemical manipulation of brain states to normalize nosological markers, using them as breadcrumbs that lead to one diagnosis over another. Psychopharmacological treatment differs accordingly. In depth psychological models, treatment is focused on intrapsychic and intersubjective complexities, and a process of stabilizing and integrating any vulnerabilities through varying psychodynamic approaches to therapy, which includes: a focus on fantasy, affect, avoidances, past experience, interpersonal relationships, and the transference and countertransference relationship with the therapist (Shedler, 2010; Summers & Barber, 2010; Cabaniss, 2011). It is unfortunate that the current landscape of mental health has polarized these two essential contributors to understanding and valuing a complete human being. Mills (2017) summarized it well:

> [T]here is very little encouragement among mental health disciplines to promote psychotherapy for the psychotic. And any discussion of personality structure, the attachment system, desire and defence, developmental trauma, interpersonal matrices, the social link, and the psychological needs and conflicts informing mental functioning are eclipsed for reductive explanations fixated on the neurology of a thought disorder. (p. 81)

Mills (2017) challenged the medical model as genetic essentialism and determinism without any nuanced appreciation of trauma and attachment theories. However, neither branch has done an adequate job of incorporating the importance of varying perspectives, as evidenced by a fissure in diagnostic distinctions that will be explored below.

Scientific advances

Divergent paths of research

The mid-twentieth century was a time of remarkable change and inroads within both fields, the effects of which are still felt in the field of analytical psychology, specifically, and in the treatment of mental illness, generally. Both depth psychology and the medical field utilized new research, and each, within their own fields, became increasingly specialized. Placing Jung's scope of work within this era is important, especially as unique schools of practice within the Jungian community began to surface. Jung's own work took a decided turn toward interdisciplinary studies that were often sparked within the conferences at Eranos in Ascona, Switzerland.[1] Jung was developing an increased interest in quantum physics, most especially inspired through his collaborations with Wolfgang Pauli, which began around 1933 (Meier, 2001). His moves at the time, which resulted in extrapolations on the initial notion of a collective unconscious into a realm of a decidedly non-localized understanding of a human psychological experience, contrasted with an increasingly nuanced focus by another group of Jungian-trained analysts. This group, now labeled the *developmental school*, moved further into the human interaction between infant and caregiver, as explored through psychoanalytic object-relations theories and research on infant attachment patterns (Downing & Mills, 2017; Solomon, 2008). So a trend begins, in the mid-twentieth century, that moves one branch of Jungian thought further and further out into the cosmos, per se; and one branch deeper and deeper into the unique experience of the biological human over the course of development. Each has a view of scientific advance in their pockets, but each uses them in decidedly different fashion and yields differing conclusions. This fissure has yet to be reconciled. In an ironic twist, the same science of essentialism and reduction so challenged in depth psychology today is the very same data used to challenge Jung's work on the collective unconscious.

It is important to note that the trajectory of scientific discovery began to arc just as Jung was nearing the end of his life. Four years before he died, Jung (1958/1960) wrote:

> It will assuredly be a long time before the physiology and pathology of the brain and the psychology of the unconscious are able to join hands. Till then they must go their separate ways. But psychiatry, whose concern is the total man, is forced by its task of understanding and treating the sick to consider both sides, regardless of the gulf that yawns between the two aspects of the psychic phenomenon. Even if it is not yet granted to our present insight to discover the bridges that connect the visible and tangible nature of the brain with the apparent insubstantiality of psychic forms, the unerring certainty of their presence nevertheless remains. May

this certainty safeguard investigators from the impatient error of neglecting one side in favour of the other, and, still worse, of wishing to replace one by the other. For indeed, nature would not exist without substance, but neither would she exist for us if she were not reflected in psyche. (p. 271 [CW 3, para. 584])

His caution seems most directed toward the medical field: "Nobody need write an apology for the meaning of the brain since it can actually be put under the microscope. The psyche, however, is nothing, because it is not sufficiently physical to be stained and mounted on a slide" (Jung, 1952/1976, p. 350 [*CW* 18, para. 828]). Yet, as will be explored below, the lack of physical data—the inability to "see psyche"—is as problematic for depth psychologists as it is for those in the medical field.

Medical model

Two things happened in the mid-twentieth century that had long-term ramifications in the medical study of severe mental illnesses. One was the rise of psychopharmacological interventions; the other was technological advances allowing researchers to study the live brain. A medical understanding of severe mental illness has been, to a certain extent, a retroactive one. In fact, the specialized use of psychopharmacology began by accident:

The earliest effective treatments for schizophrenia and other psychotic illnesses arose from serendipitous clinical observations more than 60 years ago, rather than from scientific knowledge of the neurobiological basis of psychosis, or of the mechanism of action of effective antipsychotic agents. Thus, the first antipsychotic drugs were discovered by accident in the 1950s. (Stahl, 2013, p. 131)

As yet, there was no understanding of how to "stain and mount" a mental condition. Ideas came as pharmacological treatments for other physical illnesses were seen to affect mental functioning related to mood and orientation. Insights into psychosis became possible at first only because chemical properties of drugs either amplified or minimized symptoms. From there it became a process of understanding the chemical properties of drugs and making inferences as to how these chemical properties interacted with the brain. Conclusions were then made related to causality and inference: the chemical properties and actions of the medication act in a particular way, so the targets of these drugs must be implicated in the illnesses being treated.

A popular television spot during the 1980s in the United States, during Ronald Reagan's presidential administration's so-named "war on drugs," showed a simple egg as it is cracked into a sizzling hot frying pan. The message: "This is your brain (egg); this is drugs (hot frying pan), and this is your brain on drugs (bubbling, frying egg)."[2] It was meant as a caution over the negative impact of recreational drug use and the pain of addiction, but at its simplest it is a statement of a change in brain function when different substances are introduced. The medicalized field of treatment for severe mental illness could reverse the commercial and suggest that the psychotic mind is the sizzling, frying egg. The psychopharmaceutical eases it back into a well-contained shell. These early medications have been called *conventional antipsychotics*, or *typical antipsychotics*. The use of such medications was seen as an advance over the inexact nature of electrical shocks, and clearly a better solution than the failed attempts at treatment with prefrontal lobotomies that were first tried in 1935 (Finger, 1994).

However, as more and more came to be known about the actions of these conventional antipsychotics and their side effects, neuropharmacology became more knowledgeable and less dependent on chance, creating a new class of antipsychotic agents, *atypical* or *second-generation* antipsychotics. A different class of drugs, called *mood stabilizers*, work specifically to manage relapse and recurrence of depressive and manic episodes in bipolar disorders. The action of these mood stabilizers is still largely a mystery. However, the efficacy of these drugs has been so well established, they continue to be used even as the exact mechanisms of their action are not entirely understood. Specific drugs and their properties will be explored in more detail in Chapter 5, but a particular note relates to the shroud of mystery or the incomplete nature of knowledge that accompanies much of what happens in the medical field. As a guinea pig in this arena, I can say it is no small gamble, and history tells us that approaches can sometimes be flawed at best, or cruel and inhumane at worst. But science, overall, follows this trend of working from incomplete knowledge as a quest toward an increased scope of understanding. Phenomena are labeled and explored as available. There is a satisfaction in what has been replicable, incomplete though it may be, insofar as it substantiates the need for more exploration.

The second major contributor to the study of severe mental illness was the ability to study the live human brain. Anatomical exploration of the human brain post-mortem has existed since interest in human anatomy began but, historically, humans primarily used animals as a means of carrying out brain research on live tissue (Finger, 1994). For example, the study of neuronal tissue was advanced through work on frogs (beginning in the eighteenth century), rabbits, and dogs (nineteenth century). Theodor Schwann (1810–1882) and Camillo Golgi (1843–1926) both pioneered innovative ways in which to view cell structure, using common textile dyes (cell staining) and silver nitrate, the chemical compound used to develop black and white photographs. In fact, the term *chromosome* was created through the linking of the Greek root words *chromos* and *soma*, color and body, because of what the staining process allowed scientists to uncover. We can attribute much of our information regarding the structure and functioning of neurons to the study of a species of giant squid, the North Atlantic *Loligo*, and the invention of the oscilloscope in 1936, which allowed a visual means of studying electrical charges (Kolb & Whishaw, 2009). Capra and Luisi (2014) highlighted that "the basic structure of biological molecules was discovered in the early 1950s through the confluence of three powerful methods of observation: chemical analysis, electron microscopy, and X-crystallography" (p. 41). While these advances contributed to the discovery of the structure of DNA in 1953, it took another ten years before this discovery came to deeper fruition:

> It took another decade to understand the basic mechanism through which DNA carries out its two fundamental functions of self-replication and protein synthesis .... These twin achievements—the discovery of the DNA structure and the unraveling of the genetic code—have been hailed as the greatest scientific discovery of the twentieth century. Advancing to even smaller levels in their exploration of biological life, molecular biologists found that the characteristics of all living organisms—from bacteria to humans—were encoded in their chromosomes in the same chemical substance, using the same code script. (Capra & Luisi, 2014, p. 41)

The technological growth in electroencephalography (EEG), functional magnetic resonance imaging (fMRI), electron microscopy, and nuclear magnetic resonance (NMR) continued to transform the ongoing study of live brain activity, allowing a peek into what a "psychotic brain" is doing and what happens once pharmacological intervention is in place.

While advances in medical models of treating severe mental illness began by accident, advances in the burgeoning field of biomedicine in the 1990s ushered in a new era of unprecedented research into the causes and treatment of severe mental illness. This era has been referred to as the "molecular medicine revolution" (Goodwin & Jamison, 2007, p. 463). Neurogenetic research is one such example. Neurogenetics looks at biological anomalies and chromosomal linkages among families with a history of mood disorders, and analyzes genetic patterns at a cross-cultural level through the process of *association* and population-level patterns of genotype expression (Calladine, Drew, Luisi, & Travers, 2004; Goodwin & Jamison, 2007; Kolb & Whishaw, 2009; Tallis, 2011). Most recently, this genetic research has been finding inroads to which types of medications are more likely to be efficacious depending on which markers are present (Oedegaard et al., 2016). The 1990s brought rise to other increasingly specialized fields, such as neuropsychology and neurobiology. Like neurogenetic research, each of these fields utilizes their own specialized modes of inquiry. For example, neuropsychological research has focused on test batteries that measure sensorimotor or cognitive functioning at differing episodes of the bipolar disorder cycle and how affective states are represented in the brain during these cycles. The field of neurobiology includes experimentation with amines (noradrenergic, dopaminergic, cholinergic, GABAergic, glutamatergic), neuroendocrines, neuropeptides, and the multitude of signaling pathways in our brains. There are more scientific specialties related to the study of the brain than just those highlighted above. Neuroscience also includes neuroanatomy, neuroendicronology, neuropshycics, and molecular neuroscience. Furthermore, neuroscientists "draw on the expertise of physicists, chemists, biochemists, pharmacologists, immunologists and molecular biologists, to name only a few" (Tallis, 2011, p. 16). Tallis (2011) referred to neuroscience as "the queen of the natural sciences."

Depth psychology

New interest in childhood psychological development also began in the mid-twentieth century. Hunt (1994) described the movement as a "common quest [to discover] the processes by which the psychological acorn becomes a psychological oak" (p. 351). Study in this field moved back and forth between interest in tracking more psychically neutral activities related to visual, spatial, and mental processing, with the exploration of how these motor and cognitive functions related to the development of more psychologically nuanced decision-making and emotional reaction patterns. Piaget and Erikson are both notable in this respect, but the work that remains most present within the post-Jungian developmental school is that of John Bowlby (Solomon, 2008). One of the most influential theorists of the time, Bowlby pioneered observational studies of infants and toddlers in institutional settings, leading to new hypotheses about the effect that varying degrees of caregiver–infant attachment patterns can have on later personality development. Hunt (1994) noted Bowlby's move into the mainstream solidly within this transformative period of the mid-twentieth century:

> This has been a leading topic of developmental research ever since 1952, when the World Health Organization published *Maternal Care and Mental Health* by the English psychoanalyst John Bowlby, who studied children raised in institutions, found them deficient in emotional and personality development, and attributed that to their lack of maternal attachment. (p. 368)

The impact of human interactions in early developmental stages remains a cutting edge of departure for scientific research.

The other primary influence on the developmental school of post-Jungian theory was also part of the psychoanalytic legacy: object relations theory. Mentioning Bowlby, Solomon (2008) highlighted:

> It happened that a number of outstanding clinicians and theoreticians, including Anna Freud, Melanie Klein, Wilfred Bion, Donald Winnicott, and John Bowlby, were based in London and published major contributions during the 1940s, 1950s, 1960s, and later. Klein, Bion, and Winnicott became central figures in the development of the "object relations

school" which grew up within the British Psycho-Analytical Society during those decades and has continued to develop thereafter. (p. 129)

Solomon continued:

> At the same time, in London, during the decades when object relations theory was being developed, Dr. Michael Fordham and some of his colleagues trained as Jungian Analysts founded the Society of Analytical Psychology .... They read with interest the innovative psychoanalytic contributions and began researches that sought to elaborate a coherent theory of infantile development consistent with the Jungian tradition, while able to benefit from and to some extent incorporate the relevant new object relations findings and techniques, in particular those pertaining to early infantile development and the transference and countertransference. (pp. 130–131)

Observations and theoretical extrapolations on attachment continued to morph along with technological and scientific advances over the second half of the twentieth century.

The end of Jung's legacy

The above serves as a brief sketch of the ways in which two different theoretical models of understanding mental dis-ease have come to utilize an influx of scientific inquiry based in modern technology. What were once broad strokes of inference based in clinical observation have seemingly now been captured in images and extrapolation of the most miniscule of human physiological functions. These scientific extrapolations have implications for the continuation of Jung's legacy as it stood when he died. At the time of Jung's death, it is safe to say that he was hopeful an enhanced understanding of severe mental illness would come through collaboration in the two fields. This commitment was honored within the medical field. For example, Jung was invited to serve as the Honorary President for the first *Symposium on Chemical Concepts of Psychosis* that was showcased at the second International Congress for Psychiatry, in Zurich, Switzerland, held on September 2 and 3, 1957. Satinover (1995) noted this event as "the scientific congress that launched the biological-psychiatry revolution" (p. 351).

The chairman of the symposium, Max Rinkel, described its purpose:

> The nature and causes of mental illness, especially the schizophrenias, the over-all topic of the Congress, are still unknown .... Although great progress is being made in the humane treatment of the mentally ill .... no etiotropic therapy is known. Chemistry, biochemistry, pharmacology, neurophysiology and experimental psychiatry within less than the past

ten years have created new methods for the investigation of the causes, treatment and prevention of mental illnesses; methods which may ultimately lead to a solution of the problem of the endogenous psychoses. (Rinkel & Denber, 1958, p. vii)

In his opening remarks to the symposium, Jung highlighted his psychological perspective on psychotic disorders, most especially schizophrenia: "But it was just my psychological approach that had led me to the hypothesis of a chemical factor ... I arrived at the chemical hypothesis by a process of psychological elimination rather than by specifically chemical research" (Rinkel & Denber, 1958, p. xxi). Jung was 82 years old.

Diagnostic guides

Jaspers

Advances in codification of nomenclature in the early twentieth century in Europe are often attributed to Karl Jaspers, a German psychiatrist whose original publication of *General Psychopathology* (Jaspers 1913/1964) was widely used as a means of differentiating types of mental disorder (Gask, 2004). The rise of Nazi Germany in the 1930s left Jaspers' work in the shadows because he was married to a Jewish woman. However, much of his nomenclature can be seen in the modern compendiums. Phenomenological exploration of mental illness led Jasper to codify three major categories of mental disorder: (1) cerebral illnesses; (2) the three major psychoses; and (3) personality disorders, or *psychopathien*. The three major psychoses included: (a) genuine epilepsy, (b) schizophrenia, and (c) manic-depressive illnesses. He wrote that these three psychotic disorders "remain as the chief big problem for psychiatry [and] to this group belong the vast majority of mental hospital patients" (p. 606). He found this grouping of illnesses unique from purely somatic disorders, but also distinct from personality disorders. Jaspers believed that although these disorders were not of an entirely somatic nature, "one must, however, assume that many of the psychoses have a somatic base which one day will be known" (p. 607), and that "the hereditary link is a concrete reality" (p. 608). He continued:

> The nuclear cases of the three major psychoses (...) form perhaps something *entirely unique* in pathology. We are concerned with several modes of the organism in its totality, with events which are simultaneously somatic and psychic in character without the one taking precedence over the other. We cannot find any anatomical focus and no somatic cause nor any psychic cause. The totality of the phenomena is linked together in an unending complexity both in the individual basic features as well as in their combination. (pp. 607–608)

This was Jung's position, as well:

> The problem has two aspects, physiological and psychological, for the disease [schizophrenia], so far as we can see today, does not permit of a one-sided explanation. Its symptomatology points on the one hand to an underlying destructive process, possibly of a toxic nature, and on the other—inasmuch as a psychogenic aetiology is not excluded and psychological treatment (in suitable cases) is effective—to a psychic factor of equal importance. Both ways of approach open up far-reaching vistas in the theoretical as well as the therapeutic field. (Jung, 1958/1960, p. 255 [*CW* 3, para. 552])

In cases of what was then termed hysteria, Jung considered symptomatology to be first and foremost of a psychogenic and not biological cause, meaning that the causal factor arose from emotional triggers in the outside world: "It may, for instance, be a psychic shock, a grueling conflict, a wrong kind of psychic adaptation, a fatal illusion, and so on" (Jung, 1928/1960, p. 226 [*CW* 3, para. 496]). Jung (1907/1960) wrote:

> In order to prevent misunderstandings, I must add at once that the continued predominance of a strong complex in normal psychic life can lead merely to hysteria. But the symptoms produced by the hysterogenic affect are different from those of dementia praecox. We must therefore suppose that the disposition for the origin of dementia praecox is quite different from that for hysteria. (p. 36 [para. 75])

Unfortunately, Jung wrote very little specifically on manic-depression. His only paper devoted to manic mood disorders was published in 1903 (Jung, 1903/1970), a mere 20 years after psychotic disorders were split between dementia praecox and manic-depressive insanity. An understanding of the unique presentation of the illness, then, would have been just beginning. With the benefit of 100 years of study regarding bipolar disorders, it is likely that, for the most part, the manic mood disorder Jung focused on in 1903 would be considered *bipolar II disorder*, with hypomanic presentation, not manic. His case examples are also complicated by the comorbidity between substance abuse and bipolar disorders, which, today is estimated at close to 50 percent (APA, 2013).

DSM

The origins of the diagnostic and statistical manuals for mental illnesses lay in early attempts at common nomenclature during the beginning of the twentieth century. There are differing trajectories between the United States and Europe, although they have become increasingly aligned through the World Health Organization's (WHO) *International Statistical Classification of Diseases*, now in the planning of its eleventh revision (ICD-11; WHO, 2018). The American Psychiatric Association's (APA) *Diagnostic and Statistical Manual of Mental Disorders* (APA, 1952, 1968, 1980, 1987, 1994, 2000, 2013) has had five editions and two revisions over the past 60 years, the impetus for many of which were meant to keep pace with new medical research and changes in the ICD. The move toward a uniform nomenclature in the United States is noted in the late 1920s:

> In the late twenties, each large teaching center employed a system of its own origination, no one of which met more than the immediate needs of local institutions .... There resulted a polyglot of diagnostic labels and systems, effectively blocking communication and the collection of medical statistics. (Raines, 1951, p. v)

In the first edition of the DSM (APA, 1952), manic depression and schizophrenia were part of the section on *diseases of the psychobiologic unit*. The second edition (APA, 1968) discarded that term, but kept both manic depression and schizophrenia separate from neuroses and personality disorders, and linked them more closely with a listing of other brain disorders. Over the revisions, mood disorders have moved in and out of close connection with schizophrenia.

The fifth edition of the *Diagnostic and Statistical Manual of Mental Disorders (DSM-5)* (APA, 2013) acknowledges burgeoning research that links bipolar disorders more closely to schizophrenia by shifting these illnesses away from inclusion within generalized mood disorders as found in *DSM-IV-TR* (APA, 2000):

> Bipolar and related disorders are separated from depressive disorders in DSM-5 and placed between the chapters on schizophrenia spectrum and other psychotic disorders and depressive disorders in recognition of their place as a bridge between two diagnostic classes in terms of symptomatology, family history, and genetics. (APA, 2013, p. 123)

A new model of mental disorder, the *continuum disease model* (Marneros & Angst, 2000; Stahl, 2013), has now been proposed:

> The continuum disease model proposes that psychotic and mood disorders are both manifestations of one complex set of disorders that is expressed across a spectrum, at one end schizophrenia ... and at the other end bipolar/mood disorders. Proponents of the continuum model point out that treatments for schizophrenia overlap greatly now with those for bipolar disorder, since second-generation atypical antipsychotics are effective in the positive symptoms of schizophrenia and in psychotic mania and psychotic depression. (Stahl, 2013, p. 245)

It should be noted that the continuum disease model does a great deal more than simply place schizophrenia and bipolar disorder on a spectrum. Placing mental disorders of all kinds on a spectrum is a current trend. For example, the continuum disease model shifts from only two types of bipolar disorder (bipolar I and bipolar II) to at least ten (Stahl, 2013). However, this proposal is still widely debated (Marneros & Angst, 2000; Paris, 2009; Stahl, 2013).

Recent trends: RDoC and PDM

There are two other efforts related to diagnostic uniformity. Looked at together, they highlight the widening gap between medical and depth psychological models of diagnosis and treatment of mental illness. First, citing the need for more nuanced approaches to mental health, a collaborative effort brought about the creation of a *Psychodynamic Diagnostic Manual (PDM)* (PDM Task Force, 2006). Summarizing the rationale for the manual, editors wrote: "Mental health comprises more than simply the absence of symptoms. It involves a person's overall mental functioning, including relationships; emotional depth, range, and regulation; coping capacities; and self-observing abilities" (p. 2). The influence of the manual on the understanding of personality disorders is evidenced in an abridged inclusion of its diagnostic approach in an appendix of *DSM-5*. However, in response to the APA's (2013) most recent revision of the diagnostic criteria, the National Institute of Mental Health (NIMH) has decided to build its own diagnostic tool, *Research Domain Criteria* (RDoC), out of concern that the APA does not have sufficient quantitative data to support its diagnostic conclusions (Sisti, Young, & Caplan, 2013). Of this NIMH effort, Sisti et al. (2013) wrote: "The RDoC seem to be structured around the concern that the only way to find objectivity in the classification of diseases or disorders of psychiatry is to begin with biology and work back to symptoms" (p. 1). The underexplored dilemma is where the two tracks of understanding intersect and where they diverge.

Framing the dilemma: personal onset

In order to highlight the difficulties that sit in an uncomfortable gap between the depth and medical models of psychosis, I will try to lay out my first psychotic episode and subsequent diagnosis of bipolar I disorder as a frame. The timing of the psychotic episode was the winter break between the first and second semesters of my freshman year of college, in January 1989. Of course it is difficult to state my own take on such a thing without sounding defensive, but mine was a solidly neurotic experience, by which I mean I remember my transition from high school to college as a natural, though painful, occurrence with feelings of insecurity around interpersonal relationships and making new friends. I went straight to college out of high school, which was the norm in my social circle. I chose the University of Wisconsin-Madison.

The entire city felt vibrant and progressive. There was something about its energy—the history of Bascom Hill, the description of the freezing Wisconsin winter winds rushing up the expanse of lawn leading to its steps, and the collective woe of freezing noses and hustling students—it excited me. I was 17. Certainly, my own confidence went through the woes and growing pains of a brand new experience. But my roommate and I immediately got along, and the girl in the room across the hall remains a dear friend and confidant to this day, even though our time getting to know one another was cut short. By the time of my eighteenth birthday, which came in September of that first semester, I felt embedded in a lovely group of friends that centered mostly around people on our floor of the dormitory, and some from random parties and excursions. Classes were fine, but huge: introductory, required, full of freshmen and sophomores in a school with an undergraduate student body of 30,000-ish. It was mostly a distant professor and some semi-accessible teaching assistants. So I studied, along with my friends, in the library or the dorm, but it was non-descript studying based in time spent, not material learned. So what happened?

Whatever happened, I can say that it began well before my return to school in mid-January; that it began somewhere right around Christmas, because I was having all sorts of old types of fun in new ways. I was sleeping less, I was loving everyone more. I was staying out late more, hugging my reserved brother more, drinking more, smoking more. My roommate and another friend would come meet me in Cleveland at the tail end of the holiday break, and we would drive back to campus together. By the time we packed into the car to go back to Madison, I was losing perspective in the reality plane of ego orientation. I made it back to school as planned, but never began classes. I would be involuntarily hospitalized my first week back at the dorms during our registration week.

Etiology

Genetic research

From a medical perspective, a comprehensive meta-analysis of research on bipolar disorder suggests that the average age of onset for the illness is between 15 and 19 years of age, and that a familial history of a mood disorder increases the risk of illness at a rate ten times that of the general population. This risk is increased if the history of mental illness is on the maternal side of the family (Goodwin & Jamison, 2007). My experience was typical of these findings, both in terms of age and family history: my mother's maternal aunt was lobotomized in the late 1940s; her uncle committed suicide. My personal opinion about onset is one of an epigenetic trigger related to a lack of sleep and excessive marijuana use during my finals week. I had a genetic predisposition to the disorder (explored in more detail below), and the predisposition took hold due to behaviors affecting physiological regulation (Stahl, 2013).

The APA (2013) broadly summarized the current state of best practices when they wrote: "Schizophrenia and bipolar disorder likely share a genetic origin, reflected in familial co-aggregation of schizophrenia and bipolar disorder" (p. 130); and "The risk alleles identified to date [in schizophrenia] are also associated with other mental disorders, including bipolar disorder" (p. 103).

O'Donovan, Craddock, and Owen (2009) noted, "The major psychotic illnesses, schizophrenia and bipolar disorder (BD) are among the most heritable common disorders" (p. 3). They also reiterated points of commonality in the two illnesses:

> For the past 100 years, psychosis occurring in the absence of an organic brain disorder has subdivided into two categories corresponding to the modern diagnostic equivalents of schizophrenia and bipolar disorder (BD). At a mechanistic level, the causes of psychoses are almost completely unknown. They are familial disorders, first degree relatives of an affected individual having 8–10 times the risk of the corresponding disorder in the general population which is about 1%. Most of the variance in risk for each disorder is genetic, twin studies revealing heritabilities for schizophrenia and BD around 80% or more. (O'Donovan et al., 2009, p. 3)

In light of these commonalities, O'Donovan et al. (2009) went on to highlight research that suggests the dichotomous disease model first conceptualized by Kraeplin's work may not be tenable in light of current research. They highlighted: "there is no compelling reason to believe that these diagnostic categories reflect discrete pathophysiological processes, and in reality, many of the clinical features are shared across the disorders" (p. 4). As an example, they stated:

> The largest study ever conducted, based upon over 2 million nuclear families, found that risk of both disorders was increased in family members of an index proband, regardless of whether that proband had schizophrenia or BD (Lichtenstein et al., 2009). These findings provide strong evidence that genetically, schizophrenia and BD are not discrete disorders, and as we shall see, the emerging molecular genetic data are also incompatible with the hypothesis of two distinct disorders. (p. 4)

Brain dysfunction within regions such as the hippocampus and amygdala are also common to both schizophrenia and bipolar I disorder (Avery, Williams, Woolard, & Heckers, 2013; Mamah et al., 2010).

Data used from the initial stage of research conducted for my dissertation ended in 2013. With ongoing advances in research findings, I found it prudent to add to the pool of literature since that time. New articles gathered for the purpose of this book are included where appropriate, but, in general, the scope of the literature easily confirms an ongoing reinforcement for the genetic basis of psychosis in schizophrenia and bipolar I disorder. It is beyond the scope of any literature review serving the purposes of this particular work. For example, in the EBSCO Academic search engine, I used three different key word searches, with two limiting criteria: 1) date of publication, and 2) full-text only. I initially began with 2014 as the limit criterion. However, the scope of literature from 2016–2018 was sufficient to mark the point. There were over 50 full-text articles using keywords *bipolar, genetics,* and *psychosis*. Key words *bipolar* and *genetics* had approximately 100 hits. Finally, in the two-year period, *psychosis* and *genetics* had 192 full-text results. Much of the research offers increasing specificity-related genetic loci and research into efficacy of medication as it relates to genetic markers. This will be looked at in greater detail when the specific pharmacological action of lamotrigine is explored.

Depth psychology

The depth psychological notion of psychosis focuses on a stressor, and going off to college could be seen as a perfect culprit for a breakdown in ego function. Charles (2017) noted that the developmental perspective "helps to make sense of the tendency for psychosis to manifest at points of transition, in the face of greater demands than an individual can bear" (pp. 55–56). She explained:

> We can see two early pathways to psychosis …. The first path is associated with abuse or neglect and is characterised by a lack of a consistent and organised strategy of affective self-regulation that precludes the development of a coherent, integrated self. The second path is linked to families who are struggling with unresolved trauma or loss, and is characterised by a breakdown in more generally organized and consistent strategies of affect regulation, manifesting as a self that coheres sufficiently to function relatively effectively under normal conditions but not sufficiently integrated to hold under pressure. (p. 55)

Even if we examine a psychological trigger: the stress of going to college, a new circle of friends, a new environment, a new challenge, is there a luxury of ignoring that there is a vast body of research that suggests a different phenomenon? The answer is no. We cannot stay pigeonholed in a solution of an intrapsychic dilemma. Unless, we acknowledge a very unique relationship between genetics and psychological vulnerability. This, too, supports Jung's notion of a connection between psychic experiences and physiological phenomena.

Psychoanalytic theories of psychosis rely almost exclusively on the idea that distorted object representations and limited ego strength are the root causes of psychosis, schizophrenia, and any type of severe manic-depressive fluctuation.

This position has been echoed in the literature repeatedly over 100 years of psychoanalytic literature (Jacobson, 1988; Laing, 1965; London, 1988; St. Clair, 2004). Post-Freudian psychoanalytic theory spanning the 1930s through the twenty-first century, including contributions from Klein, Fairbairn, Winnicott, Mahler, and Kernberg (St. Clair, 2004), posit an object-relations perspective on psychological development, and consider pathology to be rooted in maladaptive defensive responses to the mother–child relational dyad. St. Clair (2004) summarized:

> Frustration in the mother–child relationships keeps the child from integrating these psychological building blocks, and so these units (of self-images and object images) remain "undigested." As undigested aspects of the childish self, they can return as primitive feeling states and unintegrated emotion. (p. 16)

Psychosis, then, is the extreme expression of primitive feeling states and unintegrated emotion related to these early mother–child interactions. Summarizing Winnicott, St. Clair (2004) wrote:

> Winnicott claimed that *psychosis* results from an early privation or failure of the environment. This failure of environmental provisions disturbs maturational processes to such a degree that the child is unable to achieve the crucial maturational processes of integration, personification, and object relating. (p. 79)

St. Clair (2004) noted that Mahler attributed psychosis to "faulty or failed individuation" (p. 99).

Manic states have also been characterized as a primitive desire to return to the fused mother–child dyad:

> It is like the dream of a small child, with the wish fulfillments of the narcissistic pleasure ego. This view postulates that the ecstatic mood state of the patient relives the nonverbal experience of union at the mother's breast and is a defense against the painful frustrations and disappointments of life. (MacKinnon, Michels, & Buckley, 2006, p. 426)

But we have to wonder, why does the approximate 1 percent of the population suffering from severe mental illness repeat these psychodynamically defined challenges, over time, in an alarmingly repetitive fashion?

An example of complementarity

Although a differentiation between severe mental illnesses as separate from personality disorders is overlooked in St. Clair's (2004) review, one of the theorists he devotes attention to, Otto Kernberg, has done extensive clinical observation and research into their differential diagnosis. Most recently, Kernberg and Yeomans (2013) addressed this differential diagnosis in two ways: first, by looking at the differing presentations of depression, elevated mood, and suicidality between bipolar I disorder and personality disorders; and, second, through a comparison of object relations and identity diffusion. They found that nosological characteristics of depression differ in environmental triggers, duration, underlying feeling tones (borderline rage versus bipolar de-valuation), and physiological changes. Regarding identity diffusion and object relations, they highlighted that:

> Cases of pure bipolar symptomatology do not show severe pathology of object relations during periods of normal functioning, and even chronic bipolar patients, who suffer from both manic and major depressive episodes, maintain the capacity for relationships in depth, stability in their relations with others, and the capacity for assessing themselves and the most significant persons in their life appropriately. (pp. 3–4)

This is not true of borderline patients, who show "a marked incapacity to assess others in depth, a lack of integration of the concept of self, with severe, chronic discrepancies in the assessment of self and others, and chronic interpersonal conflicts" (p. 4). Summarizing this difference, Kernberg and Yeomans stated: "In short, the presence of a consistent and marked immaturity of all object relations, and emotional immaturity in general, *outside* bona fide episodes of manic, hypomanic, or depressive symptomatology is characteristic of borderline personality disorder" (p. 4). This clinical research provides an example of the fissure between psychoanalysis, with its undeniable expertise in personality disorders, and an acknowledgement of the separate etiological existence of severe mental illness.

A move into collective material

Remarkably, the medical establishment has their own reference to collective material. The collection of nosological data for the DSM began in 1952, and now spans over six decades. Lacking interest in the nuances and content of psychotic material that depth psychology holds, *DSM-5* (APA, 2013) has inadvertently offered six archetypal categories of thematic content, highlighted in Table 3.1 below.

Beginning most clearly with the 500-mile drive from Cleveland back to Madison, I began to experience *referential* delusions. For example, the truckers on the highway were stationed to protect our car. They jockeyed front, back, side, depending on whose turn it was and how they were communicating to one another. Back at school, dorm lights from across the quad were turned on and off in order to cue that they were there, watching and protecting me. I was important. I was a powerful witch.

That I was so important to warrant such attention highlights the category of *grandiosity* that is codified in the APA summary. As a witch, I also carried seductive powers, the *erotomanic* delusional category, from a perspective that I could charm and gain sway over others, not for my own sexual pleasure, nor was it related to one particular person. It was a role in the ferment of political change and upheaval to come: tests for the wicked or unworthy. Here are vestiges of *nihilistic* delusional content; for, in my delusion, the world was on the brink of overthrowing what was at that time a Republican nation (George H. W. Bush was in office). It went further than that, because I, in fact, believed I was going to become pregnant with the savior. I took a small opal and silver necklace charm and placed it snugly in a silk-covered jewelry box. I closed the box, and the gestation began. My friends would ultimately get me to willingly go to the hospital emergency room in order to get a pregnancy test.

I went to the hospital with my friend, Chelsea, as my companion, even though one of the reasons I qualified for a mandatory admittance to the

Table 3.1 Psychotic delusions by type (APA, 2013)

Type	Definition
Persecutory	Delusions that one is going to be harmed or harassed in some manner.
Referential	Delusions that one is the primary referent for environmental cues (including comments, gestures, current events, etc.).
Grandiose	Delusions of exceptional abilities, wealth, or fame.
Erotomanic	Delusions that one is sought after or loved by another.
Nihilistic	Delusions that a major catastrophic event will occur.
Somatic	Delusions related to physiological illness.

inpatient psychiatric ward was because I had threatened to kill her. Apparently, I also kicked her. By this time, I was becoming aware that my friends were concerned about me, and I believe I felt trapped and concerned. It could be counted as a *persecutory* delusion, except their desire to enforce their will in a way I would not have acquiesced to leaves it more real than delusional. But I do remember the threat. We were all sitting on the floor of our dorm room, talking earnestly, I thought, about the pending political coup. I told Chelsea (who espoused a somewhat radical, anarchist perspective) that if, in fact, she carried out an assassination that was not a part of the "grander plan," I would have to kill her. It was a straightforward political statement on my end. Nothing personal. However, the persecutory delusions followed me everywhere, which is only natural when the whole of society is intent on protecting me. If I weren't at risk of persecution, there would neither be a need for truckers to protect my vehicle, nor for dorm lights to flick on and off as if meant for Paul Revere.

I recall leaving the dorm room and my gathering of friends at one point, with real but also inflated fears of persecution, and going to take a shower to ground myself. I was quite aware of an odd and disconnected state of being; I just had nothing to attribute it to, nor did I appreciate feeling judged or corralled by my friends. I recall standing alone in the bathroom after my shower, in front of the mirror over the sink, naked, conscious of feeling altogether strange and other-worldly. Describing the scene in a piece of creative non-fiction, I wrote:

> I got face to face with me, feeling glorious in my naked, wet state. A goddess embodied. But I was more intrigued, and not satisfied, by what I saw, because I wasn't quite sure of who I was looking at. Me, but not me. I stood shivering from the cold tile on the floor and looked into my eyes. I was interested. My long-lashed green eyes were slits—slits rimmed with red puffy lids. I was tickled by what these eyes might be—my eyes, my windows to my soul. I saw a life-force between my red puffy lids, a power darting toward my reflection, that excited my showered serenity into proud and calculated stillness, like a cat waiting to pounce. I tried to open these eyes wider. Still slits. I shivered again and sound escaped through my chattering teeth, like a hissing snake's. It echoed through the empty bathroom, and I did it again, this time on purpose, still intrigued by this reflection, the witchiness in my eyes, the hisses. But fear began creeping in, looking at me in the mirror hissing like a snake, the 18-year old that was me and not me. The life force was darting *back* from the mirror now—it was no longer my own. I was no longer cat, but prey. I stared myself down, challenged my red-slitted eyes, and lost. "Dear God" I whispered, "the Devil is here." (Durchslag, 2004, p. 6)

It could not have been long after that when Chelsea took me to the hospital for my "pregnancy test." I have a memory of standing in the stairwell at the hospital, holding Chelsea's hand, asking if people were watching us through the lighting on the ceiling. She was reassuring and calming, and said no. I remember being in the examination room with a doctor and a police officer, and then I was admitted. The entire shift in my state of being would have been no more than a few weeks, and my decompensation at school prior to hospitalization just a few days. I remained hospitalized for several weeks. My parents came to pick me up and take me back to Cleveland.

Moving forward

Commenting on the status of analytical psychology, Satinover (1995) wrote:

> At the time [Jung] formulated his hypothesis about the brain-based mechanisms that he believed must correlate with many, if not all, psychic phenomena, he had nothing to go on but his observations and his intuition. It took a good seventy years for hard science to catch up with him, and in the meantime his followers have been able to elaborate with precision only on the psychological side of the brain–psyche relation. (pp. 350–351)

Instead, Jung worked from an intuitive sense of the partnership between our psyche and our physiology. Von Franz (1992) highlighted Jung's acknowledgement of this limitation:

> During this period of his discoveries Jung left the question of the relation of these archetypes to the bodily processes open, and proceeded next to study the phenomenology of the psyche from the hypothesis that it is an entity existing for itself, whose nature we do not, however, understand. (p. 180)

Jung's intuition came five decades before its time. His theoretical trajectory did not have the benefit of most of the discoveries to come.

It is the nature of the dialectic to hold two aspects of a phenomenon in order to increase an understanding of each. There is dire need in the depth psychological community to find a more nuanced appreciation of the two interrelated but essentially unique processes in the manifestation of psychosis. Depth psychological notions of intrapsychic reorganization are powerful, valid, and essential to what can be a development in strength and progress in an individual's psyche. However, while there is certainly an overlap, severe mental illnesses must be considered as something that forces a psychic journey that exists beyond one of fragmentation and re-organization. If not, why does 1 percent of the population seem to have such difficulty with these psychological impasses? So much difficulty, in fact, these reorganizations occur over and over again; and not with unique unconscious material, but with the same unconscious material. This material is the subject of the following chapters.

Notes

1 The inception of the Eranos conferences lay in the passion of Olga Fröbe-Kapteyn, the owner of the venue. Joseph Campbell (1968) described these conferences as: "successive companies of the greatest scholars of our time ... that have inspired, and are inspiring still, the cultural evolution of mankind" (p. xi). An overview can be found in *Spring: A Journal of Archetype and Culture*, vol. 92 (Bernardini & Cater, 2015).
2 This television commercial first appeared in 1987, through the Partnership for a Drug-Free America, as a piece of what Nancy Reagan labeled the "Just Say No" campaign. The interested reader can find multiple references online, for example Rossen (2017). The post includes a YouTube video of the commercial.

References

American Psychiatric Association (APA). (1952). *Diagnostic and statistical manual of mental disorders (DSM-I)*. Washington, DC: American Psychiatric Association.

American Psychiatric Association (APA). (1968). *Diagnostic and statistical manual of mental disorders (DSM-II)* (2nd ed.). Washington, DC: American Psychiatric Association.

American Psychiatric Association (APA). (1980). *Diagnostic and statistical manual of mental disorders (DSM-III)* (3rd ed.). Washington, DC: American Psychiatric Association.

American Psychiatric Association (APA). (1987). *Diagnostic and statistical manual of mental disorders (DSM-III-R)* (3rd ed., text revision). Washington, DC: American Psychiatric Association.

American Psychiatric Association (APA). (1994). *Diagnostic and statistical manual of mental disorders (DSM-IV)* (4th ed.). Washington, DC: American Psychiatric Association.

American Psychiatric Association (APA). (2000). *Diagnostic and statistical manual of mental disorders (DSM-IV-TR)* (4th ed., text revision). Arlington, VA: American Psychiatric Association.

American Psychiatric Association (APA). (2013). *Diagnostic and statistical manual of mental disorders (DSM-5)* (5th ed.). Washington, DC: American Psychiatric Publishing.

Avery, S. N., Williams, L. E., Woolard, A. A., & Heckers, S. (2013). Relational memory and hippocampal function in psychotic bipolar disorder. *European Archives of Psychiatry and Clinical Neuroscience*, 264(3), 199–211. doi:10.1007/s00406-013-0442-z.

Bernardini, R., & Cater, N. (Eds.). (2015). *Spring, a journal of archetype and culture, vol. 92, Spring 2015, Eranos: Its magical past and alluring future: The spirit of a wondrous place*. New York, NY: Spring Journal and Books.

Cabaniss, D. L. (2011). *Psychodynamic psychotherapy: A clinical manual*. Oxford: Wiley-Blackwell.

Calladine, C. R., Drew, H. R., Luisi, B. F., & Travers, A. A. (2004). *Understanding DNA: The molecule and how it works* (3rd ed.). San Diego, CA: Elsevier Academic Press.

Campbell, J. (Ed.). (1968). *The mystic vision: Papers from the Eranos yearbooks*, vol. 6. (R. Manheim, Trans.). Princeton, NJ: Princeton University Press.

Capra, F., & Luisi, P. L. (2014). *The systems view of life: A unifying vision*. New York, NY: Cambridge University Press.

Charles, M. (2017). Working with psychosis: Contextualising and integrating fragments of meaning. In D. L. Downing & J. Mills (Eds.), *Outpatient treatment of psychosis: Psychodynamic approaches to evidence-based practice* (pp. 55–78). London: Karnac Books.

Downing, D. L., & J. Mills, J. (Eds.) (2017). *Outpatient treatment of psychosis: Psychodynamic approaches to evidence-based practice*. London: Karnac Books.

Durchslag, H. B. (2004). *Unpublished manuscript*. 33.

Ellenberger, H. F. (1970). *The discovery of the unconscious: The history and evolution of dynamic psychiatry*. New York, NY: Basic Books.

Finger, S. (1994). *Origins of neuroscience: A history of explorations into brain function*. New York, NY: Oxford University Press.

Gask, L. (2004). *A short introduction to psychiatry*. Retrieved from https://ebookcentral.proquest.com.

Goodwin, F. K., & Jamison, K. R. (2007). *Manic-depressive illness: Bipolar disorders and recurrent depression*. New York, NY: Oxford University Press.

Hunt, M. (1994). *The story of psychology*. New York, NY: Anchor Books.

Jacobson, E. (1988). On psychotic identifications. In P. Buckley (Ed.), *Essential papers on psychosis* (pp. 131–142). New York: New York University Press.

Jaspers, K. (1913/1964). *General psychopathology* (J. Hoenig & M. W. Hamilton, Trans.). Chicago, IL: University of Chicago Press.

Jung, C. G. (1903/1970). On manic mood disorder. In H. Read, M. Fordham, & G. Adler (Eds.), *Psychiatric studies: The collected works of C. G. Jung*. (R. F. C. Hull, Trans.) (2nd ed., Vol. 1, pp. 109–134). Princeton, NJ: Princeton University Press.

Jung, C. G. (1907/1960). The psychology of dementia praecox. In H. Read, M. Fordham, G. Adler, & W. McGuire (Eds.), *The collected works of C. G. Jung* (R. F. C. Hull, Trans.) (Vol. 3, pp. 3–151). New York, NY: Pantheon Books.

Jung, C. G. (1928/1960). Mental disease and the psyche. In H. Read, M. Fordham, & G. Adler (Eds.), *The collected works of C. G. Jung*. (R. F. C. Hull, Trans.) (Vol. 3, pp. 226–230). New York, NY: Pantheon Books.

Jung, C. G. (1952/1976). Foreword. In H. Read, M. Fordham, G. Adler, & W. McGuire (Eds.), *The collected works of C. G. Jung*. (R. F. C. Hull, Trans.) (Vol. 18). Princeton, NJ: Princeton University Press.

Jung, C. G. (1958/1960). Schizophrenia. In H. Read, M. Fordham, & G. Adler (Eds.), *The collected works of C. G. Jung* (R. F. C. Hull, Trans.) (Vol. 3, pp. 256–271). New York, NY: Pantheon Books.

Kernberg, O. F., & Yeomans, F. E. (2013). Borderline personality disorder, bipolar disorder, depression, attention deficit/hyperactivity disorder, and narcissistic personality disorder: Practical differential diagnosis. *Bulletin of the Menninger Clinic*, 7(1), 1–23.

Kolb, B., & Whishaw, I. Q. (2009). *Fundamentals of neuropsychology*. New York, NY: Worth.

Laing, R. D. (1965). *The divided self*. Harmondsworth, UK: Penguin Books.

London, N. J. (1988). The phenomenology of psychosis. In P. Buckley (Ed.), *Essential papers on psychosis* (pp. 1–48). New York: New York University Press.

MacKinnon, R. A., Michels, R., & Buckley, P. J. (2006). *The psychiatric interview in clinical practice* (2nd ed.). Washington DC: American Psychiatric Publishing.

Mamah, D., Wang, L., Csernansky, J. G., Rice, J. P., Smith, M., & Barch, D. M. (2010). Morphometry of the hippocampus and amygdale in bipolar disorder and schizophrenia. *Bipolar Disorders*, 12, 341–343.

Marneros, A., & Angst, J. (Eds.). (2000). *Bipolar disorders: 100 years after manic depressive insanity*. Boston, MA: Kluwer Academic.

Meier, C. A. (Ed.). (2001). *Atom and archetype: The Pauli/Jung letters 1932–1958*. Princeton, NJ: Princeton University Press.

Mills, J. (2017). Rethinking psychosis: Attachment, developmental trauma, and the psychotic spectrum. In D. L. Downing & J. Mills (Eds.), *Outpatient treatment of psychosis: Psychodynamic approaches to evidence-based practice* (pp. 79–122). London: Karnac Books.

O'Donovan, M. C., Craddock, N. J., & Owen, M. J. (2009). Genetics of psychosis; insights from views across the genome. *Human Genetics*, 126, 3–12. doi:10.1007/s00439-009-0703-0.

Oedegaard, K. J., Alda, M., Anad, A., Andreassen, O. A., Balaraman, Y., Berrettini, W. H., ... Kelsoe, J. R. (2016). The pharmacogenomics of bipolar disorder study (PGBD): Identification of genes for lithium response in a prospective sample. *BMC Psychiatry*, 16, 129–144. doi:10.1186/s12888-016-0732-x.

Paris, J. (2009). The bipolar spectrum: A critical perspective. *Harvard Review of Psychiatry*, 17(3), 206–213. doi:10.1080/10673220902979888.

PDM Task Force. (2006). *Psychodynamic Diagnostic Manual*. Silver Spring, MD: Alliance of Psychoanalytic Organizations.

Raines, G. N. (1951). Foreword. In American Psychiatric Association. *Diagnostic and statistical manual of mental disorders* (pp. v–xi). Washington, DC: American Psychiatric Association.

Rinkel, M., & Denber, C. B. (Eds.) (1958). *Chemical concepts of psychosis*. New York, NY: McDowell, Oblensky.

Romanyshyn, R. (1989). *Technology as symptom & dream*. London: Routledge.

Rossen, J. (2017, May 18). The most famous anti-drug ad turns 30. Any questions? *Mental Floss*. Retrieved from https://www.mentalfloss.com/article/500800/most-famous-anti-drug-ad-turns-30-any-questions

Satinover, J. (1995). Psychopharmacology in Jungian practice. In M. Stein (Ed.), *Jungian Analysis* (2nd ed., pp. 349–371). Chicago, IL: Open Court.

Shedler, J. (2010). The efficacy of psychodynamic psychotherapy. *American Psychologist*, 65(2), 98–109. doi:10.1037/a0018378.

Sisti, D., Young, M., & Caplan, A. (2013). Defining mental illnesses. *BMC Psychiatry*, 13(346), 1–5. Retrieved from http://www.medscape.com.

Solomon, H. M. (2008). The developmental school. In Young-Eisendrath, P., & Dawson, T. (Eds.), *The Cambridge companion to Jung* (pp. 125–146). New York, NY: Cambridge University Press.

Stahl, S. M. (2013). *Stahl's essential psychopharmacology: Neuroscientific basis and practical applications*. New York, NY: Cambridge University Press.

St. Clair M., (Ed.). (2004). *Object relations and self psychology: An introduction* (4th ed.). Australia: Brooks/Cole CENGAGE Learning.

Summers, R. F., & Barber, J. P. (2010). *Psychodynamic therapy: A guide to evidence-based practice*. New York, NY: The Guilford Press.

Tallis, R. (2011). *Aping mankind: Neuromania, Darwinitis and the misrepresentation of humanity*. Bristol, CT: Acumen.

Von Franz, M. (1992). *Psyche and matter*. Boston, MA: Shambhala.

World Health Organization (WHO). (2018). *International classification of diseases for mortality and morbidity statistics ICD-11* (11th revision). Retrieved from https://icd.who.int/browse11/l-m/en.

Chapter 4

Thematic alignment in psychosis

> An elephant is true because it exists. The elephant, moreover, is neither a conclusion nor a statement nor a subjective judgment of a creator. It is a phenomenon. But we are so used to the idea that psychical events are wilful and arbitrary products, even inventions of the human creator, that we can hardly liberate ourselves from the prejudiced view that the psyche and its contents are nothing but our own arbitrary invention or the more or less illusory product of assumption and judgment. The fact is that certain ideas exist almost everywhere and at all times and they can even spontaneously create themselves quite apart from migration and tradition. They are not made by the individual, but they rather happen—they even force themselves upon the individual's consciousness. This is not platonic philosophy but empirical psychology.
>
> (Jung, 1938, from *The Terry Lectures*, pp. 3–4)

Stripping down terminology

At the end of Chapter 3, I highlighted how the onset of my psychosis was easily recognizable in the categories that the APA (2013) has found to exist amongst psychotic delusions (see Table 3.1). The primary nosological compendium for the medical model of mental illness, pooled across time and culture, has highlighted six primary categories of delusional material: persecutory, referential, grandiose, erotomanic, nihilistic, and somatic. Delusions situate one as a primary referent for environmental cues, convinced of exceptional abilities, wealth, desire, or fame; and distracted over a major catastrophic event to come. This cursory and overly simplistic survey notes content that sits quite well within an idea of archetypal patterns that transcends any one individual. The term *transpersonal* carries a heavy load that can extend into debates about higher powers of a spiritual or religious nature. But stripped down, the prefix *trans*, which originates from the Latin, means simply "across" or "beyond." It can sit on its own to suggest something that seems to exist outside of a unique, individualized experience.

At its basest, the collective unconscious simply named such an idea. It was an idea that transpersonal material could be conceptualized as existing *somewhere*: an *a priori* construct, named to note something that we can intuit and frame through form and content, not because we view *it*. Concretizing the collective unconscious as an "it" is dangerous. We long to see this pool, this dwelling place, and how it came to exist. This applies to the term *archetype* as well, which is a label for some type of carrier, or "visible maker" of repetitive and seemingly transpersonal patterns. The term came to be used to name something that becomes visible from something that can only be intuited. How it becomes visible, how it might possibly be patterned in order to become visible in the first place; this demanded a continual return for Jung to "What if...?" or "Perhaps..." or "We could describe it as..." or "This scientific paradigm might...." We have something becoming visible from something yet to be located. This is problematic in any paradigm. And yet, we can return again and again to data that support something that aligns with Jung's original intent. In summary, moving forward in this chapter, the terms *collective unconscious* and *archetypal* are being used for purely utilitarian purposes, to continue the legacy of noting something that is seen to replicate itself transpersonally. The collective unconscious remains a term to denote some unknowable repository, as it were; and archetype/archetypal relate to the resulting pattern. Even the need to unpack whether archetype is an image or a form, in and of itself, or only a tendency toward a certain pattern, can be easily suspended.

Empirical inquiry

A brief mention of Jung's position in the field

The analysis of case material from patients suffering with severe mental illness led Jung to identify archetypal clusters that remain central to analytical psychology: *Anima, Animus, Shadow, Self, Mother, Rebirth*, and *Child* (Jung, 1968, 1936/1968). Within these archetypal clusters, specific stories were found to well up according to the archetype being expressed. For example: the connection to Christ when confronting the Self; the maiden, mother, or powerful sorcery of Hecate when confronting anima; or the hermaphroditic or messianic energy of the child archetype. Jung (1953) would later acknowledge that these same themes emerged in manic psychosis. He wrote: "I am dealing with it [the unconscious] from a purely empirical point of view, that is, I restrict myself to the observation of the phenomena and I refrain from any application of metaphysical or philosophical considerations" (Jung, 1938, p. 2). This comment did not preclude Jung from following up with philosophical considerations, many of which are widely considered flawed attempts. But I will use an overly glib turn of phrase when I state, don't throw the baby out with the bathwater. I am in no position to comment on the rigor or lack thereof that was exercised in Jung's philosophical exploration, but his attempts seemed focused on deepening what were, initially, solely empirical observations. The question of whether or not the mythic clusters defined as anima, animus, or Self were archetypes in and of themselves, or whether an archetype in and of itself could never be defined or understood, remains debatable.

However, this empirical data, in itself, has consistently been challenged in the post-Jungian community, for example, conclusions related to the case material based on Solar Phallus Man (Roesler, 2012) or Ms. Miller (Hogenson, 2004). However, a challenge to empirical data seems a much grander one than merely a critical piecing apart of single cases. This strategy might also need to challenge the empirical data of other psychologists and philosophers whose research was reviewed by Jung (1936/1968), as Jung's study of this material could be considered a meta-analysis of research already conducted. Jung's entire body of work continued and continuously circled back to support the hypothesis of a collective unconscious. Jung wrote:

> Had thorough investigation shown that in the majority of such cases [psychoses] it was simply a matter of forgotten knowledge, the physician would not have gone to the trouble of making extensive researches into individual and collective parallels. But, in point of fact, typical mythologems were observed among individuals to whom all knowledge of this kind were absolutely out of the question, and where indirect derivation from religious ideas that might have been known to them, or from popular figures of speech, was impossible. Such conclusions forced us to assume that we must be dealing with autochthonous revivals independent of all tradition, and, consequently, that "myth-forming" structural elements [archetypes] must be present in the unconscious psyche. (Jung, 1940/1968, p. 152 [*CW* 9i, para. 259])

Furthermore, it would have to contradict the additional research analyzed in the present piece of work (Boisen, 1936; Coate, 1965; Custance, 1951, 1954; Perry, 1953, 1975, 2005). It would, in fact, have to question qualitative data that provides evidence of consistent patterns of psychotic content identified across epochal intervals (Goodwin & Jamison, 2007; Marneros & Angst, 2000). If we start with Jung's postulations beginning in the fruitful time when severe mental illnesses were becoming delineated in Kraeplin's psychiatric work, we can follow themes by patients, themselves, spanning from the United States in the 1930s to Great Britain in the 1950s, and through a thread of research by Perry (1953, 1975, 1999, 2005) for 50 years, seemingly picking up where Jung's work ended, and extending research supporting theoretical constructs of collective material and archetypal patterns to the present day.

Anton Boisen

Anton Boisen (1936), one of the primary sources of narrative analysis for this book, was a wounded researcher, like me. In the preface to his book, he wrote: "I come to it as one who has explored the little-known country with which it deals" (p. x). He wrote:

> To be plunged as a patient into a hospital for the insane may be a tragedy or it may be an opportunity. For me it has been an opportunity. It has introduced to me a new world of absorbing interest and profound significance; it has shown me that the world throughout its entire range, from the bottommost depths of the nether regions to the height of religious experience at its best; it has made me aware of certain relationships between two important fields of human experience which thus far have been held strictly apart; and it has given me a task in which I find the meaning and the purpose of my life. (p. 1)

Boisen was a religious man, and the religiosity of many of the delusions present in his study, as well as the intensity of his own experience with delusional material, made him especially interested in imagining how mental illness and the manifestation of age-old religious struggles coincided. He clearly noted his interest:

> Certainly, I have ample reason to know that the relationship which I am pointing out between the domain of mental illness and that of religious experience has thus far been strangely ignored by psychiatrists and by theologians. If that relationship can be established there should be far-reaching consequences. (Boisen, 1936, p. x)

It led him to conduct research similar to Jung's, and his empirical observations also support the findings Jung had begun to compile a decade prior. He took the methodological process of inquiry seriously, writing:

> The ideas of my patients, even though elusive, are just as properly objects of empirical observation as their pulse rate or blood pressure. And any definite utterances of theirs are much more direct and objective indications of what is going on in their minds than are mere descriptions of their behavior. (pp. 184–185)

Continuing, he stated, "What I have tried to do in this inquiry and what seems to me central to the principle of empiricism is to deal at first hand with the raw material of some definite segment of human life" (p. 185), "an insane asylum."

That said, Boisen does highlight his position as the wounded researcher:

> The interpretation which I am giving is thus by no means free from a definite personal bias. But whatever value it has lies in the fact that it comes from one who has himself shared in the experience of which he reports and whose attempts to understand it have been no mere matter of academic interest but of life and death. (p. 116)

He is speaking here of some of the conclusions or analysis he makes in his book, and also his passion regarding the project. This is not a statement related to the narrative collections he gathered during his research. But it is worth noting here, because I, too, was driven toward understanding some type of reason, or purpose, behind my own experience. An impetus toward subject matter does not preclude empirically rigorous work to follow. It comes with scrupulous attention to personal bias, which, like any process, is central to a cautious and grounded report of the findings.

Boisen (1936) conducted a 3-year study of 173 hospitalized mental health patients. He found regularly occurring psychotic delusion that included "ideas of cosmic catastrophe," "cosmic identification," and "earthly power" (p. 32). Citing particular patient experiences, Boisen (1936) summarized:

> Here we have a group of ideas which appear over and over again in the profounder disturbances. In 57 of our cases we find ideas of impending world change of some sort and of great issues at stake. In 53 cases we find in the patient exalted ideas as to his own role. In 41 cases these two ideas are found in conjunction. One patient thus had the idea that the world is about to be destroyed and that he himself is the world. Three have the idea that the world is about to be destroyed and that its fate is entirely dependent upon them; if they die the world is ruined. Three others have received revelations that the second coming of Christ is about to take place and that they themselves are to have a central role in this great event, presumably as the present-day incarnation of the Christ spirit. Another announces that he is to be crucified. Two speak of themselves as "the Son of God" .... Another considers himself the reincarnation of Abraham. Another is the devil and he is greatly concerned lest all the Bibles be burned. Another is alternately God and the devil. (p. 33)

Moving forward, it will become increasingly apparent that content glossed over in broad hegemonic patterns of transpersonal material is, more often than not, of a suprapersonal nature, related to both a spiritual and organic continuity. This will continue to be highlighted.

Perry

Perry (1953, 1975, 1999, 2005) undertook several phenomenological studies that expanded Jung's work on severe mental illness and archetypal delusions, beginning with a single case study in 1953. Jung would write the Foreword to this initial work, highlighting the synergy in their efforts. Perry (1953) wrote:

> My most sincere gratitude goes to Dr. C.G. Jung, not only for his foreword, his many hours spent on the manuscript, and his helpful notes of comment, but even more for the rich discussions I have been fortunate enough to hear from him concerning the deeper reaches of psychic processes. (p. ix)

Jung (1953), in turn, wrote: "Psychiatry has entirely neglected the study of the psychotic mind .... Therefore I welcome Dr. Perry's book as a messenger of the time when the psyche of the mental patient will receive the interest it deserves" (p. vii). Twenty years later, with additional research into psychotic delusions, Perry (1975) wrote:

> When one does open oneself to the inner process of the psychotic individual, what one finds reveals some regularities .... They represent themselves in every kind of issue or guise: political, moral, racial, directional, etc. They clash, they reverse themselves, and they finally unite in resolution, particularly with the theme of sacred marriage. The clash of opposite world powers is accompanied by the imagery of the world destruction and world creation, which conforms to the myth and ritual motif of the cosmic conflict by which the world was created afresh .... Messianism is another of the most universal experiences. (p. 48)

Perry (2005) eventually expanded his work through the empirical study of psychotic content in twelve additional cases of schizophrenia. Throughout, he continued to note the connection between thematic material and the physiological roots of severe mental illness: "In respect to the physiological and biochemical elements in the schizophrenic syndrome, I do not mention them in this study because I take them for granted" (p. 4).

Table 4.1 lists and generally defines the ten categories (Perry, 2005) identified in his phenomenological case analysis (pp. 35–36).[1]

These categories replicated and expanded Perry's (1975) earlier qualitative research that identified themes of scared marriage, cosmic conflict, and messianism in psychotic material. Recall Boisen's (1936) work, which also noted that "The ideas of cosmic catastrophe and cosmic identification tend to occur together as a part of a constellation of ideas which includes also ideas of rebirth, previous existence, mission, and so forth" (p. 39). Discussing rebirth as an archetypal theme, Jung (1940/1968) wrote: "Rebirth is an affirmation that must be counted among the primordial affirmations of mankind. These primordial affirmations are based on what I call archetypes" (p. 116 [*CW* 9i, para. 207]). Again, a bare-bones understanding of archetype is meant to capture what Boisen and Perry discovered, as well.

54 Thematic alignment in psychosis

Table 4.1 Perry's (2005) delusional categories and definitions

Categories	Definitions
center	Delusions that focus on a cosmic center where the universe coalesces (e.g., heaven, earth, the underworld are an undifferentiated core).
Death	Delusions that suggest those experiencing them have already died and are communicating in an afterlife; often they have been sacrificed, and their bodies have been torn apart or mutilated.
Return to beginnings	Related to the delusional category of *center*, these delusions return to creation stories, for example, "Garden of Eden, waters of the abyss, early steps of evolution, primitive tribal society, creation of planets" (p. 35).
Cosmic conflict	World-wide clashes between good and evil, often alluded to as Armageddon, the Last judgment, or other mythic stories, where one overcomes the other and rules the world.
Threat of opposite	Delusions that reflect an individual struggle with opposites (e.g., turning into the opposite sex, identifying with the opposite sex as either better than or more evil than their own).
Apotheosis	The person experiencing the delusion becomes either royal or divine.
Sacred marriage	The person experiencing the delusion becomes a partner in a couple of mythic proportions (e.g., marrying a king/queen, god/goddess); can also be partnership with spirit (e.g., a delusional female becomes the virgin to couple with the Holy spirit to create divine child).
New birth	Delusion that the birth of a savior or powerful leader is imminent (e.g., "Divine Child, Infant Savior, Prince, or Reconciler of the division of the world" (p. 35)).
New society	Delusions related to the creation of a new world order that reflects a heightened and renewed sense of purpose or enlightened society (e.g., "a New Jerusalem, Last Paradise, Utopia, World Peace, a New Age" (p. 36)).
Quadrated world	Delusions where world powers, religious traditions, human races, lands, or the universe consist of four parts of a whole.

The hero

One of the biggest constellations of delusional themes relates to the mythic story of the hero and the themes of apotheosis and new birth: the former related to political embodiment; the latter to a religious one. Perry (2005) wrote: "The delusional themes are so repetitive from case to case as to make it a burden to write and even more to read" (p. 85). To organize the material, Perry charted each of 12 patients and listed whether they experienced any of six heroic themes and sub-themes. The summary of this material is listed in Table 4.2.

Table 4.2 Political or religious constellations of hero archetype in delusions of 12 psychotic patients

Categories	Number of patients
Election to either divine or royal supreme rule	7
Election as either political or spiritual savior	9
Supremacy of the goddess	4
Virgin mother giving birth to savior	9
Initiation to qualify for leadership either through death/rebirth or instructions/tests	12
World or national reform	12

The expression of the hero archetype relates to anima, cosmic conflict, apotheosis, and new society. In summary, Perry's (1953, 1975, 2005) and Boisen's (1936) research reinforces Jung's (1968; 1930/1968) initial identification of the archetypal clusters related to Self, rebirth, and child.

Supra-individual constellation

The theory of actuality

Jung (1931/1969) described the collective unconscious as "a kind of supra-individual psychic activity ... distinct from a superficial, relative, or personal unconscious" (p. 147 [*CW* 8, para. 311]). He continued:

> I cannot, therefore, discover anything fortuitous in these visions [speaking of patients' experiences of the material], but simply the revival of possibilities of ideas that have always existed, that can be found again in the most diverse minds and in all epochs, and are therefore not to be mistaken for inherited ideas. (p. 151, para. 320)

Von Franz (1992) offered this general directive note about what Jung meant when referring to a collective unconscious: "According to the Jungian view, the collective unconscious is not at all an expression of personal wishes and goals, but is a neutral entity, psychic in nature, that exists in an absolutely transpersonal way" (p. 231). One of the more lasting impressions I gained through my research is the spontaneous revelation of global concepts and new insights: a shared deepening of experience.

One example of this type of material is based in a philosophy of the human experience that came to Custance (1951, 1954), unbidden, during manic episodes. His *Theory of Actuality* is sweeping in nature, touching on vast explorations of anima, logos, eros, and cross-cultural traditions.

Custance discovered Jung's work only after his psychotic episode. Citing the competing theories of unconscious material between Freud and Jung, Custance wrote:

> While Freud in his exploration of the Unconscious traces its origins mainly to the childhood of the individual in the nursery, Jung lays his chief stress on the childhood of the race. He develops a theory of a Collective Unconscious .... Certainly my own experience bears out Jung's theories. (Custance, 1951, pp. 17–18)

He also clarified:

> At the outset I should perhaps make clear that the subjects of nature religion, orgiastic rites, Great Mother worship, occultism and so on, with which this series of fantasies was largely connected, were, at the time when they first appeared, a closed book to me. I had little or no knowledge of psychology, and I had never read Jung, whose ideas, as will be seen, correspond remarkably closely with those which seemed to be "revealed" to me. The whole experience, indeed, opened with a vision of what was undoubtedly the "anima" Jung describes. (Custance, 1951, pp. 84–85)

The Theory of Actuality was born of some type of intuitive connection, in this case, through the phenomenon known as mania:

> In the ecstasy of mania in which the Theory of Actuality first appeared to me—it was literally in a padded room—I saw this double vision on a kind of electrical analogy, as two poles of ultimate being as it were, which I was impelled to call "positive" and "negative" respectively. Broadly speaking the purely rational visible aspect of things presented to my conscious mind was "positive;" moreover it was essentially male, like the Chinese concept of Yang .... Conversely, the "negative" aspect was irrational and intuitive, darkly chaotic, essentially female, and associated with Yin, the opposite of Yang. Numerous analogies become apparent: Goethe's systole and diastole, the Apollonian and Dionysiac principles derived by Nietzsche from Greek thought, the more common opposition of Logos to Eros, that stressed by Bergson of reason to instinct; these and many others have obvious affinities to what I was trying to grasp. But the closest analogy of all is with the ideas of Jung, who uses on occasion the same terms "positive" and "negative" meaning by the latter that reverse aspect of things, the other side of the medal or coin, which in the modern world we almost invariably tend to repress or reject. (Custance, 1954, p. 16)

Custance attributed the desire for distinction between things that coalesce as an ultimate single entity to the "Positive, analytical Yang power," which refers to the cultural bias toward rationality and quantification.

Jung (1952/1976) would eventually write the Foreword to the 1952 edition of Custance's book. In it, he highlighted:

> What the author has discovered in the manic state is in exact agreement with my own discoveries. By this I mean more particularly the structure of opposites and their symbolism, the anima archetype, and lastly, the unavoidable encounter with the reality of the psyche. As is generally known, these three main points play an essential role in my psychology, with which, however, the author did not become acquainted until afterwards. (p. 351 [*CW* 18, para. 829])

While Custance created an extensive theory from material rising during his illness, others noticed or experienced a general musing over suprapersonal issues.

Other reflections

Morag Coate (1965) reflected on psychic division as well, also in line with Jung's language. She wrote: "The stimulus—at once painful and creative—of this primary psychic division gave rise to the prototype of Animus and Anima, the great figures, one male and one female, whose shadowed memory haunts the imagination of the unconscious mind" (pp. 45–46). Considering an explanation of why such things came to her, she reflected:

> Experience suggests that prototypes of such concepts as truth, beauty, balance, justice and true love have already been laid down in us while we were in the womb. We have no recollection, but we do have the capacity for recognition .... If later an experience of great intensity livens the self to full consciousness, is it not possible that the stimulus reawakens the life our sleeping embryo experienced; a phase of existence which perhaps provides the basis for the collective unconscious of the human race? This is a surmise. Beyond it lies a mystery. Somewhere within that mystery is the deeper and transcendent truth in which our spiritual life takes root. (p. 135)

Reflecting on the implications, Coate stated:

> If I, who had these experiences, had been a member of some primitive tribe, I would have woven them into a myth, embellished in detail with the history, known or imagined, of my race. And others would perhaps have adopted or adapted it and handed it on in altered form from one generation to the next. For that is surely how myths are made. (p. 47)

The language used resonates with Jung's own description of his construct.

While content of a suprapersonal nature is unwieldy, it has a clear presence within symptomatic periods of severe mental illness.

Eschatological content

As highlighted in the previous pages, Boisen (1936) found regular identification in his study of patients seeing themselves as Christ, or more generally a son of God, as prophets of a second coming, or even the devil. Coate (1965) also reflected, "At one time I took the part of the Virgin Mary, at another I was the boy David" (p. 36). My own delusions were wrought with being the virgin Mary, or sometimes God, herself. These are explored in more detail in the following chapter. Of special note here is thematic content specifically focused on eschatological content. Eschatology is a branch of theology that focuses on death, judgment, and the final destiny of the soul of mankind. Van der Leew (1949/1983) offered this definition:

> By eschatology we mean man's utterances in so far as they refer to events at the margin of the world before it was world, and after it has ceased to be world. It includes the glory of the first day but also the horror of the last day, *novissima rerum*. (p. 336)

In this way, Perry's research findings support the experience of psychosis as calling into categories aligned in eschatological explorations, not only the *return to beginnings* but also *cosmic conflicts*, the *novissima rerum*, in worldwide clashes between good and evil, Armageddon, or the Last Judgment. Perry (2005) defined the delusional category related to a *return to beginnings* as delusions of center that express themselves in the well-known mythic and Biblical creation stories, for example, "Garden of Eden, waters of the abyss, early steps in evolution, primitive tribal society, [or] creation of planets" (p. 35). Perry's category of *center* also has eschatological echoes. In this sense, it is related to "the happy primordial past, where heaven and earth had not yet split apart" (van der Leeuw, 1949/1983, p. 336).

All four autobiographical excerpts explore these creation stories on two levels: creation of the universe or earth and also the creation of the embodied human. Custance (1954) summarized his experience in this vein:

> The idea of salvation through catastrophe, which often takes the definite apocalyptic shape of a Last Judgment and a Second Coming, has dominated every manic period I have ever had .... In any event I am sure that a fundamental pattern in the Collective Unconscious must somehow be involved, and that this pattern largely controls our age. (p. 190)

There are specific Biblical passages and religious figures that move throughout all of the autobiographical material. And while some of the experiences can be seen as a connection to Biblical themes that are known to the patient, for example when Custance (1951) connected with the Book of Luke, the messages came as reinforcement of themes of Armageddon. This muddies the debate about the personal versus collective unconscious that post-Jungians debate. However, the material rises in service to general and collective impulse to explain an underlying vision of catastrophe. Furthermore, this is not always the case. In some instances, psychotic material rises first, and matches Biblical passages. This lack of personal connection to suprapersonal material is, of course, what pushed Jung into an idea of an *a priori* collective repository in the first place.

We cannot overlook the Western sample in this research and the nature of the religious material. However, scholarly study of cross-cultural exploration of eschatological themes is vast in its own right. It includes: Von Franz's (1990, 1996, 1997) body of work on myth and fairy tale; the work of Van der Leew from above; and compendiums on cross-cultural eschatological study that dwarf any connections Jung or post-Jungians have attempted, for example the *Oxford Handbook of Eschatology* (Walls, 2008). Jung retroactively began to study such connections because of the repetitive nature of material connecting the severely mentally ill with these ancient stories, but he is most certainly not alone in recognizing their archetypal patterns.

Moving forward

In his 1931 essay, "Basic Postulates of the Collective Unconscious," Jung (1931/1969) wrote:

> If it were possible to personify the unconscious, we might think of it as a collective human being combining the characteristics of both sexes, transcending youth and age, birth and death, and, from having at its command a human experience of one or two million years, practically immortal. If such a being existed, it would be exalted above all temporal change; the present would mean neither more nor less to it than any year in the hundredth millennium before Christ; it would be a dreamer of age-old dreams and, owing to its limitless experience, an incomparable prognosticator. It would have lived countless times over again the life of the individual, the family, the tribe, and the nation, and it would possess a living sense of the rhythm of growth, flowering, and decay. (pp. 349–350 [*CW* 8, para. 673])

Psychotic manifestation of eschatological debates—the apotheosis into the gods or goddesses—are extreme. It is an unfortunate dilemma to deal with the movement of eschatological debates and the discovery of replicable insights into the universe that advance and retreat in such fashion. But deal with it we must. As the conversation moves into the next chapter, challenges to what these repetitive themes can be attributed will be looked at more closely.

Note

1 Tables presented here, and in the chapters to follow, were presented in dissertation (Durchslag, 2015) and published for the first time in Durchslag (2016).

References

American Psychiatric Association (APA). (2013). *Diagnostic and statistical manual of mental disorders (DSM-5)* (5th ed.). Washington, DC: American Psychiatric Publishing.

Boisen, A. T. (1936). *The exploration of the inner world: A study of mental disorder and religious experience*. Philadelphia: University of Pennsylvania Press.

Coate, M. (1965). *Beyond all reason*. Philadelphia, PA: J. B. Lippincott.

Custance, J. (1951). *Wisdom, madness and folly: The philosophy of a lunatic*. London: Victor Gollancz.

Custance, J. (1954). *Adventure into the unconscious*. London: Christopher Johnson.

Durchslag, H. B. (2015). A narrative analysis of bipolar psychosis: An empirical relationship between neurochemistry and the collective unconscious. (Doctoral Dissertation). Retrieved from Proquest https://search.proquest.com/docview/1668380821.

Durchslag, H. B. (2016). Severe mental illness: A bridge between neurochemistry and the collective unconscious. *Psychological Perspectives*, 59(1), pp. 30–45. doi:10.1080/00332925.2016.1134210.

Goodwin, F. K., & Jamison, K. R. (2007). *Manic-depressive illness: Bipolar disorders and recurrent depression*. New York, NY: Oxford University Press.

Hogenson, G. B. (2004). Archetypes: Emergence and the psyche's deep structure. In J. Cambray & L. Carter (Eds.), *Analytical psychology: Contemporary perspectives in Jungian analysis* (pp. 32–55). New York, NY: Routledge.

Jung, C. G. (1931/1969). The structure of the psyche. In H. Read, M. Fordham, G. Adler, & W. McGuire (Eds.), *The collected works of C.G. Jung* (R. F. C. Hull, Trans.) (2nd ed., Vol. 8, pp. 139–158). Princeton, NJ: Princeton University Press.

Jung, C. G. (1936/1968). The concept of the collective unconscious. In H. Read, M. Fordham, G. Adler, & W. McGuire (Eds.), *The collected works of C. G. Jung* (R. F. C. Hull, Trans.) (2nd ed., Vol. 9, part I, pp. 42–53). Princeton, NJ: Princeton University Press.

Jung, C. G. (1938). *Psychology and religion: Based on the Terry Lectures delivered at Yale University*. New Haven, CT: Yale University Press.

Jung, C. G. (1940/1968). Concerning rebirth. In H. Read, M. Fordham, G. Adler, & W. McGuire (Eds.), *The collected works of C. G. Jung* (R. F. C. Hull, Trans.) (2nd ed., Vol. 9, part I, pp. 111–147). Princeton, NJ: Princeton University Press.

Jung, C. G. (1953). Foreword. In J. W. Perry, *The self in psychotic process: Its symbolization in schizophrenia* (pp. v–viii). Berkeley, CA: University of California Press.

Jung, C. G. (1968). The archetypes and the collective unconscious. In H. Read, M. Fordham, G. Adler, & W. McGuire (Eds.), *The collected works of C. G. Jung* (R. F. C. Hull, Trans.) (Vol. 9, part I). Princeton, NJ: Princeton University Press.

Jung, C. G. (1952/1976). Foreword. In H. Read, M. Fordham, G. Adler, & W. McGuire (Eds.), *The collected works of C. G. Jung* (R. F. C. Hull, Trans.) (Vol. 18). Princeton, NJ: Princeton University Press.

Marneros, A., & Angst, J. (2000). Bipolar disorders: Roots and evolution. In A. Marneros & J. Angst (Eds.), *Bipolar disorders: 100 years after manic depressive insanity*. Boston, MA: Kluwer Academic Publishers.
Perry, J. W. (1953). *The self in psychotic process: Its symbolization in schizophrenia*. Berkeley, CA: University of California Press.
Perry, J. W. (1975). Jung and the new approach to psychosis. *Psychological Perspectives: A Quarterly Journal on Jungian Thought*, 6(1), 37–49. doi:10.1080/00332927508409433.
Perry, J. W. (1999). *Trials of the visionary mind: Spiritual emergency and the renewal process*. Albany, NY: State University of New York.
Perry, J. W. (2005). *The far side of madness* (2nd ed.). Putnam, CT: Spring Publications.
Roesler, C. (2012). Are archetypes transmitted more by culture than biology? Questions arising from conceptualizations of the archetype. *Journal of Analytical Psychology*, 57, 223–246.
Van Der Leew, G. (1949/1983). Primordial time and final time. In J. Campbell (Ed.), *Man and time: Papers from the Eranos Yearbooks, vol. 3* (pp. 324–350). Princeton, NJ: Princeton University Press.
Von Franz, M. (1990). *Individuation in fairy tales*. Boston, MA: Shambhala.
Von Franz, M. (1992). *Psyche and matter*. Boston, MA: Shambhala.
Von Franz, M. (1996). *The interpretation of fairy tales*. Boston, MA: Shambhala.
Von Franz, M. (1997). *Archetypal patterns in fairy tales*. Toronto, Canada: Inner City Books.
Walls, J. (2008). *The Oxford handbook of eschatology*. New York, NY: Oxford University Press.

Chapter 5

The personal narrative of psychosis

The naturally occurring variable

One of the criticisms related to an exploration of a collective unconscious and its archetypal patterning is what is sometimes perceived as a contrived effort to "provide so-called scientific 'proof' for the existence of archetypes" (Mills, 2018, p. 4). For example, there were two empirical studies performed in the 1990s in which archetype was examined by looking at its constellation in images and symbols (Maloney, 1999; Rosen, Smith, Huston, & Gonzalez, 1991). First, controlling for conscious knowledge of particular symbols, Rosen et al. (1991) utilized the Archetypal Symbol Inventory (ASI) to assess whether the archetypal nature of certain symbols produced unique memory recall patterns when compared with non-archetypal symbols. The results supported "Jung's theory of the collective unconscious and the idea that it contains ancient memory traces embedded in archetypes" (p. 220). Second, Maloney (1999) utilized preference ratings for archetypal images of mother and hero with either a positive, negative, or neutral valence as chosen by the researcher. Results supported (1) a "robust" connection between archetypal imagery and adult cognition; and (2) consistency "with the hypothesis that the innate structure of the human mind produces 'apparent' content, thereby shaping human experience and culture" (p. 111). These two studies supported the presence of archetypal patterns related to anima (mother) and Self (hero) in non-delusional states.

Ignoring for a moment that all experimental designs are contrived by the very nature of their mission, my own experience was organic, and the independent variable constellated itself in the very nature of the experience. Monotherapy for bipolar I disorder is the exception: most courses of treatment include a combination of two mood stabilizers or of mood stabilizers in combination with atypical antipsychotics (Stahl, 2013). The fact that I was on monotherapy prior to my decisions to titrate off of my medication simplifies matters a great deal as this research explores the relationship between psychopharmacology and the collective unconscious. Simply, there is only one drug that can be considered the independent variable. The psychopharmacological action of *Lamictal* kept imagery from the collective unconscious fettered. The removal of the psychopharmacological action opened the gate for psychotic flooding of mythic material into consciousness.

Temporality

A core methodological step in this research was the creation of a narrative reflecting my own experience with psychosis during a specific time period during which I was no longer taking my mood stabilizer, Lamictal. My initial dose of Lamictal was 400 mg daily (200 mg BID). The titration schedule suggested by my psychiatrist was to decrease the dosage by 25 mg per week. I began this process on April 11, 2006. Email correspondence, journal entries, psychiatric progress notes, and my yearly planner for 2006 were analyzed for the 5-month period between April and September 2006. The portion of the narrative used for data analysis is primarily limited to the brief period of time in July 2006, during which my medication levels fell below 50 mg of Lamictal, which, according to the sources gathered, began on July 10, 2006. This is the point at which regular life seemed to come to a standstill. Prior to this, I was still working, attending meetings, communicating with friends and family, making plans for the future, going to my psychiatrist, my analyst, and accomplishing daily tasks of living. Emails I sent prior to this period seemed unremarkable for the most part, and were answered in equally unremarkable fashion (Durchslag, 2016). I was hospitalized 9 days after I fell below 50 mg of Lamictal, on July 19, 2006.

Thematic analysis

The final transcript of this stream of consciousness narrative was approximately 12,000 words. Coding for content, I found approximately 70 instances which fell into the archetypal patterns explicated in the previous chapter. Table 5.1 highlights the thematic replication in the autobiographical narratives according to Perry's (2005) categories outlined in Chapter 4.

Although there are no references to sacred marriage or the birth of the savior in the narrative of the time from July 10–July 19, 2006, stream of consciousness writing spanning the time from my admittance to the hospital in Massachusetts until my discharge in Cleveland (July 19–September 2, 2006) has multiple references to both, along with continued delusions related to death, apotheosis, cosmic conflict, world and national reform, return to beginnings, and new society. Three of the general archetypal categories—cosmic conflict, apotheosis, and new society—were repeated between 8 and 18 times throughout the narrative. Death, although only surfacing twice, was a strong theme toward the end of the narrative. Specifically related to the constellation of the hero archetype, two categories, initiation to qualify for leadership and world or national reform, occurred over five times. In many respects, the separation of these categories is difficult to maintain. Themes of cosmic conflict were directly related to world and national reform, as well as to new society.

64 The personal narrative of psychosis

Table 5.1 Coding of delusional content in personal narrative

General categories	
Categories	References in text
center	3
Death	2
Return to beginnings	2
Cosmic conflict	8
Apotheosis	10
Sacred marriage	none
New birth	3
New society	18
Quadrated world	none
Political or religious constellations of hero archetype	
Categories	References in text
Election to divine or royal supreme rule	None
Election as either political or spiritual savior	3
Supremacy of the goddess	4
Virgin mother giving birth to the savior	none
Initiation to qualify for leadership	5
World or national reform	11

Table 5.2 highlights how these themes compared with thematic content in the other autobiographical accounts (Boisen, 1936; Coate, 1965; Custance 1951, 1954).

My narrative aligned with others' in 7 out of 10 categories. Three additional references were made more specifically related to the eros of mother earth and anima identified in Boisen's, Custance's, and Perry's (2005) case analyses, which will be expanded upon below.

Synopsis

Without interruption of categorical alignment, a sketch of the psychotic storyline is as follows: I am convinced that the hegemonic power structure in the United States is going to be challenged. The marginalized and disenfranchised Black culture is positioned and ready to overthrow the Federal government—the seat of White hegemonic culture—in an orchestrated coup, a coup in which I play a central role. White Nationalist neo-Nazis are aligned as the military arm of the Federal government. The battle is of Biblical proportions: the country is going to be flooded and burned. There is a younger generation of Americans that has known this has had to happen for quite some time, but they have been waiting for our generation to take action. In

Table 5.2 Replication of Perry's (2005) delusional categories in autobiographical selections

Categories	Autobiographical accounts			
	Boisen	Custance	Coate	Durchslag
center	•	•	•	•
Death				•
Return to beginnings	•	•	•	•
Cosmic conflict	•	•	•	•
Threat of opposite				
Apotheosis		•	•	•
Sacred marriage		•		
New birth	•	•	•	•
New society	•	•	•	•
Quadrated world				

the meantime, they have been the quiet Resistance across the country. This youth movement was most recognizable in the fluid nature of fashion trends and gender identification. When the fighting and destruction is over, my hometown of Cleveland Heights, OH will be the new seat of government.

I am responsible for leading "innocents" to safety on Martha's Vineyard, MA, off of the mainland of the United States, where we will wait until it is safe to return. On July 18, 2006, after performing several rituals to prepare for battle and leaving instructions for those who would be fortifying the city, I leave in my car to begin the caravan. The war has begun. As my 700-mile journey continues, I realize that the neo-Nazis have been tipped off about the coup. They have begun to mobilize and have come out onto the highways. I increasingly realize that the coup has failed and that I, personally, have failed in my military responsibility. I am despondent and believe I have lost the right to live. I wait to be killed by my own army. When my car breaks down, I get out and begin walking down the median of the highway, convinced that my body will soon fade out of existence entirely, that I am moving into the realm of the otherworld, what it looks like I don't know.

Thematic analysis using Perry's categories

Cosmic conflict, national reform, and new society

The cosmic conflict at hand was based in political issues in the United States as I saw them: a clash between a white ruling class and a minority population. Referential and nihilistic delusions began to pervade the environment in which I lived:

There is an assisted living facility across the street. It is an apartment building, like mine, but it has a grand circular driveway where the special medical transport vehicles line up and wait for their next group to take to the grocery store, the doctor's office, wherever. They are mostly black faces in the driver's seats. I can see them from above. The proof of a minority service class that takes care of all things for the ruling class. The white class. Nurses aides, drivers, orderlies, there they are, right across the street fulfilling indispensable duties for minimum wage. The vans are lined up to do their jobs. But I also know they are waiting for us. Waiting for the signal. They will ride out like the warrior convoy that they are. The meek shall inherit the earth. The white man will wither in the unfettered heat of the sun blasting through without the protection of the ozone layer. White men did that, too. They will burn first. They will die first. And the time of the brown skin can rise again. These vans will move on you. The ancient lands on the edge of the lake will be taken by the righteous once again. This land will belong to the righteous once more, and a new breed of the white race, returned to the ancient brown skin of things, will blend humanity through the deepening of things, a return of the deep colors of soul. We are the inhabitants of ancient glacial lands from the continent that held the beginning of things [Cleveland]. We will do our deed as the final stronghold after the floods, when the meek shall inherit the earth, and as the leaders in battle, we will hold court from above.

Any institution that seemed related to a hegemonic power structure was scoffed at, including the police. For example, driving by a police cruiser at the start of my journey to Martha's Vineyard, the narrative stated:

A police cruiser rolls by going the opposite way. We both have our windows open, it's a beautiful night, so we see one another quite clearly as we pass, but he has no idea what has been put in motion. It's too late, I think. You guys are fucked.

The effort to secure the roads to allow the righteous to make it to Martha's Vineyard was threatened by the white race. In response to increasing traffic on the road, the narrative read:

We have got to move out. The highway is getting crowded now. Full of people. Traffic is slow and full in both lanes. If we don't move now, we won't get everybody over. The roads are bottlenecking, and these Aryan stone white fuckheads are going to catch wind. They are not that stupid.

The "browning of things" cited above related to the idea of a blending of all things. There would no longer be racial divides and clashes, but a new culture that reflected the positive attributes of both white and minority groups. The

Aryan subgroup of white culture reflected the extreme perversity of what unintegrated society becomes.

This lens of cosmic conflict, world reform, and new society pervaded many of the personal interactions I had in ways that align with the APA's (2013) generalized category of referential delusions (see Table 5.1). For example, a man I met at a writer's conference became someone enlisted to defend the eastern seaboard (he was moving to North Carolina). A custodian I knew from the apartment building next door was enlisted as someone similar to what the Secret Service would be for a politician.

My vision of a new society aligned with Perry's (2005) definition of a new world order that reflected an enlightened society or Utopia, a new world age of peace. A local coffee shop represented this enlightened society:

> I go inside and order coffee at the counter. The young, 20-something man that serves me is in full black eyeliner and mascara. He is friendly, intense, unabashed. We look at each other and smile. I scan the scene behind the counter. Other young hipsters in heavy black eye makeup—young men and women—piercings, tattoos, spiked hair, messy hair, sweet smiles. They are all versions of one another, male or female, radical individuals among radical individuals. An underlying peace to them, an underlying knowing that they are starting something. That the revolution has been brewing for a few years now .... They have grown up with this energy. We are older and have had to reconnect to it. I think to myself, this is how it is all becoming. We are at the Phoenix [the name of the coffee house], where the new rises from the ashes, and it is a new androgyny, where boys can be in full makeup and girls can sport crewcuts and combat boots. The sexuality has mixed and no one seems bothered. They are at one with both the masculine and the feminine. It is a group energy now. The music is playing in the background, the servers and baristas simply doing what they do, in the model of the world that is going to come.

The androgyny of the coffee baristas reflected the idea of comfort with gender identity and sexuality outside of rigid stereotypical norms.

A final way in which the new society and world reform expressed itself in the psychotic narrative was through a blending of religions and religious stereotypes. For example, to prepare for battle, "I use what I've learned from the last vestiges of a noble ruling class," which "model inconspicuous fortune." I categorize this as "the Christian way." In contrast, I write, "As a Jew, I know about flash and consumption." There is the undertone here that Jews have something to learn from stereotypical images of the white Anglo-Saxon protestant, which, for me, were representative of the ruling class. However, the narrative places Jews as the leaders of the revolution:

> The leaders that have taken their rightful throne on the promised land of Martha's Vineyard are not from the Christian ruling class. This couple is

Jewish .... They are the Judaic equivalent of Zeus and Hera. They are the immortals.

This blending of religion is explored in more detail below related to apotheosis and messianism. The fact that I am Jewish did nothing to keep me from identifying with either being the messiah or giving birth to the messiah, nor did it keep me from identifying with Christ's journey to the cross.

My psychotic self believed that Cleveland would be "the new site of the country's brain trust." Its residents would be spared from the flood. It could be seen as the New Jerusalem. The place of refuge during the flood would be a community center:

> I look down at the basketball courts and bleachers below. I see African-American faces, mothers, children, young men, grown men. They sit on the bleachers and watch the world go by. I know that this is the shelter for everyone to come to for safety. I know they know this is their safe space. They will all rally here on higher ground, protected, waiting for the worst of the fighting to be over, waiting for the flood waters to recede and begin anew. It is a beautiful sight, a reassuring sight. We are moving, coming out of hiding, the troops are waiting for our signal.

The day before my hospitalization, I walked out of the community center with the idea that the message about the start of the revolution had been received:

> As I walk out the doors of the community center, a tall, thin, black man comes in. He is clearly a runner. He has the body of a marathon runner, like the ones we see from Kenya. Long, lanky, sinewy. As we pass each other in the doorway, I look him in the eyes and he looks in mine. We hold eye contact as we pass each other. He has come. The messenger has made it to safety. He will deliver his message to general-god, and will most likely have to be on his way again. Running, sending messages.

I even asked one of the orderlies in the hospital in Massachusetts if "he had people in Cleveland" I could help bring to safety.

Initiation to qualify for leadership

There were several different scenarios related to proving myself worthy for my leadership role in the revolution. For example, during the time period after my medication had dropped below 50 mg of Lamictal, I choked on a piece of food while having dinner with a friend who became amplified into the role of "general-god." The narrative read, "Later, I realize this was training for when I actually had to swallow the blank rune [representing a type of amulet]." The night I left for Martha's Vineyard (July 18, 2006), after I had swallowed several amulets (including the rune mentioned above, an opal, and an acorn) I also had to perform a ritual bath:

> I've made a shallow bath, just enough to skim over the tops of my thighs and up to my belly button. I am sitting in the silence, breathing, and again know what I have to do. I realize that when I submerge my head, I am risking death. I can picture myself under the bath water with my eyes open, staring up at the bright, high ceiling. Does the universe support me or doesn't it? I know this is a test. If I am truly ready for this journey, I will drown and survive. I lay flat and long on the bottom of the porcelain tub and just lean back, resting my head on the porcelain tub bottom. And then we will see. Radical trust. My heart is beating.

I left my apartment shortly after the bath and began the 700-mile road trip to Martha's Vineyard. The narrative captured five different rest stops along the way. I was taken to an emergency room approximately 130 miles away from Woods Hole, MA, which is the site to catch the ferry to Martha's Vineyard.

Apotheosis, national reform, and new society

The category of apotheosis relates to the psychotic delusion that the person has become either royal or divine. Apotheosis is a central element of the archetypal stories of the hero. At times, the narrative reflected the belief that I would be a political leader, for example, the connection to the building custodian mentioned above. The narrative read, "I lean forward and ask him if I can count on him. I tell him, every Jewish white girl in politics needs a black man standing guard." Later, the narrative reads, "I can't tell if I'll be 'the woman behind the man,' organizing dinners and get-togethers of the power brokers within the new order, or whether I'll be the leader, herself. It bounces back and forth." APA (2013) criteria define this type of delusion as grandiose, a delusion that someone has exceptional abilities, wealth, or fame. It also verges on persecutory because there is belief that a body guard will be necessary. However, these broad categories miss the connection to the archetypal myth of the hero.

The narrative of this psychosis also captured the divine pole of the hero archetype. I was a political leader at times, but at other times, I was the messiah. The narrative read:

> I think some people realize that the messiah is now walking amongst them, others are clueless. But those that are aware keep it to themselves, like when a famous person is trying to be inconspicuous and they are surrounded by like-minded people who wish to offer the space they require. Many have seen [my] car .... It is a remarkable thing, I think to

myself, that this is happening. How can this be? Can we really be on the verge of something wonderful? It's time. It's really time.

The political nature of the journey and the strategic importance and symbolism of Martha's Vineyard is reinforced as the passage above continues:

> We will settle in there just fine. After all, the Kennedys have had a compound there for decades. People used to see Jackie on a little motor boat in their lagoon. People just drive by on their way to work, carpenters, gardeners, shop owners, and say, yep, Jackie's out today. And of course the Clintons, although they were not low key, but they were not meant to be. They inhabited the official seat of government. Of course, the Vineyard seems a perfectly natural spot. The officially unofficial court of kings. For the democrats, of course. The republicans use Maine. They have the stronghold now.
>
> But we have the power gods in place. Olympus is lording and there's no more need for subtlety, at least on the unofficial court of kings. Until we can cleanse the rest and move back to the mainland.

A reference to the egalitarian nature of the new society is also seen in the easy coexistence of "political royalty" and the middle or working classes.

The last stop I made before being taken to the hospital was in Massachusetts. This portion of the narrative shows the confluence between the multiple categories of delusional content. In the following passage, my role of messiah and the cosmic conflict story of the Last Judgment come together as they are connected to the need for national reform:

> I'm in Massachusetts now. The vistas are wider. I am grateful to have made it this far. Once over the New York border, it's only 200 miles to the ferry. It's within reach. I pull over to a rest area. Time to connect to this landscape, the renewed openness and freshness of things.
>
> I get closer to the main building, and I see a lovely little area with a fountain, some benches, landscaping. I think, how beautiful, what a perfect balance, a wonderful compromise and accommodation for the necessary ugliness of concrete interstates and parking lots. And people are actually sitting on the benches, enjoying this retreat and respite. This makes me happy. I go to revel in the respite, as well.
>
> The fountain has been created like a small stream that flows into a pool. There are landscaped banks around this pool, benches and such, but there is room to sit right on the ground, wood-chipped mulch I think. Maybe just dirt. But not grass, at least not where I chose to sit down, because once I sat down I was able to run my fingers through the earth, pick up the mulch or the dirt or both, run it through my fingers, revel in the rootedness to nature. Did I splash in the water? I'm not sure. The water might have been what set me off.

Because soon I begin to feel the perversion of it all, the disappointment. My stomach sinks inside of itself and turns black, cavernous. The people on the benches are looking at me, no love in their hearts. Coldness. The caricatures of all that is wrong with our American culture. Fast-food fed, strip-mall clothed, mass-media duped, close-minded fools with no idea how to appreciate truth, earth, love. These eyes around me are cold eyes, greasy eyes, self-satisfied eyes with folded arms resting on fat folds of stomach. There is a deity sitting amongst them, a key to their saving grace here, in the dirt, hoping for the peace of the place, the resurrection of the twisted culture that has enveloped us, the very reason we are on this journey at all. To root it out. To flood it out. To burn it out.

I begin to see the water for what it is: chemical-laden, thick with its additives. The pool is plastic at the bottom, meant to look blue. It is the degradation of what's left of our appreciation. This is probably nature to these people. This is enough for them. A poisoned pool in the middle of a parking lot. I am disgusted. And I am angry.

My heart begins to pound, slowly, purposefully, deeply, like a drum beat. My gut is pulsing with it. My blood is coursing and alive. My eyes are slits, powerful, mean, but inside my heart is breaking. I am shaking my head from side to side in my mind's eye. You have failed. You have failed. You have disrespected the beauty of the savior among you with your mean cold distant stares.

The narrative traces my action of going into a bathroom in the main building to wash myself off (I had been sitting in the dirt). Again, it references a final judgment and a conflict on a cosmic scale:

For a moment I feel as though I must clean up my mess. And then I realize, fuck you. Clean up your own fucking mess you horrible mass of ants. Your earth is going to shake. And when you realize what you've done, when you realize that the savior has been walking amongst you and you have shunned it, you will have the flash of fear before you die, thinking, please, I'll never do it again, but it's too late. Judgment comes swift and hard.

Themes of becoming the messiah and/or a prime political figure persisted throughout the entire period leading into my second hospitalization in Cleveland. Even more specifically, these were Christian images of the messiah, of Christ, and of new birth of the divine child (also part of Perry's delusional categories). Such broad Christian images were clearly figures I was conscious of in my normal scope of experience. However, I was raised in a secular Jewish household with very little exposure to Biblical scripture. These archetypal themes belonged more to my psychotic delusions than to anything from my personal life.

Death

The delusional category of death that showed up in my psychosis was not something that was identified in the narrative analysis of the other autobiographies (Boisen, 1936; Coate, 1965; Custance, 1951, 1954). However, my own narrative reflected Perry's (2005) category in which the person experiencing the delusion has already died and is communicating in an afterlife. The psychotic story was of a failed offensive to get people to safety on Martha's Vineyard. The narrative read: "The roads have been compromised .... It will not be as clean as we'd hoped." My own role in the offensive was over:

> I feel an overwhelming sense of sadness, but also fear. Fear of death, fear of disappointing my family of gods with my cowardice. But this is nothing new. These are the tests I have already faced with courage, and this is just another. I am a goddess, and I have performed with the bravery that was needed as a leader of troops. And now I need to step aside for a new tactic .... I will join them soon enough, or I will be sacrificed. This is their choice and I am ready to sacrifice myself for the cause. This is the work of the savior. To face sacrifice, death, for the hopes of a new order.

I believed that I had already died prior to being put into an ambulance and taken to the hospital. There was an indeterminate time during which I was walking along the median of the highway before being picked up. The narrative reads:

> Will I just continue walking? When will I become invisible and simply meld off out of my human form? Or maybe this is meant to be the long, hot journey, naked, alone, the martyr, or the fallen, like carrying the cross and posing a final test to the passer-bys. Kindness brings you salvation. Leers and mean laughter damnation.

When I was finally admitted to the psychiatric ward from the emergency room, I thought the other patients I met were the gods and goddesses of Olympus.

Aftermath

Obviously, I did not disappear into the ether. I remained quite visible. As referenced above, on July 19, 2006, I was picked up by an ambulance while walking naked on a stretch of median on Interstate 90-East, approximately 200 miles from Martha's Vineyard. I was hospitalized for 20 days. I refused medication at the hospital, although they forcibly sedated me on multiple occasions. On or about July 27, I was threatened with becoming a ward of the State of Massachusetts unless I began the medication regime being advised by the psychiatrist.[1] I acquiesced and was finally released, as officially noted in medical notes, "against doctor's orders," on August 7. I immediately threw out my medications and drove back to Cleveland, OH. I was re-hospitalized just 13 days later, on August 21, 2006. I was on some combination of atypical antipsychotics and mood stabilizers throughout what would become a 12-day hospitalization. I initiated legal proceedings to petition for my release and was finally discharged, again against doctor's orders, on September 1, 2006. At the time of discharge, I was taking Abilify (aripiprazole), 30 mg QD (daily). Hospital discharge notes stated:

> The patient was initially manic on admission, was extremely irritable, grandiose, and entitled. At time of discharge she was much more friendly, she was apologetic for previous interactions stating that she felt well .... She was talkative, pleasant, and her speech was within normal limits on discharge.

This is not to say that I was functioning normally, only that my behavior had become less symptomatic based on diagnostic criteria. There was no longer sufficient evidence to keep me hospitalized. Discharge notes used a Global Assessment of Functioning (GAF) scale (APA, 2000). On a scale of 0–100, my GAF was 40, which still marks major impairment in reality testing, judgment, mood, ability to work, and ability to maintain healthy social or familial relationships. In fact, I remember still experiencing referential and grandiose delusions after release, although these delusions were qualitatively different from those I experienced without medication. There was no connecting theme or narrative, just isolated distortions that rose for brief moments and faded.

The challenge moving forward

Overall, I spent five of the seven weeks between July 19 and September 3, 2006 hospitalized. I had not been hospitalized since the onset of my illness 17 years prior; nor have I been hospitalized in the 12 years since. Clearly, I am asking the reader to consider that a determining factor in this psychotic upheaval was due to the removal of my pharmaceutical medication. I doubt the reader need entirely abandon the psychodynamic frame to acknowledge the medical perspective has enough weight to examine. Before moving ahead to the next chapter, which will focus on pharmaceutical action more specifically, I will repeat a challenge from Chapter 3. First, if psychosis sits most heavily within attachment and trauma, the critic must find answer as to why my neurotic, but relatively stable, ego crumbled when medication was discontinued, and why, after medication was replaced, I went back to my neurotic pathologies of the past. Second, we must contend with a reinforcement of material that is transpersonal and collective in nature.

Jung's notion was to imagine and label a repository that might hold and somehow offer the consistent patterns of psychological story and insight. Any acknowledgment of pharmaceutical action on the narrative content explored in this and the previous chapter demands consideration of a connection between our physiology and these themes. A growing body of post-Jungian literature questions if such a thing is feasible in light of quantitative research on the human brain and how it functions (Knox, Merchant, & Hogenson, 2010; Goodwyn, 2010a, 2010b, 2012, 2013; Haule, 2011; Merchant, 2006, 2009; Tresan, 1996, 2013). Post-Jungian arguments utilize the increasingly crowded data on brain development and biological functions to highlight the sheer impossibility of a brain which "contains" or "holds in its stores" the complex storylines and imagery posited to exist in the unknown realm of the collective unconscious. Brooke (2015) highlighted:

> It is true that Jung's attempt to situate the archetypes in the structure of the brain violates his methodological and epistemological limits; and it is true that between salts, fatty acids, genes, and neurons, on one hand, and experience and meaning on the other is an unbridgeable ontological and conceptual chasm. (p. 149)

Many post-Jungians engaged in the debate have reached the conclusion that Jung's conceptualization of archetype is not supported because the human brain has no means of carrying complex images prior to consciousness. Therefore, according to these trends, the transpersonal themes explored in this book thus far are linked to my, and others', personal unconscious of implicit memory. Merchant (2006) summarized the broad implications of this theoretical shift: "it collapses the 'sacred heritage' approach to archetypes and it removes the conceptual division between the collective and personal unconscious" (Merchant, 2006, p. 51)

My research, which captures the impressions and research done by others more so than my own, challenges this notion.

Note

1 In practice, the term voluntary only suffices to contrast it with involuntary hospitalization: with the former, you have legal recourse to petition for release; with the latter, you have no legal recourse and release is at the sole discretion of the institution.

References

American Psychiatric Association (APA). (2000). *Diagnostic and statistical manual of mental disorders (DSM-IV-TR)* (4th ed., text revision). Arlington, VA: American Psychiatric Association.

American Psychiatric Association. (2013). *Diagnostic and statistical manual of mental disorders (DSM-5)* (5th ed.). Washington, DC: American Psychiatric Publishing.
Boisen, A. T. (1936). *The exploration of the inner world: A study of mental disorder and religious experience.* Philadelphia: University of Pennsylvania Press.
Brooke, R. (2015). *Jung and phenomenology.* New York, NY: Routledge.
Coate, M. (1965). *Beyond all reason.* Philadelphia, PA: J. B. Lippincott.
Custance, J. (1951). *Wisdom, madness and folly: The philosophy of a lunatic.* London: Victor Gollancz.
Custance, J. (1954). *Adventure into the unconscious.* London: Christopher Johnson.
Durchslag, H. B. (2016). Severe mental illness: A bridge between neurochemistry and the collective unconscious. *Psychological Perspectives*, 59(1), 30–45. doi:10.1080/00332925.2016.1134210.
Goodwyn, E. D. (2010a). Approaching archetypes: Reconsidering innateness. *Journal of Analytical Psychology*, 55, 502–521.
Goodwyn, E. D. (2010b). The author replies. *Journal of Analytical Psychology*, 55, 550–555.
Goodwyn, E. D. (2012). *The neurobiology of the gods: How brain physiology shapes the recurrent imagery of myth and dreams.* Hove, UK: Routledge.
Goodwyn, E. D. (2013). Recurrent motifs as resonant attractor states in the narrative field: A testable model of archetype. *Journal of Analytical Psychology*, 58, 387–408.
Haule, J. R. (2011). *Jung in the 21st century: Evolution and archetype* (Vol. 1). London: Routledge.
Knox, J., Merchant, J., & Hogenson, G. B. (2010). Response to Erik Goodwyn's "Approaching archetypes: reconsidering innateness." *Journal of Analytical Psychology*, 55, 522–549.
Maloney, A. (1999). Preference ratings of images representing archetypal themes: An empirical study of the concept of archetypes. *Journal of Analytical Psychology*, 44(1), 101–117.
Merchant, J. (2006). The developmental/emergent model of archetype, its implications and its application to shamanism. *Journal of Analytical Psychology*, 51, 125–144.
Merchant, J. (2009). A reappraisal of classical archetypal theory and its implications for theory and practice. *Journal of Analytical Psychology*, 54, 339–358.
Mills, J. (2018). The essence of archetypes. *International Journal of Jungian Studies*, 10(3), 199–220. doi:10.1080/19409052.2018.1503808.
Perry, J. W. (2005). *The far side of madness* (2nd ed.). Putnam, CT: Spring Publications.
Rosen, D. H., Smith, S. M., Huston, H. L., Gonzalez, G. (1991). Empirical study of associations between symbols and their meanings: Evidence of collective unconscious (archetypal) memory. *Journal of Analytical Psychology*, 36(2), 211–228.
Stahl, S. M. (2013). *Stahl's essential psychopharmacology: Neuroscientific basis and practical applications.* New York, NY: Cambridge University Press.
Tresan, D. (1996). Jungian metapsychology and neurobiological theory. *Journal of Analytical Psychology*, 41(3), 399–436.
Tresan, D. (2013). A commentary on "A structural-phenomenological typology of mind-matter correlations" by H. Atmanspacher and W. Fach. *Journal of Analytical Psychology*, 58, 245–253.

Chapter 6

The brain and pharmaceutical actions

The difficult dilemma of the brain

The human brain has been subjected to dissection and analysis since the humans that utilize it began to self-reflect from a scientific perspective. Its mysteries continue to enchant and to daunt. Within post-Jungian discourse, it is also seen to hold the demise of Jung's notion of a collective unconscious. Jung's attributions to the brain and to archetype over the course of his lifetime were often changeable. But there is enough consistency to allow it to remain a constant point of return. For example, in Jung's essay, "The Psychological Foundations of Belief in Spirits," originally written in 1919, he offered the following, which I will quote at some length:

> The other part of the unconscious is what I call the impersonal or collective unconscious. As the name indicates, its contents are not personal but collective; that is, they do not belong to one individual alone but to a whole group of individuals, and generally to a whole nation, or even to the whole of mankind. These contents are not acquired during the individual's lifetime but are products of innate forms and instincts. Although the child possesses no inborn ideas, it nevertheless has a highly developed brain which functions in a quite definite way. This brain is inherited from its ancestors; it is the deposit of the psychic functioning of the whole human race. The child therefore brings with it an organ ready to function in the same way as it functioned throughout human history. In the brain the instincts are preformed, and so are the primordial images which have always been the basis of man's thinking—the whole treasure-house of mythological motifs. (Jung, 1948/1969, pp. 310–311 [*CW* 8, para. 589])

Jung moved specifically into looking at severe mental illness and schizophrenia:

> These contents can be seen most clearly in cases of mental derangement, especially in schizophrenia, where mythological images pour out in astonishing variety. Insane people frequently produce combinations of

ideas and symbols that could never be accounted for by experiences in
their individual lives, but only by the history of the human mind. It is
an instance of primitive, mythological thinking, which reproduces its own
primordial images, and is not a reproduction of conscious experiences.
(p. 311 [*CW* 8, para. 589])

So the reader can look back at the narrative categories and threads from the previous chapters and insert Jung's definition above.

Fast-forwarding 40 years, in one of Jung's last essays before his death in 1961, "Symbols and the Interpretation of Dreams," he stated much the same:

Just as the human body represents a whole museum of organs with a long evolutionary history behind them, so we should expect the mind to be organized in a similar way rather than to be a product without history. By "history" I do not mean the fact that the mind builds itself up through conscious tradition (language, etc.), but rather its biological, prehistoric, and unconscious development beginning with archaic man, whose psyche was still similar to that of an animal. This immensely old psyche forms the basis of our mind, just as the structure of our body is erected upon a generally mammalian anatomy. (Jung, 2011, pp. 107–108, para. 522)

So even without the purported moves related to Jung's definitions, his predilection to associate transpersonal material to the human brain remained close by.

However, as referenced at the end of the previous chapter, several post-Jungian arguments posit that through the lenses of cognition, brain development, the formation of image schema, and implicit and explicit memory, there is no means of understanding how mythic material could be transmitted as a common thread throughout the evolution and history of races and cultures. This demands critiques of even earlier models, including Lamarckism, nativism, and Darwinism (Atmanspacher & Fach, 2013; Hogenson, 2004; Knox, Merchant, & Hogenson, 2010; Merchant, 2006, 2009; Rensma, 2013; Saunders & Skar, 2001; Tresan, 1996, 2013). Erik Goodwyn (2010a, 2010b, 2019) has explored brain function and mythological imagery from the broadest perspective, including extensive research compiled in his book, *Neurobiology of the Gods* (Goodwyn, 2012), which attends to, addresses, and adds to most aspects of this complicated debate.[1] Most recently, the discussion has been renewed from a philosophical standpoint (Mills, 2018a, 2018b, 2019). Overall, the debate within the field is difficult. Tresan (1996) offered a challenge to the depth community almost 15 years ago:

In fact, it is my hope that by rethinking the brain, an organ necessary for the processing of individual realities, all psyches will recognize a totem ancestor which at the outset of life is neither Jungian or Freudian nor of

British Middle School extraction but simply an incredibly plastic, extraordinarily organized, three pounds of wondrous biological material that we each carry in our skulls. It is to be hoped that the common possession of this organ by each of us and the increasing ability to arrive at common agreements about how it works will diminish the nasty partisanship in the name of truth that has characterized the field of depth psychology from the time of its inception in the early 1900s to the present, but I doubt it. (p. 427)

The hopes for this book is to move debate forward from a different perspective, specifically through the lens of pharmacological action and its influence on the presence or absence of transpersonal material.

The brain: Action over system

Physiological focus

As analytical psychology is increasingly questioning the viability of Jung's work in an age of the brain, it is important to pay due attention to what is happening in the brain during the pharmacological interventions that mediate the complex rise of what seem to be a sort of gestalt eruption of once foreign collective material. Genetic research is fast becoming a key component of studying and understanding severe mental illness, but the treatment for these illnesses focuses on changing some type of movement between different pieces of the brain. We need look no farther than the fleeting trend of lobotomization, an intervention focused on manipulating the brain, itself, to see that the solution is not contained in brain matter, but in its complex networks of action. To highlight the active nature of the phenomena we are looking into, I have chosen to use the term *physiological* instead of *biological*. Definitions of biology suggest implanted systems over time, and can include explorations of most living creatures and systems. Physiology remains in the realm of activity, and is most often especially and uniquely human. It is considered a subset of biology, and looks at function and activity, especially related to cellular and chemical phenomena (Wolf, 1977). This caveat is meant to highlight the interest in the brain as a source of transmission, or the means of physiological activity, much more so than the exploration of particular parts of the brain and their unique functions. There are two ways in which the body transmits information: one is chemical, the other is electrical. Targets for atypical antipsychotic medications are primarily focused on the former; mood stabilizer on the latter.

Structure

Today, scientists can look at images of the brain from a bird's-eye view (dorsal); from the left or the right (lateral views); from the bottom up (ventral view); and from the inside out, like a cauliflower sliced in half (medial view)

(Kolb & Whishaw, 2009). Science has labeled four lobes—temporal, frontal, parietal, and occipital—and each of those can be looked at from any of the four angles above. We continue to be enchanted by what Tresan (1996) called "three pounds of wondrous biological material" (p. 427). For a cursory perspective, Kolb and Whishaw's (2009) image of the human fist serves the purpose. If we stare at the right fist so that we can see our fingers wrap round themselves, we can imagine the left hemisphere of the brain:

- The portion of our thumb that wraps around the tops of our fingers is the *temporal lobe*.
- The *frontal lobe* is the flat plane created on the exposed portion of our fingers in our fist, from our wrapped thumb to the knuckles.
- Our knuckles themselves are the *parietal lobe*.
- Our *occipital lobe* rests where our wrist begins.
- Tucked underneath, in the fold of our palm, rest the *cerebellum* and the *upper brainstem*.

Brainstem

We can imagine the wrist as our *upper brain* or *diencephalon* (Latin for "between brain," referring to its position between the oldest and newest pieces of our brain). This region includes the *epithalmus* ("upper room"); *thalamus* ("inner room or chamber"); *hypothalamus* ("lower room"); and *pituitary gland*. The size of the hypothalamus has been estimated to be the size of four peas (Diamond, Scheibel, & Elson, 1985). Yet this region, which is as small as four peas, or only 0.3 percent of our brain's weight, "takes part in nearly all aspects of motivated behavior, including feeding, sexual behavior, sleeping, temperature regulation, emotional behavior, movement, and through its interactions with the pituitary gland, endocrine function" (Kolb & Whishaw, 2009, p. 69).

The midbrain includes the *tectum* ("roof") and *tagmentum* ("floor"). Differing areas of these structures process visual and auditory stimuli, influence motor function, and modulate pain responses and "species-typical behaviors (for example, sexual behavior)" (Kolb & Whishaw, 2009, p. 69)

The hindbrain is most recognizable as the *cerebellum*. The cerebellum plays a major role in coordination, complex movement, balance, posture, and muscular integration. The *pons* and the *medulla* are the final gateway into the narrow spinal column. Diamond et al. (1985) summarized:

> The lowest part of the hindbrain, the *medulla oblongata,* is continuous with the spinal cord. This 2.5-centimeter-long region controls such vital functions as respiration and heart rate. Just above the medulla is the *pons*, which serves as part of a relay between the cerebral hemispheres and the *cerebellum*. (Plate 1–2)

Overall, the hindbrain regulates internal processes such as heart rate, as well as externally visible processes central to physical mobility and muscle movement.

Forebrain

The forebrain includes the *basal ganglia*, the *limbic system*, and the *cerebral cortex* (sometimes called *neocortex* in reference to its late evolutionary appearance). Over the centuries, increasingly advanced means of exploring the forebrain have led to an increasingly detailed and accurate parsing of brain function. The first unsuccessful attempt rested in the flawed theory of phrenology and cranial size. The rest has come slowly, over time, with the increased specializations of neuroscience. Hearing, vision, motor control, speech, cognition, behavior, and stimulus–response patterns all reside in this complex portion of the brain. The forebrain includes structures that are primary sites for inquiry into severe mental illness and the psychopharmacological manipulation of neurochemical communication between parts of the brain described above.

Pathways and communication

Overview

Out of a dozen or more neurotransmitters that have been identified in the human body, dopamine (DA) is one of five most often manipulated by psychotropic medications. The other four are serotonin (5HT), norepinephrine (NE), glutamate (GLU), and (5) y-aminobutyric acid (GABA). Psychopharmacological interventions have been honed through a system of trial and error that has explored how different medications seem to affect specific neurotransmitters and their receptor sites, the effects of which are seen in mediating behaviors attributed to different parts of our brains. Medical models look broadly at mood and affect, hypothesize about how they manifest, and attempt to shift the "faulty phone line." Matching symptoms with neural pathways has become similar to a game of pin the tail on the donkey. Stahl (2013) literally offers a figural depiction of mania with the heading: "Match each diagnostic symptom for a manic episode to hypothetically malfunctioning brain circuits" (p. 279).

Dopamine

Dopamine (DA) is synthesized through the amino acid, tyrosine, and a tyrosine pump. Tyrosine becomes DA through the work of enzymes (TOH and DDC). Once the enzymes have completed their tasks, a vesicular monoamine (VMAT2) moves the DA into the presynaptic vesicle until it is needed. DA has its own transporter, DAT, that acts as its metaphoric bodyguard. DAT ushers DA back and forth between the synapse and the terminal. If DAT cannot usher excess DA back to safety, the presynaptic cell often takes action and destroys it through the action of other enzymes (MAO-A, MAO-B). Sometimes, excess DA can escape both the neuron and its enzymes, but then another enzyme, COMT, or sometimes another neurotransmitter, norepinephrine (NE), neutralizes it. The transmission of DA can be controlled by blocking the gates out of the presynaptic cell, or by blocking the receptors on the postsynaptic cell. Five different receptors are examined most often, numbered D_2 through D_5. D_2 is best understood because it is the primary binding site for most anti-psychotic drugs. D_2 is also unique because it acts as the block in the presynaptic neuron.

Serotonin

Serotonin, also known as 5-hydroxytryptamine (5HT), is also synthesized through an amino acid, in this case, tryptophan, which travels from our plasma into the brain. Tryptophan becomes 5HT through the work of enzymes (TRY-OH and AAADC). The same vascular monoamine that transports DA, VMAT2, also transports 5HT to the synaptic vesicle of the presynaptic neuron for "stand-by" for transport to the postsynaptic neuron. Like DA, 5HT has a designated "bodyguard," the presynaptic transporter SERT. It pumps 5HT out of the synapse, and also can usher it back into the originating nerve terminal for future use. The MAO enzyme can neutralize or destroy 5HT in similar fashion as the MAO-A and MAO-B enzymes neutralize DA.

As with the regulation of DA, regulation of 5HT can happen pre- or post-synaptically through various 5HT receptors that rest in the presynaptic cell, the postsynaptic cell, or both. These receptors are labeled with subscripts containing both numbers and letters A through D (e.g., $5HT_{1A}$, $5HT_{2A}$). These are powerful receptors, as they have the ability to gate or receive many of the neurotransmitters, the regulation of which seems to be affected through different atypical antipsychotic medications.

Norepinephrine

A specific type of neuron, the noradrenergic neuron, utilizes norepinephrine (NE) as its neurotransmitter. NE initially has the same properties of DA, and is synthesized with the same amino acid, tyrosine. However, in noradrenergic neurons, there are additional genetic instructions. Like DA, the enzymes TOH and DDC act on the amino acid. If the neurotransmitter were in a DA neuron, that would be the end of it. However, in the specialized NE neuron, tyrosine is acted upon by an additional enzyme, dopamine β-hydroxylase (DBH), which converts the DA to NE. Like DA, NE action can be terminated by the enzymes MAO-A or MAO-B, which can sit in the presynaptic noradrenergic neuron or in the synapse after release. An additional enzyme, COMT (catechol-O-methyl-transferase), can terminate NE in the synapse. One enzyme, NET, acts as the bodyguard for NE. Although it does not escort NE out of the presynaptic terminal as do the transporters for DA and 5HT, NET does act as a vacuum to suck excess NE out of the synapse and back into the presynaptic terminal for future use. The NE receptors are labeled either α or β accompanied by numeric and alphabetic subscripts (e.g., $α_{1A}$, $α_{1B}$, $α_{2A}$, $β_1$, $β_2$, etc.). Again, depending on where the receptors are located (pre- or postsynaptic neuron) these receptors can act as either gatekeepers for NE release or as receptor sites. Certain antipsychotic medications have the ability to mimic these receptors, thus regulating how much NE is transmitted.

Glutamate

Glutamate (GLU) is, itself, an amino acid, and is of major importance for protein synthesis. It acts as a neurotransmitter when it is located in glial cells, specific types of cells that support neuronal functioning (Diamond et al., 1985). Stahl (2013) summarized:

> Glutamate is the major excitatory neurotransmitter in the central nervous system and sometimes considered to be the "master switch" of the brain, since it can excite and turn on virtually all CNS neurons. The synthesis, metabolism, receptor regulation, and key pathways of glutamate are therefore critical to the function of the brain. (p. 96)

GLU moves from the glutamate neurons to glia through an excitatory amino acid transporter, EAAT. Once GLU is inside the postsynaptic neuron, GLU is converted into glutamatine by the enzyme glutamine synthetase. This conversion allows GLU to be used specifically as a neurotransmitter versus generalized use for the creation of proteins. GLU is then transported out of the glia with an amino acid transporter, SNAT, returned to the glutamate neuron, and converted back into glutamate through the enzyme, glutaminase. Finally, it is transported back into the synaptic vesicle by the presynaptic transporter vGluT (vesicular GLU transporter) for future use. SNAT accompanies GLU from the presynaptic neuron to the glia and back, thereby earning a designation as a reverse transporter. However, EAAT sometimes "takes back" the glutamine from the SNAT, and returns it to the glia for future use. GLU has receptors that function in several different ways depending on how it will be used. Both EEAAT and vGluT are considered receptors, and there are receptors specific for protein production (more than eight different receptors). One receptor only functions for GLU if it is attached to additional amino acids, glycine (GlyT2) or NMDA (N-methyl-$_D$-aspartate). In general, GLU is unique in that it has a role in a different group of pharmaceuticals used to treat mood disorders, namely, the anticonvulsants (as compared with atypical antipsychotics), which will be briefly discussed below. One of these anticonvulsants, lamotrigine, is the focus of the empirical data in the body of this research.

Y-aminobutyric acid

Y-aminobutyric acid (GABA) is an amino acid transmitter, like GLU. Kolb and Whishaw (2009) call GLU and GABA "'the workhorses of the nervous system,' because so many synapses use them" (p. 121). They continued: "In the forebrain and cerebellum, glutamate is the major excitatory transmitter and GABA is the main inhibitory neurotransmitter" (p. 121). GABA is synthesized from GLU through the action of the enzyme, GAD. Like the other neurotransmitters, it has its own transporters (VIAATs) and it can be terminated through the action of particular enzymes (GAT and GABA-T). Receptor sites for GABA are denoted with alphabetic subscripts (e.g., $GABA_A$, $GABA_B$, $GABA_C$). These receptors act along both ligand-gated channels and voltage-sensitive calcium channels (to be explored below). There are extensive subtypes of receptors related to each of the above, sometimes called *isoforms* (Stahl, 2013). These isoforms utilize subscripts α, β, γ, ρ, Θ, ε, and π, each with their own alphabetic subscripts. Clearly, the action of GABA is extremely complex and specialized, and its role in both the expression and treatment of severe mental illnesses is vast.

Monoamine neurotransmitter system

DA, 5HT, and NE in particular are considered three primary neurotransmitters in mood disorders. They have been grouped as the *monoamine neurotransmitter system* because of their complex interactions and strong implication for treatment. In no uncertain terms, Stahl (2013) wrote: "Essentially all known treatments for mood disorders act upon one or more of these three systems" (p. 255). Looking at depressive or manic symptoms in bipolar disorders, for example, research has suggested that irregular transmission of DA or NE can reduce *positive* affect, leading to symptoms that include "loss of happiness (joy), loss of interest/pleasure, loss of energy/enthusiasm, decreased alertness [and] decreased self-confidence"; especially on pathways running from the prefrontal cortex to the basal ganglia (p. 278). The combination of NE dysfunction with 5HT dysfunction can lead to an increase in *negative* affect, which would include symptoms of depression such as "guilt/disgust, fear/anxiety, hostility, irritability, and loneliness" (Stahl, 2013, p. 278). These types of insights regarding the five primary neurotransmitter targets and pathways from differing brain regions are the basis of most pharmacology today.

Example: Dopamine pathways

Using animal studies and clinical trials, reductive methods in the natural sciences hone in on minute alterations and correlations between brain activity and mood. For example, depressive and manic symptoms are categorized in terms of: (a) whether symptoms are positive or negative; (b) where in the brain these symptoms are thought to occur; and (c) how they are transmitted.

Following the movement of just one of these neurochemicals, dopamine (DA) offers a glimpse into the complicated circuitry in the brain. There are five major dopamine pathways through the brain, each related to certain identifiable behavioral patterns:

- The *nigrostriatal* pathway moves from the substantia nigra in the midbrain to the basal ganglia in the forebrain. Manipulation of this pathway seems to relate to motor function and movement.
- The *mesolimbic* pathway runs from the tagmentum in the midbrain into the nucleus ambiens, situated in the limbic system of the forebrain. This is thought to affect pleasurable sensations and contribute to the euphoria of drug abuse, as well as contribute to the manifestation of delusions and hallucinations.
- The *mesocortical* pathway also begins from the tagmentum, but communicates primarily with the prefrontal cortex of the forebrain, affecting both cognition and affect.
- The *tuberinfundibular* pathway runs from the hypothalamus to the pituitary gland inside the upper brainstem, which is thought to relate to the secretion of prolactin.
- Very little is known about the final pathway. DA travels from multiple sites of the brain, all directed toward the *thalamus*.

The hypothesis is that positive or negative symptoms of severe mental illness correlate with the transmission of these neurochemicals along certain pathways between parts of the brain. For example, the mesolimbic pathway is not only implicated in delusions and hallucinations, but also in disorganized speech, disorganized behavior, catatonic behavior, and agitation. These are all considered positive symptoms that are correlated with types of psychosis, schizophrenia, and mania (Stahl, 2013). The mesocortical pathway is thought to relate to the negative symptoms of these disorders, including blunted affect, reduced emotional responsiveness, reduced interest, and reduced socialization. The mesolimbic pathway is not only implicated in delusions and hallucinations, but also in disorganized speech, disorganized behavior, catatonic behavior, and agitation. These are all considered positive symptoms that are correlated with types of psychosis, schizophrenia, and mania (Stahl, 2013).

In summary, the medical model of understanding symptom and symptom relief pertains to pathways from one part of the brain to another. Stahl (2013) succinctly described the sum total of neurotransmitter activity:

> The message of chemical neurotransmission is transferred via three sequential "molecular pony express" routes: (1) a presynaptic neurotransmitter synthesis route from presynaptic genome to the synthesis and packaging of neurotransmitter and supporting enzymes and receptors; (2) a postsynaptic route from receptor occupancy through second messengers all the way to the genome, which turns on postsynaptic genes; and (3) another postsynaptic route starting from the newly expressed postsynaptic genes transferring information as a molecular cascade of biochemical consequences throughout the postsynaptic neuron. (p. 27)

There are specialized ways in which neurotransmitter receptors and amino acids distribute themselves according to different brain regions.

Therapeutic targets in antipsychotic medications

The current understanding of psychopharmacology has become increasingly nuanced with technological advances that aid neurological research into brain regions, their functions, and the unique nature of the neural pathways implicated in the neurochemical communication from one region to another. The second-generation, atypical antipsychotic drugs mentioned in Chapter 3 have become increasingly able to pinpoint and manipulate the transmission of specific neurotransmitters (especially the monoamine neurotransmitters); to specific brain regions; along specific neuropathways that either *antagonize* or *inhibit* movement from cell to cell; thereby either blocking or opening presynaptic and postsynaptic receptor sites. The point is to target specific physical and behavioral symptoms in severe mental illnesses. Combinations of the drugs are used to target circadian rhythms, mood, racing thoughts, motor disturbances, olfactory hallucinations, or disorganized speech. Psychiatrists try different doses in different combinations until they see stabilization of each of these symptoms.

Stahl (2013) categorizes atypical antipsychotic medications into four groups—the pines, the dones, two pips, and a rip—based on their effects on neurochemical transmission. Each of these groups binds to different receptor sites. Furthermore, within each class, different drugs have different binding profiles. The pines (peens), for example, include several different drugs (clozapine, olanzapine, and quetiapine) that act as serotonin–dopamine antagonists. The goal of these medications is to block up to 60 percent of D_2 receptor sites through the manipulation of DA, 5HT, and the related receptor sites:

Despite its complex pharmacology, these atypical properties were linked particularly to the presence of $5HT_{2A}$ antagonism added to the dopamine D_2 antagonism of conventional antipsychotics, and this has become the prototypical binding characteristic of the entire class [the pines] of atypical antipsychotics, namely $5HT_{2A}$ antagonism with D_2 antagonism. (Stahl, 2013, p. 180)

As an example, when 5HT is released in the cortex, it binds to its $5HT_{2A}$ receptors that sit on certain glutamatergic neurons, which then connect to and stimulate GABA, bind to dopaminergic neurons, and limit DA release. As a contrast, binding to a $5HT_{1A}$ receptor (versus $5HT_{2A}$) on a neural pathway from the brainstem to the cortex will inhibit GLU production, thereby limiting GABA, which then allows DA to flow freely. This is quite exacting because although this process can be manipulated moving from the brainstem *to* the cortex, it cannot function in reverse. These nuances apply to each of the neural pathways most implicated in DA and 5HT transmission, and each utilizes GLU, GABA, and NE differently. The practice of combining "pines," "dones," and "pips" can be seen in the course of my pharmacological treatment while hospitalized. Table 6.1 organizes the medication regime I was on when discharged after my first hospitalization, which included a "pip," a "pine," and a "done."

My medication regime after my release from my second hospitalization was also primarily atypical antipsychotics. (The drug, Neurontin, is a mood stabilizer.)

Table 6.1 Medications at time of discharge

Medication	Dose
Risperidone (Costa)	25 mg IM (long-lasting, 2-week injection)
Olanzapine (Zyprexa)	15 mg QHS (bedtime)
Aripiprazole (Abilify)	15 mg QAM (morning)
Neurontin	600 mg QHS/QAM

Pharmacological action of mood stabilizers

Electrical stimulation

Neurochemistry is one of two primary modes of physiological communication in the human body. The other primary mode of physiological communication is electricity. Three factors contribute to the electrical communication: a concentration of ions; voltage gradient; and the structure of the membrane. Ions are simply molecules that separate into two parts when dissolved in water, where one keeps the positive charge, the other the negative. Kolb and Whishaw (2009) used the simple example of sodium chloride (NaCl), or common table salt, to illustrate the process. When placed in water, NaCl separates into positively charged sodium (Na+) and negatively charged chloride (Cl−). The concentrated cluster of ions disperses like ink in water: at first, the ink sits dark and clumpy on the surface of the water. Gradually, it expands and diffuses, turning the black clumps on top of the water into water that is well-mixed and of a semi-grayish hue. This illustrates the first factor in electrical movement: concentration. The second factor in electrical stimulation is voltage, measured through the number of positively charged (cations) and negatively charged ions (anions). Sodium (Na+) and potassium (K+) are cations; chlorine (A−) and chloride (Cl−) are anions. The third factor is the structure of the cell membrane itself, which is actually a bi-layer of heads and tails called phospholipids (fatty acids and water). They remain stable because the heads are hydrophilic (Greek for "water loving"), while the tails are hydrophobic ("water phobic"). They rest in mutual attraction–distaste for one another, keeping the intracellular fluid in place. When there is a sufficient gathering of anions and cations (Na+, K+, A−, Cl−) either inside or outside of the intracellular fluid, a spike in electrical current can trigger channels, pumps, or gates to open, allowing a potential leapfrog through dendrites and axons into the presynaptic vesicles.

This electrical activity has five components: (1) resting potential, (2) graded potential, (3) action potential, (4) nerve impulse, and (5) saltatory conduction. At resting potential, the negative charge inside the cell matches the positive charges outside of the cell. Neither the sodium on the outside of the cell nor the negatively charged proteins on the inside of the cell can permeate the cell membrane. This is because the cells are big and there are no membrane channels to let them out. However, the resting potential must be considered as "energy stored," not lack of energy. Therefore, if the membrane's barrier is for some reason removed, the four types of anions and cations will want to move. Graded potential is a brief blip in the homeostasis, like a small ripple in a pond without much effect (Kolb & Whishaw, 2009). This movement, although slight, is enabled through the hyperpolarization or depolarization allowed by gates or channels in the membrane. Action potential, on the other hand, is a larger flip in polarity that has enough voltage to enable a massive flux of ions. Kolb and Whishaw (2009) likened the movement to a flushing of a toilet— with a flush (voltage-sensitive gates, pumps, or channels), water is sucked out of the toilet bowl, and then it slowly re-fills. The voltages of such electrical charges were discovered and measured thanks to the giant North Atlantic squid, *Loligo*, previously mentioned, and the invention of the oscillope in 1936. Voltage has been measured at −70mV at resting potential. At action potential, this voltage jumps to +30mV. This happens when threshold potential (a big enough ripple in the pond) hits −50mV, and opens the voltage-sensitive channels. This leads to what we know as nerve impulses, where the voltage-sensitive channels open like a domino effect in one direction, down the axons, myelin sheaths, and nodes of Ranvier. We can imagine these sheaths and nodes of Ranvier as an insulated cover over the axons, interrupted in ways that look like the joints in balloon animals. The process of saltatory conduction (from Latin, *saltare*, or "to leap") speeds up the process, allowing these impulses to travel from node to node with increasing speed.

Two primary types of openings operate according to electrical charge and voltage: *voltage-sensitive sodium channels* (VSSCs, also called voltage-gated sodium channels, or VGSCs) and *voltage-sensitive calcium channels* (VSCCs). There are three additional types of channels that regulate ion movement: ligand-gated ion channels, ionotropic receptors, and ion-channel-linked receptors. Unlike VSSCs and VSCCs, which function through electrical stimulation, these three channels are opened and closed through neurotransmitters. Psychopharmacological medications can affect all types of communication. Some medications affect the voltage-sensitive gates, some the neurochemical gates. There seems to be consensus that the action of VSSCs and VSCCs is implicated to a greater degree in mood stabilizers than that of ligand-gated ion channels, ionotropic receptors, and ion-channel-linked receptors, which are often sites of action in the differing classes of atypical antipsychotics. Re-stating the difference between the two: VSCCs and VSSCs are opened and closed by electrical impulses; the latter three are operated by neurotransmitters. All of these channels, gates, and pumps inhibit or allow the movement of ions that leads to signal transduction cascades. This contrasts with the action of atypical antipsychotics, which focus on the antagonism or deregulation of neurotransmitters.

Mood stabilizers: Lithium and anticonvulsants

While neurochemical communication is the primary target with the atypical antipsychotics, mood stabilizers are thought to function through electronic transmission. Mood stabilizers are drugs that work specifically to manage relapse and recurrence of depressive and manic episodes in bipolar disorders. Atypical antipsychotics are increasingly being used in this fashion, but best practices for bipolar disorder continue to be lithium or anticonvulsants. In my own experience with psychopharmaceutical treatment, atypical antipsychotics have proven invasive and ineffective. Except for medication regimes during my hospitalizations and for a brief time immediately after, I have always used mood stabilizers to manage my bipolar I disorder: (1) *lithium*; and two from the class of drugs called *anticonvulsants*, namely, (2) *lamotrigine* and (3) *valproic acid*. Unlike the specificity related to the psychopharmacological properties of the antipsychotic medications, the action of these mood stabilizers is still largely a mystery. However, the efficacy of these drugs has been so well established, they continue to be used even as the exact mechanisms of action are not entirely understood.

In general, the actions of these mood stabilizers seem to be related to signal transduction cascades, otherwise known as the molecular pony express, described in the previous section. These transduction cascades are the roots of chemical neurotransmission highlighted in this chapter, but they are rooted in, and begin with, the chemical and electrical stimulation of sodium (Na+), calcium (Ca), potassium (K+), and chloride (Cl−) (Calladine, Drew, Luisi & Travers, 2004; Kolb & Whishaw, 2009; Stahl, 2013). This electrical transduction moves through intracellular membranes via (a) channels, (b) gates, or (c) pumps. Channels are openings; gates change shape like a key into a door lock; and pumps need sufficient energy to suck or flush substances across the threshold of the membrane. The neurotransmitters are ushered through, from presynaptic neuron to postsynaptic neuron, at which point chemical transmission becomes electrical stimulation once again.

Overview of lithium bicarbonate

Lithium bicarbonate (Li_2CO_3) is an ion created from the base metal, *Li*, and has been used for the treatment of bipolar disorders for 50 years. It is still considered the "gold standard" for treatment of bipolar disorder (Goodwin & Jamison, 2007; Hirschowitz, Kolevzon, & Garakani, 2010; Stahl, 2013). However, as stated previously, very little is understood about how this ion mediates bipolar symptoms:

> Although lithium is the oldest treatment for bipolar disorder, its mechanism of action is still not well understood .... Lithium may work by affecting signal transduction, perhaps through its inhibition of second-messenger enzymes ... by modulation of G proteins ... or by interaction at various sites within downstream signal transduction cascades. (Stahl, 2013, p. 372)

Reiterating earlier explanation, ions are created when an electrical impulse becomes strong enough to separates electrons from protons and neutrons, leaving either a positive or negative charge. These shifts alter the amount of energy that passes between other atoms and molecules in highly reactive ways (Stwertka, 2002, p. 27). Additional lithium bicarbonate in the body seems to rebalance the reactive nature of these ions and stabilize symptoms of bipolar disorder.

Valproic acid

Unfortunately, nuanced commonalities in the actions of mood stabilizers have not been easy to identify. Fountoulakis et al. (2012) summarized: "Each anticonvulsant may possess a very distinct mode of pharmacologic action and should be considered separately. The mode of action of anticonvulsants in BP [bipolar] has not been fully elucidated" (p. 58). In general, however, the focus on mood stabilizer action relates more to the electrical signals than to the neurochemical translation of these electrical messages. Stahl (2013) highlighted three potential ways in which *valproic acid* might work: (a) by limiting the number of ions that flow through the voltage-sensitive or voltage-gated sodium channels (the VSSCs or VGSCs), thereby diminishing neurotransmitter activity, most likely GLU; (b) by manipulating GABA, either by increasing release, decreasing uptake, or inactivating it; or (c) by affecting downstream transduction cascade through the manipulation of enzyme and protein synthesis.

Lamotrigine

Lamotrigine (my monotherapy) is thought to affect the activity of voltage-sensitive sodium and calcium channels, which may affect the transmission of the neurotransmitter, GLU. It is thought to function differently from other anticonvulsants, because it affects not only sodium ion activation and inactivation, but the excitability of potassium (K+) and calcium (Ca+), as well. It is an anticonvulsant that is also used in the treatment of epileptic disorders because of the role of VGSCs (equivalent to the acronym VSSC) in neuronal excitability. Mantegazza, Curia, Biagini, Ragsdale, & Avoli (2010) summarized the action:

> VGSCs are closed at resting potentials .... In response to membrane depolarization, they open within a few hundred milliseconds (a process termed activation), resulting in an inward sodium ion (Na+) current, and then convert within a few milliseconds to a non-conducting inactivated state. (p. 413)

Excessive neuronal excitation is thought to be at the root of epileptic seizures. The structures of these channels are extremely complex with intricate extracellular loops of amino acids. Stahl (2013) summarized the complexity when he stated:

> Voltage-gated ion channels have a more complicated structure than just a hole or a pore in the membrane. These channels are long strings of amino acids, comprising subunits, and four different subunits are connected to form the critical pore. (p. 68)

There are also regulatory sub-proteins that affect opening and closing of the channels. Only some of these subunits have been discovered and studied. However, even within the limited scope of experimentation, at least three different genetic mutations have been identified that contribute to neuronal excitability and abnormal functioning (Mantegazza et al., 2010).

Burgeoning research

Research on genetic loci, and increasing specificity related to cell type and function, continues to add to the literature regarding the action and efficacy of mood stabilizers. For example, Kaminsky et al. (2015) found increasing evidence targeting the dysregulation of ion channel function in a specific category of potassium voltage-gated channels. Qiao, Sun, Clare, Werkman, and Wadman (2013) identified a distinct α-subunit related to voltage-activated Na+ channels, and found a relationship to differing responsiveness to anti-epileptic drugs. Research focused on genetic functioning of two genes, *KCNQ2* and *KCNQ3*, the loss of electrical inhibition, and "neuronal hyper-excitability" in bipolar disorders. Highlighting the action of anticonvulsant drugs, the authors supported the notion that this excitability might be an underlying pathophysiological feature of the illness.

Oedegaard et al. (2016) published the protocol for a 2-year longitudinal study on genetic predictors for lithium monotherapy in a sample of 700 bipolar patients. In the study protocol, authors cited:

> There is much evidence to suggest that genetic factors play a strong role in the variation in response to lithium. Several studies have indicated that lithium-responsive patients are more likely to have a stronger family history of bipolar disorder than lithium non-responders. (p. 4)

The researchers see potential for growth in both diagnostic categories and treatment protocol:

> The long-term goal of this project is to better understand the mechanism of action of lithium and variation in the genome that influences response. Practically, the hope is that this understanding may lead to a DNA test that would aid physicians in selecting mood stabilizers. It also may add to our understanding of bipolar disorder by distinguishing a genetically distinct form. (p. 4).

Although generalized reference to genetic research was highlighted in Chapter 3, it is hoped that this chapter allows a greater understanding of research in the field and its targets. For example, Zhang et al. (2010) studied nucleotide polymorphism (SNP) markers in 737 families and found significant correlation between the expression of bipolar disorder and a chromosome related to the action of voltage-gated potassium channels. In a meta-analysis of genome research into schizophrenia and bipolar disorders, O'Donovan et al. (2009) cited associations to loci for the *zinc finger binding protein 804A (ZNF804A)* and for the *calcium channel, voltage dependent L type, alpha 1C subunit (CACNA1C)* for both bipolar disorder and schizophrenia. There have been multiple genetic mutations identified in the abnormal functioning of other channels involved with electrical stimulation, including anomalies at *SCN2A, SCN9A, SCN3A,* and *SCN1B* (Mantegazza et al., 2010). These findings have now been replicated in a review of genome wide association studies (GWAS), some of which have been highlighted above (Gupta et al., 2012; Insel, 2011; Kaminsky et al., 2015; Krug et al., 2014; Qiao et al., 2013; Seifuddin et al., 2013; Sklar et al., 2011; Wessa et al., 2010).

Moving forward

In his essay on "The Significance of Constitution and Heredity in Psychology," Jung (1929/1969) wrote: "In the opinion of scientists today, there is no doubt that the individual psyche is in large measure dependent on the physiological constitution; indeed, there are not a few who consider this dependence absolute" (p. 107, para. 220). Science is becoming increasingly enamored of this position: ninety years later, mood and emotion are coming ever closer to being linked to brain function and brain function alone. Change your cognition, change brain patterns, change mood. The Westernized version of meditation, or mindfulness, is one such example. There is less and less need of an exploration of psychic content, we can simply release ourselves from its pull by changing our brainwaves. This, in and of itself, is not problematic. It is the one-sided abandonment of the other side. Depth psychology is one of few remaining disciplinary approaches that values the meat and substance of unconscious imagery and story. Jung highlighted the relative autonomy and difference between body and the elusive psyche:

> I would not like to go as far as that myself, but would regard it as more appropriate in the circumstances to grant the psyche a *relative* independence of the physiological constitution. It is true there are no rigorous proofs of this, but then there is no proof of the psyche's total dependence on the constitution, either. We should never forget that if the psyche is X, constitution is its complementary Y. Both, at bottom, are unknown factors, which have only recently begun to take on clearer form. But we are still far from having anything approaching a real understanding of their nature. (Jung, 1929/1969, p. 107 [*CW*8, para. 220])

Von Franz (1992) highlighted:

> The fact, though, that there are psychogenic illnesses and psychogenic cures of physical pathological symptoms permits us from the start to conjecture a connection with the bodily somatic processes, about which, we know just as little or as much as does psychosomatic medicine as a whole, that is we know that a connection *does* exist, but we cannot yet give an accurate causal description of its details or of the laws governing its functioning. (p. 180)

Medical science agrees. There is no finality related to current understandings of severe mental illness, nor the medications that treat them. What we are left with at this juncture is that my physiological constitution Y intersected and influenced psyche X around the fulcrum of the pharmaceutical action of Lamictal, a chemical compound created by bonds between carbon, hydrogen, chlorine, and nitrogen: $C_9H_7Cl_2N_5$.

Note

1 One example in particular highlights the internal struggle in the post-Jungian community captured through extensive contributions to the discussion of archetype published in *The Journal of Analytical Psychology* (JAP) (Tresan, 1996; Saunders & Skar, 2001; Merchant, 2006, 2009; Goodwyn, 2010a, 2010b, 2012; Tresan, 2013). It should be noted that all of the authors cited below are considered especially well-versed in the constructs surrounding the debate (Goodwyn, 2010a, 2010b, 2012, 2013; Hogenson, 2004; Knox, 2003; Knox et al., 2010; Merchant, 2006, 2009). Goodwyn (2010a) wrote: "Most recently, with the advent of genetic research and the human genome project, the idea that psychological structures can be innate has come under even harsher criticism even within Jungian thought. There appears to be a growing consensus that Jung's idea of innate psychological structures was misguided, and that perhaps the archetype-as-such should be abandoned for more developmental and 'emergent' theories of the psyche. The purpose of this essay is to question this conclusion, and introduce some literature on psychological innateness that appears relevant to the discussion" (p. 503). Goodwyn's choice of literature included consideration of Evolutionary Psychology (EP), innatism, and nativism, and the potential conflict these theories have with more constructionist, subjectivist viewpoints, specifically emergentism and the work of Jean Knox, who, as mentioned above, has also written extensively on the subject, and has created her own theory of archetype, the image schema model, which is rooted in emergent models of mind (Knox, 2003).

Knox, along with two other authors well-versed in the subject—Hogenson (2004) and Merchant (2006, 2009)—were asked to write responses to Goodwyn's (2010a) article. Goodwyn's position was summarized as "an implicit assumption that there is a ground plan or blueprint of the human psyche inherited in our genes and that this blueprint contains the potential for specific types of imagery, such as the archetypes of the collective unconscious" (Knox et al., 2010, p. 522). Knox (2010) challenges this assumption due to "a failure to appreciate the nature of epigenetic processes" (p. 523). According to Knox, these "blue prints" cannot exist:

"Domain-specificity not only does not have to be pre-existent, it cannot be pre-existent. The emergence of new developmental capacities depends on the information contained in the preceding developmental level of phenotypical organization, rather than in pre-existing genetic or environmental instructions" (Knox, 2010, p. 523). Merchant (Knox et al., 2010), in his response to Goodwyn's (2010a) article, wrote: "Any argument for innate archetypes must take into account the growing body of neuroscience research which indicates that humans are born with extensive neuroplasticity and little specialization so that the final sculpting of mind/brain structures is dependent on developmental experience in the environment" (Knox et al., 2010, p. 541). Merchant attributes the misguided belief that psyche has some sort of evolutionary thread to confusion about when and how mythic representations begin: "The problem is that once these mind/brain structures are functionally in place, it can look as if they are innate when in fact they have been developmentally acquired. This can create a particular problem for higher or later levels of investigation like evolutionary psychology on which Goodwyn relies" (Knox et al., 2010, p. 541). Hogenson (Knox et al., 2010) suggested that this misguided belief might partially be due to an idealized transference toward Jung. Specifically related to Goodwyn's (2010a) work, Hogenson wrote: "Regretfully, as I read Goodwyn's paper I have to say he has failed to come to terms with the arguments presented … and has seriously misrepresented the positions taken by myself, as well as others who work in the area of emergent and developmental theories of archetype" (Knox et al., 2010, p. 548). Not surprisingly, Goodwyn (2010b), in his reply, wrote: "The above authors accuse me of misrepresenting their position. Interestingly each is equally guilty of misrepresenting mine" (p. 550).

References

Atmanspacher, H., & Fach, W. (2013). A structural-phenomenological typology of mind-matter correlations. *Journal of Analytical Psychology*, 58(2), 219–244.

Calladine, C. R., Drew, H. R., Luisi, B. F., & Travers, A. A. (2004). *Understanding DNA: The molecule and how it works* (3rd ed.). San Diego, CA: Elsevier Academic Press.

Diamond, M. C., Scheibel, A. B., & Elson, L. M. (1985). *The human brain coloring book*. Oakville, CA: Coloring Concepts.

Fountoulakis, K. N., Kasper, S., Andreassen, O., Blier, P., Okasha, A., Severus, E., … Vieta, E. (2012). Efficacy of pharmacotherapy in bipolar disorder: A report by the WPA section on pharmacopsychiatry. *European Archives of Psychiatry and Clinical Neuroscience*, 262, 1–48. doi:10.1007/s00406-012-0323-x.

Goodwin, F. K., & Jamison, K. R. (2007). *Manic-depressive illness: Bipolar disorders and recurrent depression*. New York, NY: Oxford University Press.

Goodwyn, E. D. (2010a). Approaching archetypes: Reconsidering innateness. *Journal of Analytical Psychology*, 55, 502–521.

Goodwyn, E. D. (2010b). The author replies. *Journal of Analytical Psychology*, 55, 550–555.

Goodwyn, E. D. (2012). *The neurobiology of the gods: How brain physiology shapes the recurrent imagery of myth and dreams*. Hove, UK: Routledge.

Goodwyn, E. D. (2013). Recurrent motifs as resonant attractor states in the narrative field: a testable model of archetype. *Journal of Analytical Psychology*, 58, 387–408.

Goodwyn, E. D. (2019). Jung and the mind-body problem. In J. Mills (Ed.), *Jung and philosophy* (pp. 67–85). New York, NY: Routledge.

Gupta, A., Schulze, T. G., Nagarajan, V., Akula, N., Corona, W., Jiang, X-y. … Detera Wadleigh, S. D. (2012). Interaction networks of lithium and valproate molecular targets reveal a striking enrichment of apoptosis functional clusters and neurotrophin signaling. *The Pharmacogenomics Journal*, 12, 328–341. doi:10.1038/tpj.2011.9.

Hirschowitz, J., Kolevzon, A., & Garakani, A. (2010, September/October). The pharmacological treatment of bipolar disorder: The question of modern advances. *Harvard Review of Psychiatry*, 18(5), 266–278. doi:10.3109/10673229.2010.507042.

Hogenson, G. B. (2004). Archetypes: Emergence and the psyche's deep structure. In J. Cambray & L. Carter (Eds.), *Analytical psychology: Contemporary perspectives in Jungian analysis* (pp. 32–55). New York, NY: Routledge.

Insel, T. (2011, November 28). Psychiatric genetics: More pieces of the puzzle. *National Institute of Mental Health.* Retrieved from http://www.nimh.nih.gov.
Jung, C. G. (1929/1969). The significance of constitution and heredity in psychology. In H. Read, M. Fordham, G. Adler, & W. McGuire (Eds.), *The collected works of C.G. Jung* (R. F. C. Hull, Trans.) (2nd ed., Vol. 8, pp. 107–113). Princeton, NJ: Princeton University Press.
Jung, C. G. (1948/1969). The psychological foundation of belief in spirits. In H. Read, M. Fordham, G. Adler, & W. McGuire (Eds.), *The collected works of C.G. Jung* (R. F. C. Hull, Trans.) (2nd ed., Vol. 8, pp. 159–233). Princeton, NJ: Princeton University Press.
Jung, C. G. (2011). *The undiscovered self: With symbols and the interpretation of dreams.* Princeton, NJ: Princeton University Press.
Kaminsky, Z., Jones, I., Verma, R., Saleh, L., Trivedi, H., Guintivano, J., … Potash, J. B. (2015). DNA methylation and expression of KCNQ3 in bipolar disorder. *Bipolar Disorders*, 17, 150–159. doi:10.1111/bdi.12230.
Knox, J. (2003). *Archetype, attachment, analysis: Jungian psychology and the emergent mind.* London: Routledge.
Knox, J., Merchant, J., & Hogenson, G. B. (2010). Response to Erik Goodwyn's "Approaching archetypes: reconsidering innateness." *Journal of Analytical Psychology*, 55, 522–549.
Kolb, B., & Whishaw, I. Q. (2009). *Fundamentals of neuropsychology.* New York, NY: Worth.
Krug, A., Witt, S., Backes, H., Dietsche, B., Nieratschker, V., Shah, N., Nothen, M., Rietschel, M., & Kircher, T. (2014). A genome-wide supported variant in CACNA1C influences hippocampal activation during episodic memory encoding and retrieval. *European Archives of Psychiatry and Clinical Neuroscience*, 264(2), 103–110.
Mantegazza, M., Curia, G., Biagini, G., Ragsdale, D. S., & Avoli, M. (2010). Voltage-gated sodium channels as therapeutic targets in epilepsy and other neurological disorders. *The Lancet Neurology*, 9(4), 413–424. doi:10.1016/S1474-4422(10)70059-4.
Merchant, J. (2006). The developmental / emergent model of archetype, its implications and its application to shamanism. *Journal of Analytical Psychology*, 51, 125–144.
Merchant, J. (2009). A reappraisal of classical archetypal theory and its implications for theory and practice. *Journal of Analytical Psychology*, 54, 339–358.
Mills, J. (2018a). The essence of archetypes. *International Journal of Jungian Studies*, 10(3), 199–220. doi:10.1080/19409052.2018.1503808.
Mills, J. (2018b). The myth of the collective unconscious. *Journal of the History of the Behavioral Sciences*, 55(1), 40–53. doi:10.1002/jhbs.21945.
Mills, J. (Ed.). (2019). In J. Mills (Ed.), *Jung and philosophy.* New York, NY: Routledge.
O'Donovan, M. C., Craddock, N. J., & Owen, M. J. (2009). Genetics of psychosis: insights from views across the genome. *Human Genetics*, 126, 3–12. doi:10.1007/s00439-009-0703-0.
Oedegaard, K. J., Alda, M., Anad, A., Andreassen, O. A., Balaraman, Y., Berrettini, W. H., … Kelsoe, J. R. (2016). The pharmacogenomics of bipolar disorder study (PGBD): Identification of genes for lithium response in a prospective sample. *BMC Psychiatry*, 16, 129–144. doi:10.1186/s12888-016-0732-x.
Qiao, X., Sun, G., Clare, J. J., Werkman, T. R., & Wadman, W. J. (2013). Properties of human brain sodium channel α-subunits expressed in HEK293 cells and their

modulation by carbamazepine, phenytoin, and lamotrigine. *British Journal of Pharmacology*, 171, 1054–1067. doi:10.1111/bph.12534.

Rensma, R. (2013). Analytical psychology and the ghost of Lamarck: Did Jung believe in the inheritance of acquired characteristics? *Journal of Analytical Psychology*, 58(2), 258–277.

Saunders, S., & Skar, P. (2001). Achetypes, complexes and self-organization. *Journal of Analytical Psychology*, 46, 305–323.

Seifuddin, F., Pirooznia, M., Judy, J. T., Goes, F. S., Potash, J. B., & Zandi, P. P. (2013). Systematic review of genome-wide gene expression studies of bipolar disorder. *BMC Psychiatry*, 13, 1–19. Retrieved from http://www.medscape.com/viewarticle/811759.

Sklar, P., Ripke, S., Scott, L. J., Andreassen, O. A., Cichon, S., Craddock, N., ... Holmans, P. A. (2011). Large-scale genome-wide association analysis of bipolar disorder identifies a new susceptibility locus near ODZ4. *Nature Genetics*, 43(10), 977–983.

Stahl, S. M. (2013). *Stahl's essential psychopharmacology: Neuroscientific basis and practical applications*. New York, NY: Cambridge University Press.

Stwertka, A. (2002). *A guide to the elements*. New York, NY: Oxford University Press.

Tresan, D. (1996). Jungian metapsychology and neurobiological theory. *Journal of Analytical Psychology*, 41(3), 399–436.

Tresan, D. (2013). A commentary on "A structural-phenomenological typology of mind matter correlations" by H. Atmanspacher and W. Fach. *Journal of Analytical Psychology*, 58, 245–253.

Von Franz, M. (1992). *Psyche and matter*. Boston, MA: Shambhala.

Wessa, M.Linke, J., Witt, S. H., Nieratschker, V., Esslinger, C., Kirsch, P., ... Rietschel, M. (2010). The CACNA1C risk variant for bipolar disorder influences limbic activity. *Molecular Psychiatry*, 15, 1126–1127.

Wolf, H. B. (Ed.). (1977). *Webster's new collegiate dictionary*. Springfield, MA: G. & C. Merriam.

Zhang, P., Xiang, N., Chen, Y., Sliwerska, E., McInnis, M. G., Burmeister, M., & Zollner, S. (2010). Family-based association analysis to finemap bipolar linkage peak on chromosomes 8q24 using 2,500 genotyped SNPs and 15,000 imputed SNPs. *Bipolar Disorders*, 12, 786–792.

Chapter 7

Radiating outward and the collective unconscious

> The hypothetical possibility that the psyche touches on a form of existence outside space and time presents a scientific question mark that merits serious consideration for a long time to come.
> (Jung, 1934/1969, p. 414 [CW 8, para. 814])

Continuing the hermeneutic circle

Part of the journey with narrative analysis is the retroactive form of meaning-making that takes place as the analysis continues. As presented in Chapter 2, the basic questions of who, what, where become increasingly honed into the question of why such a thing is important. Explication deepens. The chapters that follow reflect this process. First, it bears repeating that as this method progresses, certain perspectives rise well over the horizon, while others move down into darkness. As highlighted in the previous chapter, the pharmacological actions of mood stabilizers are still little understood and largely hypothetical, as is acknowledged by those who research them and those who prescribe them. Therefore, any extrapolations I make are also provisional in nature.

An entirely new era of diagnostic nuance is likely to burgeon in the not so distant future. Science, itself, is provisional in nature, always one step from moving backward into revising the so-called surety of theory thus far. Furthermore, there is well-deserved caution in concretizing even what is seeable by the naked or technologically aided eye, which includes medical models of how medication works. Therefore, any attempt to frame unconscious phenomena into some sort of working model demands a metaphoric and fluid sensibility in order to avoid the concretization of a partial and potentially misdirected model. That said, there is enough medical and narrative support that allows for postulations based in a relationship between electric stimulation and altered relationships to a consensual reality.

Brain as transformer station

Consideration of energy

Jung remained within the scope of scientific advances during his lifetime, trying to progress and hone his theories along with the advance in years and innovation. Jung (1954/1969) wrote:

> There are indications that psychic processes stand in some sort of energy relation to the physiological substrate. In so far as they are objective events, they can hardly be interpreted as anything but energy processes, or to put it another way: in spite of the nonmeasurability of psychic processes, the perceptible changes effected by the psyche cannot possibly be understood except as a phenomenon of energy. (p. 233 [CW 8, para. 441])

As problematic as it is, there is a stubbornness to Jung's return again and again to the actual organ of the brain as the seat of a collective repository of transpersonal material. For example, he wrote:

> This idea has been stamped on the human brain for aeons .... I have often been asked where the archetypes or primordial images come from. It seems to me that their origin can only be explained by assuming them to be deposits of the constantly repeated experiences of humanity. (Jung, 1917/1966, p. 69 [*CW* 7, para. 109])

Jung (1931/1970) described archetypes as the "hidden foundations of the conscious mind ... inherited with the brain structure" (p. 31 [*CW* 10, para. 53]). He also stated:

> The archetypal motives presumably start from the archetypal patterns of the human mind which are not only transmitted by tradition and migration but also by heredity. The latter hypothesis is indispensable, since even complicated archetypal images can be spontaneously reproduced without any possible direct tradition. (Jung, 1938, pp. 63–64)

His postulations did begin to shift, however, as he became increasingly engaged in work with Wolfgang Pauli (Meier, 2001; Von Franz, 1992).

Correspondence between the two men moved Jung into considerations of a *psychoid* archetype, or "psychophysical whole," with two different languages or perspectives—one psychological, one material. Von Franz (1992) described it as "the same world via two different channels" (p. 248). Zabriskie (2001) explained:

> [Jung] increasingly saw psychic energy as a large field from one source, with two complementary but not incompatible conduits, the conscious and the unconscious. These exist between the subjective and objective, emerging from a mind-matter continuum that can only partially observe itself, which Jung came to call "psychoid." (p. xxxviii)

Noting the convergence of multiple streams of inquiry, Von Franz (1992) summarized: "With the emergence of all these surprising analogies, it becomes conceivable that the dimension of universal matter and that of the objective psyche are one" (p. 248). She highlighted the implications:

> If the unconscious psyche appears to be connected with the body, then it is natural to think that it is connected with the *whole* body and not just especially with processes in the brain. In more recent views, the brain appears to be just *one* of a number of sophisticated apparatuses, which is specialized in ordering our perceptions of the external world. (Von Franz, 1992, p. 3)

With this additional nuance, Jung moved outward: from a self-contained, hereditary, inherited apparatus in the human body, and into a non-contained and fluid relationship with matter.

Jung began to entertain the idea of the brain as a transformer station, not just a repository of psychic patterning. He moved beyond the brain's constraints to imagine it as a gatekeeper within a space-time continuum full of collective imprints. In a 1952 letter to John R. Smythies, Jung pondered psychic processes in this way:

> It might be that psyche should be understood as *unextended intensity* and not a body moving with time. One might assume the psyche gradually rising from minute extensity to infinite intensity, transcending for instance the velocity of light and thus irrealizing the body .... In light of this view the brain might be a transformer station, in which the relatively infinite tension or intensity of the psyche proper is transformed into perceptible frequencies or "extensions." Conversely, the fading of introspective perception of the body explains itself as due to a gradual "psychification," i.e., intensification at the expense of extension. Psyche=highest intensity in the smallest space. (Von Franz, 1992, p. 250)

In a later letter to Von Franz (1992), Jung restated:

> We might have to give up thinking in terms of space and time when we deal with the reality of archetypes. It could be that psyche is an unextended intensity, not a body moving in time. One could assume that the psyche arises gradually from the smallest extension to an infinite intensity, and thus robs bodies of their reality when the psychic intensity

transcends the speed of light. Our brain might be the transformation, where the relatively infinite tensions or intensities of the psyche are tuned down to perceptible frequencies and extensions. But in itself the psyche would have no dimension in space and time at all. (pp. 161–162)

In prescient fashion, Von Franz (1992) noted that these postulations might also align with "the new discoveries of psychopharmacologists that seem to show an intimate relationship between the psyche and the body" (p. 250). This connection is, of course, the organizing principle of this current work.

Electroconvulsive therapy (ECT)

Boisen's (1936) work would have come decades too early to have any understanding of how his pool of 173 subjects might have been affected with the treatment options that came available. However, Custance (1951) and Coate (1965) both noted the full force of medical intervention using *electroconvulsive therapy* (ECT). The initial use of electric shock for the treatment of schizophrenia was in 1938, when two Italian physicians collaborated in the treatment of a homeless schizophrenic man who had been arrested by police in Rome (Finger, 1994). After treatment, the once homeless patient was able to regain regular employment.

Coate (1965) described two separate treatment courses. Her first course of treatment while hospitalized, made her very ill over the long term, lasting weeks into her discharge. However, while still in the hospital, she reflected: "I woke one day, as my normal self, to the consciousness that I had recently been mad. I tried to hope that this was not true, that I had dreamed it, and that nothing had really happened. This hope died quickly" (p. 37). After several months, Coate relayed:

> Suddenly one day, without a moment's warning, I was taken ill again. I have no memory of this. I developed a religious delusion and spoke openly of it in a public place. I was admitted to hospital at once, and quickly recovered after a course of E.C.T. (p. 41)

Custance (1951) noted his own treatment as follows:

> The Military Hospital gave me only two convulsions. At the time I was in a state of acute mania, seeing continuous illusions, imagining everyone around me to be resurrected historical personages and convinced that I was destined to start then and there a movement that would save the world. The two convulsions were sufficient to break up the world related to the whole syndrome of vision and phantasy, and within a little more than two months I was discharged as cured. I had no recurrence for two years. (p. 250)

When Custance (1951) reflected on his experience with electroconvulsive therapy (ECT), he wrote:

> Introspectively, ECT appears to shift my observing ego from one state of consciousness to another, or using another metaphor, to push one state of consciousness below the "threshold" of observation and replace it with another .... I could actually feel the phenomenon of elation being pushed away from my consciousness. (p. 251)

Each highlights the dramatic move from one state to another.

The illnesses, themselves, were also well described as energic experiences. Both Custance and Coate experienced their symptomatic periods as altered states of energy inside of their bodies, including explicit references to voltage and electrical activity. Coate (1965) described:

> My brain was like a machine which had been adapted to function normally at a lowered voltage; with the voltage suddenly raised the change in activity and intensity of experience was dramatic, but this carried with it unsuspected dangers. Some good sedation at that stage might well have prevented serious trouble later. (p. 129)

Using a different metaphor, she wrote: "Reason clocks off and leaves the door open to the inner mind. Unconscious impulses, like a band of irresponsible children, take over the telephone exchange and play about with the controls" (p. 150). Custance (1954) echoed Coate's descriptions of heighted voltage: "I can only describe it by saying that 'the lights go up,' as if a kind of switch were turned on in my psycho-physical system. Everything seems different, somehow brighter and clearer" (p. 185). ECT fell out of favor as options increased with the rise of pharmacology in the 1950s and 1960s. However, it has become increasingly utilized in today's medical repertoire for treatment-resistant mania and depression.

Today, the use of electrodes to deliver timed and measured voltage to the brain continues to be honed, especially as it relates to placement of electrodes on either the right or left sides of the brain to study efficacy related to either depression or mania (Goodwin & Jamison, 2007); in the case of ECT, causing small brain seizures seems to be able to "reboot" the brain in a way that relieves symptoms, potentially through the manipulation of neurotransmitters. Two more recent permutations of brain stimulation have also come into use: transcranial magnetic stimulation (TMS), and deep brain stimulation (DBS) (Goodwin & Jamison, 2007; Stahl, 2013). TMS and DBS are both targeted more specifically to the stimulation of particular brain regions in the cortex and limbic system. Magnetic fields and electrical stimulation are both used to encourage polarization and depolarization, which theoretically shifts neurochemical activity. From a lay perspective of someone with a direct experience,

Coate (1965) wrote: "There is obviously a physiological factor in this kind of acute illness. The biochemical aspects of it are still little known. In practice I can sum the process up as follows: cerebral overstimulation, sectional failure of mental organisation, chaos" (p. 150).

Lamictal

My own bodily experiences of psychosis resonate with the above. To remind the reader, I began my titration off of Lamictal in April 2006. By the end of June 2006, my dose had dropped by 30 percent. In a late-night journal entry on June 21, 2006, I wrote: "First day of summer this morning and now we're in the midst of crazy thunderstorm bands. I'm not sure if the electricity in the air is keeping me up, the solstice, or what, but I am overly tired and overly stimulated …. I've been tired and not tired three nights in a row." In the stream-of-consciousness narrative created for the purpose of this research, I described it as follows:

> I am not sleeping well. I am tired, but can't seem to find rest when I lie down. I lie with my eyes closed in the dark, but I feel so much frenetic energy coursing through my insides, it's hard to drift off. I feel like a tuning fork that doesn't stop vibrating. (Durchslag, 2016, p. 43).

Another excerpt from the narrative was temporally located on July 18, 2006, one day before my eventual hospitalization. I had already left Cleveland late the night before on my travel to Martha's Vineyard, MA, and was at a rest stop just inside of New York (the excerpt includes a recollection of impressions earlier in the titration period):

> So here I am, and here the world has reached …. I am floating and ephemeral. It is remarkable the energy I feel around my body. Sheer energy. Outside of my skin yet a part of me. It is like its own magnetic frequency. I remember the first time I really began connecting to the electric frequency of it all. The boundlessness of physical body. Weeks ago, sitting peacefully on my couch in my studio, next to the open window, task lamp on the sidetable, propped on pillows, watching the small television tucked into the bookshelf against the wall. I was well on my way toward being medication free. Was it a week? Two weeks? I don't know. But I remember sitting watching the television, and the energy of the television show and my own were meeting somehow, connected and holding the space between me, the television. We are enfolded into one another. The characters on the television, they are so real. I think, this is some of the best acting I've ever seen. What a remarkable story this is, what remarkable character portrayal, I can literally see and feel the embodiment of that character, well done! I marvel at their craft. I

> remember thinking to myself how wonderful life can be—how ripe, how latent. I think to myself, so this is what it feels like to be off of my medication. This is remarkable. I can feel myself connecting to the boundlessness of it all. Exquisite. And so this is how I feel when I turn off my car and step out at the oasis. All things radiate and move together. I am moving and the world moves around me, but we are slower somehow, a thick membrane of connection in the empty spaces. The bathrooms, the food court, are all on the west-bound side of the oasis. I walk through the glass doors, down the pedestrian bridge, brown berber industrial carpet, people coming and going. I have never felt so connected to earth. I radiate up like an immovable force.

My experience of my body and my sensory perceptions changed dramatically as my medication decreased.

Both Coate and Custance offered similar impressions. Coate (1965) explained, "Colours became more vivid. I saw the sunlit countryside blaze out with the intensity of a Van Gogh" (p. 30). Custance (1954) described it in this way: "If I were asked to describe this change in the fewest possible words, I would say that the universe, the world of so-called material objects presented to my consciousness, came alive" (p. 2). He continued:

> The world in which I found myself during those ecstatic moments, or rather periods—for the abnormal phases sometimes lasted for months—was, as I have just said, a world in which everything came alive .... Animate and inanimate seemed to merge one into the other; I could speak to all things, animal, vegetable and mineral, and all things could speak to me. (Custance, 1954, p. 3)

The above narratives are meant to support the idea that shifts in brain function do manifest like an antenna out into an expansive and differing view of the world outside.

Time

The objective psyche

By the end of Jung's career, archetype became less and less situated in the human story. Jung moved farther and farther away from self-contained, subjectively activated patterns of behavior and outward into the catalyzing effects of universal patterns on the human experience. Turning the subject–object experience inside out, Von Franz (1992) wrote:

> Jung has shown that what we now call the collective unconscious has never been something psychological; it always was relegated to the

outside cosmos, to the extrapsychic cosmic sphere .... Only today do we discover the collective unconscious in the area of the inner psychic experience. (p. 150)

She reiterated: "According to the Jungian view, the collective unconscious is not at all an expression of personal wishes and goals, but is a neutral entity, psychic in nature, that exists in an absolutely transpersonal way" (p. 231). If, as some post-Jungian writers rightly identify, the term collective unconscious fell away in Jung's writing, leading to an isolated debate over archetype, much of the transition does not relate entirely to dismissal, only to a shift toward a more human-neutral tone, the *objective psyche*.

Whitmont (1969) summarized the relationship between the individual and objective psyche: "Jung's concept of the 'objectiveness' of the psyche hypostatizes it as an independent autonomous fact, prior to and regardless of consciousness, with a meaning of its own." He continued: "Its laws ... operate on autonomous terms of their own, irrespective of and at times contrary to and in opposition to consciousness, able to overrule and even to submerge the ego" (p. 55). The disconnect between subject and the function of the objective psyche had substantial implications on the nature of time. Citing the prescient dreams of a bishop that dreamt of the death of Archduke Ferdinand in June 1914 and other examples, Whitmont (1969) summarized:

> These examples illustrate the hypothetical concept or "model" of the objective psyche as a "concealed personality," a pattern of existence, space and time transcending, with an awareness and a function-potential of its own, touching upon and yet quite remote from our rational conscious functioning. (p. 55)

Questions related to the notion of time, and the influence of quantum physics, would permeate Jung's later work.

Von Franz (1992) approached the implications for the collective unconscious and a relativized concept of time in this way:

> If we define the collective unconscious as Jung did, as an omnipresent continuum of an unextended presence or an unextended everywhere, then something that happens at one point, which touches the collective unconscious, has happened everywhere simultaneously. What Jung called an omnipresence he also termed elsewhere a relativity of space-time in the deeper layers of the collective unconscious. This archetypal realm is eternal, i.e., outside time; and also everywhere, i.e., outside space. (p. 161)

As previously stated, many of these extrapolations stemmed from Jung's work with Pauli. Zabriskie (2001) described:

Jung's notion of the archetypes of the collective unconscious implied, so to speak, a supercharge, an "overplus," of energy emerging from those "fields" of interrelated experience that the human psyche is predisposed to find significant .... These exist before and beyond the only personal data of the individual time-and-space-bound ego and so further relativize it. (p. xxxii)

However, these moves did not happen in isolation. They should be seen, instead, as rising out of the cross-pollination of scientific ideas at the Eranos Conferences.

Eranos 1951

The 1951 Eranos Meeting centered around an exploration of time from multidisciplinary and multicultural perspectives (Campbell, 1957). For example, Max Knoll (1951/1957), an electrical engineer and Princeton professor, highlighted four types of time: astronomical time, biological time, psychological time, and cosmic time. Knoll was interested in an astrobiological time: the influence of planetary and universal events on human history. He differentiated astrobiological time as a phenomenon that, "must be distinguished clearly ... from physical time as perceived from 'outer' clocks in the visual cortex" (p. 287)—something different from a cognitive impression from brain activity. Jung's (1952/1969) interest in astrology remains relevant to depth psychology today, in varying forms and degrees,[1] and he utilized the work of others, including that of Knoll, as a justification for continued exploration into the subject. Eliade (1951/1957) focused on transcendence of localized time through yogic traditions. Using the ultimate model of the Buddha, Eliade described: "For him time is reversible, and can even be anticipated: for he knows not only the past but the future" (p. 188). He highlighted the physiological connection to such altered, timeless states through the use of pranayama, specialized breathwork: "There is no adept of Yoga who, in the course of breathing exercises, has not experienced another quality of time" (p. 196). While breathwork clearly influences the human brain, its place is one of a transcendent continuum that sits in opposition to the limits of personal experience. Van der Leeuw (1949/1983) discussed primordial time and final time as "the two poles of one and the same history" (p. 324). He wrote: "The riddle of time is the riddle of the beginning. We know that there can be no true beginning. Something has always gone before. In the beginning lies the whole past. The beginning is the past" (p. 325).

This Eranos conference was also the first time Jung (1951/1957) presented notions of synchronicity. Unlike the contributions above, which highlighted astronomical events or yogic practice, Jung's move into an examination of synchronicity never looked to causation. The *acausal* connecting principle was a cautious label for observable phenomena. In his early exploration of synchronicity, he concluded that "the psyche can, to some extent, eliminate the space factor" and that time "can become psychically relative" (p. 204). Jung stated, "From this it follows either that the psyche cannot be localized in space, or that space is relative to the psyche" (p. 211).

In his later work, Jung (1954/1969) borrowed conceptualizations of the necessity of subject–object observation from the field of physics:

> Physics has demonstrated, as plainly as could be wished, that in the realm of atomic magnitudes an observer is postulated in objective reality, and that only on this condition is a satisfactory scheme of explanation possible. This means that a subjective element attaches to the physicist's world picture. And secondly that a connection necessarily exists between the psyche to be explained and the objective space-time continuum. (p. 230 [*CW*8, para. 440])

Jung saw weighty effects of this for his own theory of psyche:

> If these reflections are justified, they must have weighty consequences with regard to the nature of psyche, since as an objective fact it would then be intimately connected not only with physiological and biological phenomena but with physical events too—and, so it would appear, most intimately of all with those that pertain to the realm of atomic physics. (p. 234 [*CW*8, para. 442])

Speaking from a historical perspective on the influence of quantum theory on time, Le Mouël (2009) summarized:

> Time became relative with Einstein and may simply disappear in a more fundamental description of reality, providing further support to the so-dubbed "mystic view" of a timeless reality .... If time disappears from the fundamental equation of physics, the underlying questions that will need to be answered will be these: First, what is the organizing principle of reality? Second, how do space and time emerge as a consequence of its activity? (p. 77)

Le Mouël linked these questions to Jung's work:

> At this point, a new understanding may emerge of the relationship between science and Jung's notions of how consciousness emerges from its unconscious background through the expression of archetypes. The age-old conception of a world soul or archetypal world that served as a mathematical blueprint for the creation of the universe would thereby receive a modern interpretation. (p. 77)

This description highlights the dramatic move from human evolution and into the universe.

Psychoid

Jung's late move into a psychoid archetype and the unitary nature of psyche and matter allow for consideration from a different perspective. Dating Jung's shift in thinking to 1946, Jaffé (1971) summarized:

> The concept of the psychoid archetype added an altogether new dimension, for the possibility of an archetypal "imprinting" of the physical and inorganic world, and of the cosmos itself, had also to be taken into account. Jung went even further and saw in the psychoid archetype the "bridge to matter in general." (p. 23)

She continued:

> The deeper "layers" of the psyche lose their individual uniqueness as they retreat farther and farther into the darkness. "Lower down," that is to say as they approach the autonomous functional systems, they become increasingly collective until they are universalized and extinguished in the body's materiality, i.e., in chemical substances. The body's carbon is simply carbon. Hence, "at bottom" the psyche is simply world. (p. 23)

This is an interesting statement if we consider the chemical bonds of Lamictal, the fulcrum around which I moved into and out of collective themes.

Narrative accounts seem to reference a timeless connection to the arc of universal development. Boisen (1936) noted:

> About 15 of our group of patients had ideas of previous incarnation. Their eyes had been opened so that they could see back to the beginning of all creation. They had been first one and then another historic character. Some even thought of themselves as passing through various stages of animal evolution. Several thought they were journeying around the universe, visiting Mars and Saturn and the moon and even taking a little jaunt to Arcturus. (p. 193)

Boisen, himself, had this delusional experience:

> The experience of the Psychopathic seemed to me that of passing through all the stages of individual development from the single cell onward. At the same time I seemed to be passing through all the stages in the evolution of the race. I was carried back to the period of deluge, back to the age of marshes and croaking frogs, back to an age of insects and also to an age of birds, I also visited the sun and moon .... I even roamed around the universe. (pp. 115–116)

Morag Coate (1965) shared a similar perspective:

I had been considering time past in its astronomical vastness, and seeing evolution as a visible development; in my imagination I watched it as one may watch a film taken of the opening of a flower, where the speeding up of the pictures make the blossom appear to move and grow and open out before our eyes. (pp. 29–30)

Looking specifically at the beginnings of a human life, she wrote:

> But a deeper unconscious, the preconscious memory of the flesh laid down in embryonic life, may well have more in it that we yet know. The sperm and the ovum are infinitely smaller than the baby, but the impact of their meeting, the loss of their separate identities in one another and the emergence of one single whole combining potentialities derived from both, is the real start of individual life. (p. 134)

She continued: "After that not only growth but also, deep in the living darkness of a safe environment, compressed within nine months of solar time, the recapitulation in organic terms of perhaps two hundred million years" (p. 135).

The non-synchronicity synchronicity: foreknowledge

Jung's visions of World War I

Mulling through the demanding nature of the notion of synchronicity, Jung (1952/1969) wrote: "The great difficulty is that we have absolutely no scientific means of proving the existence of an *objective* meaning which is not just a psychic product" (p. 482 [*CW* 8, para. 915]). This is a scientifically rigorous position. However, he also noted:

> Final causes, twist them how we will, postulate a *foreknowledge* of some kind. It is certainly not a knowledge that could be connected with the ego, and hence not a conscious knowledge as we know it, but rather a self-subsistent "unconscious" knowledge which I would prefer to call "absolute knowledge." It is not cognition but, as Leibniz so excellently calls it, a "perceiving" which consists—or to be more cautious, seems to consist—of images, of subjectless "simulacra." (pp. 493–494, [*CW* 8, para. 931])

Ironically, Jung never highlighted his own experience as any type of objective evidence.

Specifically, I am referring to his visions of World War I so often cited. Jung (1989) recounted this experience:

> Toward the autumn of 1913 the pressure which I had felt was in *me* seemed to be moving outward, as though there were something in the air

.... It was as though a sense of oppression no longer sprang exclusively from a psychic situation, but from concrete reality. (p. 175)

What followed were his visions of floods and destruction prior to the outbreak of World War I. He shared, "That winter someone asked me what I thought were the political prospects of the world in the near future. I replied that I had no thoughts on the matter, but that I saw rivers of blood" (pp. 175–176). He would continue to have dreams for several months, spanning from October 1913 through June of 1914. He reports feeling a sense of confusion:

I asked myself whether these visions pointed to a sort of revolution, but could not really imagine anything of the sort. And so I drew the conclusion that they had to do with me myself, and decided that I was menaced by a psychosis. The idea of war did not occur to me at all. (p. 176)

Yet, by August, World War I had begun. Jung (1989) recounted, "Now my task was clear: I had to understand what had happened and to what extent my own experience coincided with that of mankind in general." This approach began a legacy of intrapsychic focus: "Therefore my first obligation was to probe the depths of my own psyche" (p. 176). He focused his energies on his dreams and fantasies prior to his series of visions related to the war, and then on the dreams, struggles, and overpowering emotion that came after. He focused on the images, the "high rhetoric" and "bombastic" language of the archetypes. Jung took an intentional move down into active dialogue with figures and material. The essential focus became how to navigate the connection to transpersonal material as an intrapsychic phenomenon. He wrote: "The knowledge I was concerned with, or was seeking, still could not be found in the science of those days" (p. 192). He moved into a phenomenological rigor:

My science was the only way I had of extricating myself from that chaos .... I took great care to try to understand every single image, every item of my psychic inventory, and to classify them scientifically—so far as this was possible—and above all, to realize them in actual life. (p. 192)

Jung took personal responsibility for the content, but did not use it as a source of data in his own theory. This has caused a difficult legacy, leading to some serious challenges—valid challenges—to Jung's positions. He contradicted himself at many points, going round-about in order to sidle up to a point he would not simply say outright. Instead, he offered outside case material followed by postulates; for example, the material offered through Leibniz, the Rhine experiments, astrological studies, the Stockholm fire, and any other phenomena existing beside his own (Jung, 1952/1969).[2] There is a type of humility to this approach. Humility, but also a recalcitrance toward acknowledging something that could be considered on the fringes.

Instead, the experience led to the birth of active imagination and a dive inward to find personal connections to images and content. Jung never named this event as synchronistic. Nor did he use it as evidence of synchronicity as he scoured other resources related to things that were labeled as paranormal or psychic phenomena, both of which, 70 years later, continue to remain outside of the hegemonic exploration of personal psychology. For the most part, analytical psychology has remained wedded to looking into dream and fantasy as a personal, intrapsychic, and metaphoric representation of psychic dis-ease. It remains a symbolic amplification of personal material and processes. This offers a unique but exciting dilemma regarding the co-existence of each notion: metaphoric offerings and also non-personal connection to the outside world. This is explored in the chapter to follow.

Jung's fascination with the Eastern oracular instrument of the *I Ching* is another such example of remaining one step removed from any suggestion of something beyond an intrapsychic, subjective interpretation. Jung explored the *I Ching* as evidence of a notion of synchronistic phenomena, but was also afraid to name it anything beyond an acausal phenomenon. Jung (1949/1950) offered his ambivalence in his foreword to Richard Wilhelm's translation of the *Book of Changes*:

> I must confess that I had not been feeling too happy in the course of writing this foreword, for, as a person with a sense of responsibility toward science, I am not in the habit of asserting something I cannot prove or at least present as acceptable to reason. It is a dubious task indeed to try to introduce to a critical modern public a collection of archaic "magic spells," with the idea of making them more or less acceptable. (pp. xiii)

He highlighted that "according to the old tradition, it is 'spiritual agencies,' acting in mysterious ways, that make the yarrow stalks give a meaningful answer" (p. v). He never acknowledged that position in his foreword. He continued to look at his own intrapsychic, subjective projection of meaning. The rest he left floating in the ether. Even this felt an additional risk for Jung. He shared:

> I know that previously I would not have dared to express myself so explicitly about so uncertain a matter. I can take that risk because I am now in my eighth decade, and the changing opinions of men scarcely impress me anymore; the thoughts of old masters are of greater value to me than the philosophical prejudices of the Western mind. (p. xv)

Yet even as he identified taking greater risks in expounding on his use of the *I Ching* than he ever would have done earlier in his career, he still took a position once removed. He categorized the analysis of his answers from the *I Ching* as "elucidating [its] psychological phenomenology" (p. xx). He assured the reader that "nothing occult is to be inferred. My position in these matters is pragmatic" (p. xiv).

In summary, while Jung begins a theoretical exploration of a connection between internal experience and suprapersonal commentary and a nullified time–space continuum, he leaves himself out as much as possible.

My own delusions

I bring up Jung's visions of World War I as a preface to further analysis of my own psychotic experience. The goal thus far has been to highlight that my own delusional content, as well as reports from others, support transcendent collective themes. There is reason to look at the content according to the developments in Jung's thinking related to time and synchronicity, as well. I cannot claim any type of comfort with touching on the thematic lens offered below, but it offers yet another way in which to explore a physiological connection to transpersonal content. As stated, the material I have been referencing happened 13 years ago, in 2006. I could not have made my assertion below in 2012 when I began my research project. But a luxury of hindsight allows me to make an assertion about the above that I cannot find my way around, even though it puts me into a precarious position. It seems, like Jung's own prescient connection to events in 1914, I may have had my own experience with such phenomena during a lapse in my medication for bipolar I disorder. Restating the summary of content offered in Chapter 5:

> I am convinced that the hegemonic power structure in the United States is going to be challenged. The marginalized and disenfranchised Black culture is positioned and ready to overthrow the Federal government— the seat of White hegemonic culture—in an orchestrated coup, a coup in which I play a central role. White Nationalist neo-Nazis are aligned as the military arm of the Federal government .... There is a younger generation of Americans that has known this has had to happen for quite some time, but they have been waiting for our generation to take action .... This youth movement was most recognizable in the fluid nature of fashion trends and gender identification.

The high rhetoric and bombastic language of archetype is pervasive in the description of my behavior:

> As my 700-mile journey continues, I realize that the neo-Nazis have been tipped off about the coup. They have begun to mobilize and have come out onto the highways. I increasingly realize that the coup has failed and that I, personally, have failed in my military responsibility. I am despondent and believe I have lost the right to live. I wait to be killed by my own army.

Taking into consideration this overstated, rigid, and bombastic language of archetypal content, 13 years later, there are some remarkable parallels to the world as we know it now.

Since the time of my experience, the United States has elected its first African-American president. There has been renewed activism within the African-American culture; but, also, a rise in visibility of a white supremacist movement that always lurked in the shadows, felt in its most radical forms as racist extremists currently labeled as the Alt-Right. A national stage for the rights of transgender and gender-fluid identity in our culture has also expanded. Yet in many respects, the coup of recalibrating power, at least for the time being, has failed.[3] Collective categories of heroic apotheosis, cosmic conflict, and new society now seem connected to a time–space dilemma. Is it sound to relegate my psychotic delusions relating to racial conflict; attempts at dislodging power from a hegemonic white culture; and shifting images of gender identification as metaphoric offerings for an intrapsychic reorganization?

A return to the intrapsychic dilemma

The psychodynamic argument

Regardless of how someone in the field of analytical psychology makes sense of delusional content—connection to collective material or the memories of personal experience—the idea has always been one of intrapsychic transformation. Even Perry, who spent 50 years devoted to understanding archetypal patterns, returned to this model. He wrote: "In an acute psychosis individuals undergo a profound reorganization of the self, effected by a thoroughgoing reintegration through utter disintegration" (Perry, 1999, p. 26). This frame certainly aligns with psychodynamic notions of ego fragmentation and reintegration, highlighted in Chapter 3.

Case in point, Perry (2005) shared delusional material from a female client focused on environmental catastrophe. The patient's own messianic mission was described as follows:

> In the sixth week she launched into a full account of her messianic mission. She said she knew it was her duty to grow things in the earth, to plant and to sow, and to reap. Working herself into a high rage, she shouted that people should give up the evils of using metals and of working in cities. They should stop digging down into the inside of the earth to draw metals out of it; that's digging down into Mother Earth and taking things out that shouldn't be taken. All these machines and industries and cars are wrong—it should all be left in the earth, in the soil. (p. 80)

Perry reported the patient would recite "a somewhat obscure apocryphal text," which illuminated a "crazy tirade against evils of metals." He initially felt it was "a fairly confused and crazy notion emanating from her resentment of personal circumstances." However, after finding the actual Biblical text noted above he realized "it was fairly in line with a whole development of messianic thinking from the first century B.C." (p. 81): Quoting the text, he wrote:

> It says the name of the Messiah was named from before the beginning of time: "Before the sun and the planets were created, before the stars in the heavens were made, his name was named before the God of Spirits. In the blessed Days of the Messiah, 'Wisdom' will be 'as the waters [that] cover the sea.'" (p. 81)

In treating the patient, Perry (2005) admitted:

> I must confess that I found it at first a little distasteful to explore, and that I had some revulsion toward these grandiose claims. It was easy to regard them as a kind of parody of the adolescent fantasies accompanying the idealistic urge to reform the human race. (p. 79)

However, he shared that his revulsion lessened once he shifted his understanding of the delusions to a process of self-reorganization.

Perry (2005) remarked:

> As soon as we translate these images and processes into inner experience, there is nothing especially crazy about them—they are just like dreams, essentially. We may translate for "world," the "inner world"; for "war," the inner "conflict of opposites"; and now for "messianic calling" we may say "the inner hero image which has a special mission in the psyche to bring transformation of one's inner world"; and for "new society" we may say "the inner subjective culture that stands in need of change; that is, one's structure of values and meanings, outlook and design of life." (p. 78)

Regardless of the attribution to a subjective frame, Perry (2005) reiterated his patient's messianic calling as an archetypal pattern: "Item by item, this person's psyche appears to be spelling out the imagery of the messianic theme just as it had been two thousand years ago" (p. 82).

The amplification of these developmental struggles aligned with Jung's notion of a collective unconscious. Perry (2005) summarized:

> This indicates the difference between a personal and a collective mental content; that is, between an image derived from the personal circumstances and figures of the person's own life, and one from the general archaic heritage of images expressing universal emotional experiences of mankind. There are many kinds of evidence for the prevalence of this

theme of the reformed society and its messianic agencies, not the least of which is the fact that persons in this schizophrenic process sound much like one another. Another is the evidence of history. Not only that of a couple of millennia ago, but also that of today and the cultural movements that are being stirred up in the present psychic setting. (p. 83)

The question is whether we can remain entirely in Perry's, and even Jung's, safe zone of exploring material as manifesting for the sole purpose of an intrapsychic ego-reintegration.

A return to the collective

Why, in psychotic states, do those suffering from severe mental illness move into social commentary? Boisen (1936), for example, echoed environmental concerns:

Although I had never given any serious thought to such a subject, there came flashing into my mind, as though from a source without myself, the idea that this little planet of ours, which has existed for we know not how many millions of years, was about to undergo some sort of metamorphosis. It was like a seed or an egg. In it were stored up a quantity of food materials, represented by our natural resources. But now we were like a seed in the process of germinating or an egg that had just been fertilized. We were starting to grow. Just within the short space of a hundred years we had begun to draw upon our resources to such an extent that the timber and the gas and the oil were likely soon to be exhausted. In the wake of this idea followed others. (p. 3)

Recall my own narrative moved into sorrow and anger about the environment and social commentary. There is a mystery of a collective energy—as indelibly captured in the experience of the psychotic and carefully exemplified here in the first-hand narratives of those who have experienced it—which seems to be both a recollection of the past, somehow, and also a pre-cognition of a potential future.

In her analysis of archetypal patterns in fairy tales, Von Franz (1997) described the collective unconscious as an electromagnetic field, and archetypes as "excited points, points in which energy in the field is bundled, so to speak" (p. 40). In our childhood art projects, the glitter of emotionally charged personal experience gets stuck to the glue of archetypal patterns. Considering the brain as a transformer station, perhaps, in the electrical confusion and physiological diffusion described by people suffering from severe mental illness, the electromagnetic field of glitter becomes glued to collective shifts and energy. Whether expressed eschatologically, politically, or at a cosmic and universal level, delusional content might pick up on the objective psyche's commentary of the time. I cannot claim any exceptional connection to this collective material. In fact, the whole purpose of the exploration of my psychotic narrative above is to link its manifestation to the presence or absence of my medication for the genetic disorder, bipolar I disorder.

Why, with 400 mg of Lamictal each day, do I maintain an ego orientation? If I take my medication, I walk around in my singularly intrapsychic, neurotic world. Perhaps, as I am proposing in the current hermeneutic, bipolar I disorder, in its neuronal excitability and energic shifts, marks a connection to the time–space, psyche–matter diffusion. The genetic nature of the disorder suggests a deeply rooted sensitivity toward this type of permeability. The deeper the root, the more connected it becomes to a transpersonal realm, even without the seat of the mnemonic brain.

Jung (1948/1969) wrote about this is in some detail in his essay, "The Psychological Foundation of Belief in Spirits." In it, he contrasted a rise of intrapsychic complexes with a differing, collective tone. He wrote:

> So far as I can judge, these experiences occur either when something so devastating happened to the individual that his whole previous attitude to life breaks down, or when for some reason the contents of the collective unconscious accumulate so much energy that they start influencing the conscious mind. (p. 314 [*CW* 8, para. 594])

As explanation, Jung returned to a notion of a non-localized repository of energy, this one pertaining to the general tenor of a cultural epoch or societal feel:

> It seems to me, however, that external circumstances often serve merely as occasions for a new attitude to life and the world, long prepared in the unconscious, to become manifest. Social, political, and religious conditions affect the collective unconscious in the sense that all those factors which are suppressed by the prevailing views or attitudes in the life of a society gradually accumulate in the collective unconscious and activate its contents. (p. 314, para. 594)

Custance (1951) offered the collective move in dramatic fashion:

> It seems to be possible to detect in the periodicity of history something in the nature of a two-thousand year rhythm .... If this is so, must not the time be ripe, and overripe, for a great reversal of the Positive revolution of the first millennium B.C.?
>
> The whole course of my visionary experiences has forced this view on my rational consciousness. Cold or hot, World War III must and will be fought to a finish, and it will be a war of the Negative against the Positive in which the victory of the Negative is as necessary and inevitable as that the horned moon will rise tonight. (pp. 203–204)

The epochal nature of collective history is front and center.

Both Jung (1948/1969) and Perry (1999) considered psychological connection to such energy as a particular type of permeability which often manifested in psychosis. Jung (1948/1969) suggested that such individuals might be "gifted with particularly strong intuition." He stated, "Nevertheless, the mental state of the people as a whole might well be compared to a psychosis" (*CW* 8, p. 315 [para. 595]). Perry (1999) looked at three different options when working with psychotic individuals: (1) the person might be especially equipped for social, religious, or cultural leadership, which "is making its first appearance in a 'psychotic' turmoil; (2) the intrapsychic self-reorganization described in detail above; or (3) the person "might be in the throes of a disintegrative process that will lead gradually into the downhill course and chronicity of true 'schizophrenia'" (p. 29).

Subjective mud

As referenced above, Perry (1999) was inclined to treat psychotic episodes without medication even though the results often led into "the downhill course and chronicity of true 'schizophrenia' after six months" (p. 29), Perry felt that "going through the whole experience [psychosis] without medication allows the image process to proceed" (p. 27). Narrative accounts of this type of psychotic material show how this often occurs from an amplification of a real-world event glimpsed through a psychotic mind. For example, Coate (1965) described:

> Suddenly a number of events took place which were of great significance. A submarine under the ice above the pole. Trapped miners seeking a way of escape. A moving and impressing burial at sea. A major earthquake in the part of the world that had specific spiritual associations for me. I knew without doubt what this meant; the liberation of hell was at hand. At the same time a spiritual migration of free souls was taking place. Earth for them was a temporary stopping-place.... No one else noticed, but I recognised them at once. I made no comment, there was no need; it was enough to know. (p. 55)

She continued:

> For the next few days life was normal. Then by degrees elements from the other world began to slip through and interweave themselves into daily life. There was a tall, dark, distinguished, bearded stranger about the place, and I recognised him as a younger version of Wotan the Wanderer. Events must certainly be stirring in the unseen for him to arrive on earth. (p. 79)

Here, regular life is taking on archetypal amplification. Coate is able to reflect on the increasingly disorganized nature of these amplifications and her fall into overlapping myths, characters, and events. She described how her visions of Armageddon and the Last Judgment became tangled with:

> racial intolerance, the spurious sunrise of an atomic explosion, deep-sea diving, mermaids, and the faded flowers of Persephone. Weaving through it was the resistance movement of the underworld, the smuggling of souls back across the Styx, and the unsolved mystery story of the Holbein Christ at Basle. (p. 84)

These increasingly disjointed musings still show traces of archetypal patterns. However, there is something about the increasing severity of psychosis that increases the firing of mythic material, one story on top of the other.

At its worst, while in the depths of his psychosis in a mental hospital, Custance (1951) described inanimate objects—like pillow-cases, billiard balls, and towels—as personified at the archetypal level, for example, "the god Baal, with a cruel mouth like a slit" or "Hecate, who used generally to appear in pillows" (p. 72). He highlighted the fear involved:

> A crumpled pillow is quite an ordinary object, is it not? So is a washing-rag, or a towel tumbled on the floor .... Yet they can suggest shapes of utmost horror to the mind obsessed by fear .... With these visions surrounding me it is not strange that the material world should seem less and less real. I felt myself gradually descending alive into the pit by a sort of metamorphosis of my surroundings. (p. 72)

The observing ego by all accounts is compromised to such a degree that sense and distinction become impossible. This clearly is what happened to me, as well. By the time I was hospitalized, my gurney could fly, the nicotine patches left in the shower were listening devices, and the way my washcloth was positioned on the sink served as a message left by one of the orderlies.

As Perry (1999) outlined: "The third group, because of the impoverished state of our knowledge at present, needs medication early to prevent damage to brain functioning and undo chronicity" (p. 30). But perhaps there is no "group," per se, only a continuum of connection. This is explored in the next chapter.

Notes

1 See for example, works written by authors Liz Green, Keiron Le Grice, and Richard Tarnas. These include original pieces of work, and also edited collections on Jung's own work on astrology.
2 The effect of Jung's ambivalence on his writing and theory was first sparked for me during a presentation by Cynthia Poorbaugh at the 2017 conference on holism held at Essex University: "The Anxiety of Holism with Regard to Astrology."

3 Black Lives Matter and the modern permutation of the Alt-Right rose in tandem as polar reactions in the time period of 2012–2014. Black Lives Matter attributes its rise to the shooting of teenager, Trayvon Martin, with the official statement by the movement: "In 2013, three radical Black organizers—Alicia Garza, Patrisse Cullors, and Opal Tometi—created a Black-centered political will and movement building project called #BlackLivesMatter. It was in response to the acquittal of Trayvon Martin's murderer, George Zimmerman" (https://blacklivesmatter.com/herstory/). Hankes and Amend (2018) noted: "The alt-right movement is largely traced to 2012–14, with the killing of black teenager Trayvon Martin and the 'Gamergate' harassment campaign that targeted female game developers and journalist for entering the male-dominated space" (p. 31). According to *The Washington Post* (Barrett, 2018): "Reported hate crimes in America rose 17 percent last year, the third consecutive year that such crimes increased, according to newly released FBI data that showed an even larger increase in anti-Semitic attacks. Law enforcement agencies reported that 7,175 hate crimes occurred in 2017, up from 6,121 in 2016. That increase was fueled in part by more police departments reporting hate crime data to the FBI, but overall there is still a large number of departments that report no hate crimes to the federal database. The sharp increase in hate crimes in 2017 came even as overall violent crime in America fell slightly, by 0.2 percent, after increases in 2015 and 2016."

References

Barrett, D. (2018, November 13). Hate crimes rose 17 percent last year, according to new FBI data. Retrieved from *The Washington Post*. https://www.washingtonpost.com/world/national-security/hate-crimes-rose-17-percent-last-year-according-to-new-fbi-data/2018/11/13/e0dcf13e-e754-11e8-b8dc-66cca409c180_story.html?wpmk=1&wpisrc=al_news__alert-national&noredirect=on

Boisen, A. T. (1936). *The exploration of the inner world: A study of mental disorder and religious experience*. Philadelphia, PA: University of Pennsylvania.

Campbell, J. (Ed.). (1957). *Man and time: Papers from the Eranos yearbooks*, Vol. 3. Princeton, NJ: Princeton University Press.

Coate, M. (1965). *Beyond all reason*. Philadelphia, PA: J. B. Lippincott.

Custance, J. (1951). *Wisdom, madness and folly: The philosophy of a lunatic*. London: Victor Gollancz.

Custance, J. (1954). *Adventure into the unconscious*. London: Christopher Johnson.

Durchslag, H. B. (2015). A narrative analysis of bipolar psychosis: An empirical relationship between neurochemistry and the collective unconscious. (Doctoral Dissertation). Retrieved from Proquest https://search.proquest.com/docview/1668380821.

Durchslag, H. B. (2016). Severe mental illness: A bridge between neurochemistry and the collective unconscious. *Psychological Perspectives*, 59(1), 30–45. doi:10.1080/00332925.2016.1134210.

Eliade, M. (1951/1957). Time and eternity in Indian thought. In J. Campbell, (Ed.), *Man and time: Papers from the Eranos yearbooks*, Vol. 3 (pp. 173–200). Princeton, NJ: Princeton University Press.

Finger, S. (1994). *Origins of neuroscience: A history of explorations into brain function*. New York, NY: Oxford University Press.

Goodwin, F. K., & Jamison, K. R. (2007). *Manic-depressive illness: Bipolar disorders and recurrent depression*. New York, NY: Oxford University Press.

Goodwyn, E. D. (2012). *The neurobiology of the gods: How brain physiology shapes the recurrent imagery of myth and dreams.* Hove, UK: Routledge.
Hankes, K., & Amend, A. (2018, February 5). The Alt-Right is killing people. *Southern Poverty Law Center.* Retrieved from https://www.splcenter.org/20180205/alt-right-killing-people
Jaffé, A. (1971). *The myth of meaning: Jung and the expansion of consciousness* (R. F. C. Hull, Trans.). New York, NY: Penguin Books.
Jung, C. G. (1938). *Psychology and religion: Based on the Terry Lectures delivered at Yale University.* New Haven, CT: Yale University Press.
Jung, C. G. (1949/1950). Foreword. In R. Wilhelm, *The I Ching or book of changes* (C. F. Baynes, Trans.) (pp. i–xx). New York, NY: Pantheon.
Jung, C. G. (1951/1957). On synchronicity. In J. Campbell, (Ed.), *Man and time: Papers from the Eranos Yearbooks,* Vol. 3 (pp. 201–211). Princeton, NJ: Princeton University Press.
Jung, C. G. (1917/1966). On the psychology of the unconscious. In H. Read, M. Fordham, G. Adler, & W. McGuire (Eds.), *The collected works of C.G. Jung* (R. F. C. Hull, Trans.) (2nd ed., Vol. 7, pp. 9–171). Princeton, NJ: Princeton University Press.
Jung, C. G. (1931/1969). The structure of the psyche. In H. Read, M. Fordham, G. Adler, & W. McGuire (Eds.), *The collected works of C.G. Jung* (R. F. C. Hull, Trans.) (2nd ed., Vol. 8, pp. 139–158). Princeton, NJ: Princeton University Press.
Jung, C. G. (1931/1970). Mind and earth. Civilization in transition. In H. Read, M. Fordham, G. Adler, & W. McGuire (Eds.), *The collected works of C.G. Jung* (R. F. C. Hull, Trans.) (2nd ed., Vol. 10, pp. 29–49). Princeton, NJ: Princeton University Press.
Jung, C. G. (1934/1969). The soul and death. In H. Read, M. Fordham, G. Adler, & W. McGuire (Eds.), *The collected works of C.G. Jung* (R. F. C. Hull, Trans.) (2nd ed., Vol. 8, pp. 404–415). Princeton, NJ: Princeton University Press.
Jung, C. G. (1948/1969). The psychological foundation of belief in spirits. In H. Read, M. Fordham, G. Adler, & W. McGuire (Eds.), *The collected works of C.G. Jung* (R. F. C. Hull, Trans.) (2nd ed., Vol. 8, pp. 301–318). Princeton, NJ: Princeton University Press.
Jung, C. G. (1952/1969). Synchronicity: An acausal connecting principle. In H. Read, M. Fordham, G. Adler, & W. McGuire (Eds.), *The collected works of C.G. Jung* (R. F. C. Hull, Trans.) (2nd ed., Vol. 8, pp. 419–519). Princeton, NJ: Princeton University Press.
Jung, C. G. (1954/1969). On the nature of psyche. In H. Read, M. Fordham, G. Adler, & W. McGuire (Eds.), *The collected works of C.G. Jung* (R. F. C. Hull, Trans.) (2nd ed., Vol. 8, pp. 159–234). Princeton, NJ: Princeton University Press.
Jung, C. G. (1989). *Memories, dreams, reflections* (R. Winston & C. Winston, Trans.). New York, NY: Vintage Books.
Knoll, M. (1951/1957). Transformations of science in our age. In J. Campbell (Ed.), *Man and time: Papers from the Eranos yearbooks,* Vol. 3 (pp. 264–307). Princeton, NJ: Princeton University Press.
Le Mouël, C. (2009). Spirit into matter: Exploring the myth of science. *Psychological Perspectives,* 52(1), 54–79. doi:10.1080/00332920802662260.
Meier, C. A. (Ed.). (2001). *Atom and archetype: The Pauli/Jung letters 1932–1958.* Princeton, NJ: Princeton University Press.
Perry, J. W. (1999). *Trials of the visionary mind: Spiritual emergency and the renewal process.* Albany, NY: State University of New York.
Perry, J. W. (2005). *The far side of madness* (2nd ed.). Putnam, CT: Spring Publications.

Stahl, S. M. (2013). *Stahl's essential psychopharmacology: Neuroscientific basis and practical applications.* New York, NY: Cambridge University Press.

Van Der Leeuw, G. (1949/1983. Primordial time and final time. In J. Campbell, (Ed.), *Man and time: Papers from the Eranos Yearbooks*, Vol. 3 (pp. 324–350). Princeton, NJ: Princeton University Press.

Von Franz, M. (1992). *Psyche and matter.* Boston, MA: Shambhala.

Von Franz, M. (1997). *Archetypal patterns in fairy tales.* Toronto, Canada: Inner City Books.

Whitmont, E. C. (1969). *The symbolic quest: Basic concepts of analytical psychology.* Princeton, NJ: Princeton University Press.

Zabriskie, B. (2001). Jung and Pauli: A meeting of rare minds. In C. A. Meier (Ed.), *Atom and archetype: The Pauli/Jung letters, 1932–1958* (pp. xxvii–l). Princeton, NJ: Princeton University Press.

Chapter 8

From the transpersonal to the suprapersonal

Individuation and the unavoidable dilemma

> For Jung, individuation and realization of the meaning of life are identical—since individuation means to find one's own meaning, which is nothing more than one's own connection to universal Meaning. This is clearly something other than what is referred to today by terms such as information, super-intelligence, cosmic or universal mind—because feeling, emotion, the Whole of the person, is included.
>
> (Von Franz, 1992, p. 258)

The problem of spirit

As fleetingly mentioned in Chapter 7, the use of the term *collective unconscious* is becoming increasingly obsolete, so much so that Mills (2018b) suggested dispensing with it altogether: "If an archetype is self-constituted and self-generative, the notion and validity of a collective unconscious becomes rather dubious, if not superfluous" (p. 40). It is true that with more modern post-Jungian definitions of archetype, it seems entirely unnecessary. For example, Brooke (2015) offered the following:

> Considering the evolution of the concept made it possible to sift out some of the inadequate or misleading formulations Jung had made, and to arrive at the following definition: the archetypes are the sources of typical actions, reactions, and experiences that characterize the human species. The archetypes are the primordial roots of those complexes which structure behavior, images, affects, and thoughts as these emerge in the typical situations of human life. (p. 163)

The definition above references a source, and also some type of primordial root, but passes over the continued difficulty with how such roots are transmitted and from whence they came. One of Jung's own descriptions is well captured in Brooke's summary:

> To the extent that the archetypes intervene in the shaping of conscious contents by regulating, modifying, or motivating them, they act like instincts. It is therefore very natural to suppose that these factors are connected with the instincts and to inquire whether the typical situational patterns which these collective form-principles apparently represent are not in the end identical with the patterns of behavior. (Jung (1954/1969a), p. 205 [*CW* 8, para. 404])

Over the past decade, scholarship on definitions has focused primarily on this instinctual pole in Jung's explorations (Goodwyn, 2010a, 2010b, 2012, 2013; Hogenson, 2004; Knox, 2003; Knox, Merchant, & Hogenson, 2010; Merchant, 2006, 2009). For example, Haule (2011a) examined the archetype of language; Hogenson (Knox et al., 2010), the archetype of turn-taking. This is understandable if the definition of archetype becomes aligned with behavior which is thought to be strongly influenced by instinct. A focus on archetype from the pole of instinct, alone, has shifted the definition of archetype to an analysis of primary emotions, such as rage or panic (Haule, 2011a; Knox et al., 2010). Jung opened himself to this type of instinctual and behavioral extrapolation. For example, he examined the innate behaviors of a species of ants as a means of understanding the effect of archetypal patterns (Jung, 1954/1969a). Stevens (2003) capitalized on this line of inquiry in his discussion of the behavioral patterns of birds. However, this is only a portion of Jung's intent.

The aspect of archetypal manifestation left behind is that of spirit. In one description of this relationship, Jung (1954/1969a) wrote:

> Psychologically, however, the archetype as an image of instinct is a spiritual goal toward which the whole nature of man strives; it is the sea to which all rivers wend their way, the prize which the hero wrests from the fight with the dragon. (p. 212 [*CW* 8, para. 415])

He stated:

> I must stress one aspect of the archetypes which will be obvious to anybody who has practical experience of these matters. That is, the archetypes have, when they appear, a distinctly numinous character which can only be described as "spiritual," if "magical" is too strong a word. (p. 205 [*CW* 8, para. 405])

This magic is the difficulty that underlies much of Jung's work. By dispensing with the collective unconscious, we dispense with some of the magic.

Mills (2018b) highlighted that the notion of a collective unconscious throws Jung's work into the unfortunate realm of a "transpersonal cosmogony." It places Jung's theory within a supernaturalistic debate that evokes "supernatural foundations, organizations, and mystical properties, which evoke greater metaphysical questions such as emanationism, supervenience, and the God posit" (p. 42). Mills cautioned:

> If we push this issue further, boundaries quickly become blurred to the point that the collective unconscious could be synonymous with the concept of God, the actor, and the act of creation taking place in and at the center of the cosmos. If we adopt this point of view, namely, of deifying the collective unconscious as a supernatural macroanthropos, it would be disastrous for Jungian studies, as the theoretical foundation of analytical psychology would succumb to inventing unverifiable fictions that satisfy the wishful fantasies of imagination at the expense of reason, logic, and science. (p. 41)

Whether or not it is deserved of Mills's relegation to such "isms" and harbinger of disaster, the "problem with god" inevitably rises.

This was something so tenuous for Jung that he caused much of the problem over definitions himself. He tried to answer without answering, per se. For example, Jung (1954/1969b) wrote:

> It is quite impossible to conceive how "experience" in the widest sense, or, for that matter, anything psychic, could originate exclusively in the outside world. The psyche is part of the inmost mystery of life, and it has its own peculiar structure and form like every other organism. Whether this psychic structure and its elements, the archetypes, ever "originated" at all is a metaphysical question and therefore unanswerable. (p. 101 [*CW* 9i, para. 187])

Jung (1989) wrote: "And if, by employing the concept of archetype, we attempt to define a little more closely the point at which the daimon grips us, we have not abolished anything, only approached closer to the source of life" (p. 349). Mills (2018a) challenged this liberalism, as well:

> But Jung also referred to archetypes as concepts, hypotheses, heuristic models, and metaphors (*CW* 9, p. 160) when he was backtracking from his earlier philosophical commitments under the banner of science. And he was very clear to announce that he was conducting empirical psychology, not speculative philosophy, and went to great lengths to claim that his theories had nothing to do with metaphysics (*CW* 11, p. 16) despite the fact that he was engaging ontology. This is not a convincing, let alone coherent or sustainable, argument. So where does this leave us? (pp. 200–201)

It leaves us smack in the middle of a debate from time immemorial. My educational background precludes me from entering a learned philosophical debate. However, the purpose of this book is to add to what is undeniably empirical psychological material, and to do so with an open door to Jung's underlying connection to a suprapersonal principle. In Chapter 7 the collective unconscious was explored as an aspect of energy and matter. It also suggests connection to the ephemeral notion of a suprapersonal principle.

The suprapersonal

Naming

Carefully reviewing Jung's writing from the intimate position as Jung's personal secretary, Jaffé (1971) understood Jung to be discussing "the spiritual background of the world" (p. 14), and noted that "God and the unconscious are synonymous concepts" (p. 44). However, using the term *God* can be contextualized to label a connection to anything of a divine or spiritual nature. R. D. Laing offered a useful statement:

> When it comes to the words we use, including the word spiritual, all such words are so used and abused and prostituted that I can't use any of them without having to disclaim their current useage. Similarly, the way they are understood apparently by most people who use them, and that includes the word spiritual and such words as divine, God, love, charity, compassion, time, eternity, space … all of the terms that we use to express what we think about when we say what we are thinking which refers to the whole lot. (Mullan, 1996, p. 310)

The "whole lot" might be considered a contributor to a collective unconscious, but use of the word God is not a limiting one according to religion; it can be used to denote any type of transcendent influence.

The collective unconscious, according to Jung, was a neutralized term. In his final contributions to his autobiography, Jung (1989) wrote:

> If anyone is inclined to believe that any aspect of the *nature* of such things is changed by such formulations, he is being extremely credulous about words. The real facts do not change, whatever name we give them. Only we ourselves are affected. If one were to conceive of "God" as "pure Nothingness," that has nothing whatsoever to do with the fact of a superordinate principle. We are just as much possessed as before; the change of name has removed nothing at all from reality. At most we have taken a false attitude toward reality if a new name implies a denial. On the other hand, a positive name of the unknowable has the merit of putting us into a correspondingly positive attitude. If, therefore, we speak of "God" as an "archetype," we are saying nothing of His real nature but are letting it be known that "God" already has a place in that part of our

psyche which is pre-existent to consciousness and that He therefore cannot be considered an invention of consciousness. We neither make Him more remote nor eliminate Him, but bring Him closer to the possibility of being experienced. (pp. 347–348)

In his later years, Jung allowed himself to be less careful with his language. He shared that his choice of the term *unconscious* was a calculated one, so that he might work from a more scientifically acceptable premise: "Hence I prefer the term 'the unconscious' knowing that I might equally well speak of 'God'" (p. 336). Jung (1934/1969) highlighted that the terms *soul* and *religion* are the historical language of the unconscious:

This was the standpoint of past ages, which, knowing the untold treasures of experience lying hidden beneath the threshold of ephemeral individual consciousness, always held the individual soul to be dependent on a spiritual world-system. Not only did they make this hypothesis, they assumed without question that this system was a being with a will and consciousness—was even a person—and they called this being God, the quintessence of reality. (p. 351 [*CW* 8, para. 677])

Overall, the process of naming something also substantially limits the undefinable essence that the name is meant to touch.

Narrative

Somewhere within the genetic disorders explored thus far, there is a consistent connection to religiosity or spiritual connection of some kind. This rises during acute phases of these disorders, often for the first time, or at the least, in more intensified fashion. For example, Custance (1951) stated, "Manic-depression brought to me—as it does to nearly all who suffer from it—an intense emotional religious experience" (p. 13). Later, he described it this way:

I, a very ordinary lunatic and a miserable sinner, have personally experienced something of the kind, which has not totally abandoned me. What I seem to have secured through the strange and unforgettable experiences of manic-depression is precisely the sense of purpose, the "apprehension of the altogether," of which I have written. In ordinary language it is simply faith in God, and an indefinable sense of nearness to Him. (Custance, 1954, p. 216)

Boisen (1936) echoed this connection:

These periods have, moreover, been fertile in all sorts of ideas. They have opened up, as by powerful flashes of insight, new avenues of service and new vistas into the great unknown .... I should be untrue to my trust if I did not bear witness to the fact that the idea which I have since been following out with some measure of success was given to me at the time as by an Intelligence beyond my own. It was an idea which I never before had dreamed. I believe therefore that this experience of mine, with all its pathological features, was akin to that of the prophets of old. (p. 115)

Coate (1965) described the numinosity in this way:

I was in a state of the most vivid awareness and illumination. What can I say of it? A cloudless, cerulean blue sky of the mind, shot through with shafts of exquisite, warm, dazzling sunlight .... It seemed that some force or impulse from without were acting on me, looking into me; that I was in touch with a reality beyond my own; that I had made direct contact with the secret, the ultimate source of life. What I had read of the accounts of others acquired suddenly a new meaning. It flashed across my mind, "This is what the mystics mean by the direct experience of God." (pp. 21–22)

My own personal experiences have been just as powerful.

For some reason, the overall impressions are much more easily left to John Custance, Morag Coate, and Anton Boisen. Their eloquence supersedes my own poetic facility. In past writing, however, I have tried to capture the overarching numinosity of connection to a divine presence, even if in inferior fashion. For example, in a piece of creative fiction, I wrote: "I was discovering glimmers of heaven on earth"; and held a "growing belief that the divine was held in each minute—that each traceable, measurable, predictable tick of the secondhand was laced and wound in its invisible presence." I stated: "I was into this phase where everything had to be capitalized, because everything was beginning to breathe its own essence—and the essence was demanding attention. Like Beauty with a capital 'B'" (Durchslag, 2006). I was not psychotic during the time period in which the reflection above took place, but it would likely have been diagnosed as a hypomanic episode. The time period of most importance to the current research project is the fulcrum of medication and psychosis, but an exploration of the spectrum of mania has potential to shed light on some of Jung's exploration of moves across the instinct—spirit spectrum.

Abaissement du niveau mental

A spectrum of connection

Overall, severe mental illnesses are both physiological in nature and often spiritual in nature. Furthermore, as highlighted at the end of Chapter 7, there is a movement on a spectrum of experience related to shifts in ego perspective.

The psychotic individual falls into an ever-increasing spiral of overlapping material in disordered and fragmented fashion. Archetypal amplification and mythic storylines invade commonplace objects, linear time, and attribution of meaning. Whether or not the material is considered transpersonal or suprapersonal in nature, psychosis is divorced from an orienting ego. Jung utilized this sort of sliding scale related to ego-orientation across the neurotic spectrum as well: an *abaissement du niveau mental*.

Crediting Pierre Janet, Jung (1952/1969) took this phrase to note levels of consciousness:

> Every emotional state produces an alteration of consciousness which Janet called *abaissement du niveau mental*; that is to say there is a certain narrowing of consciousness and a corresponding strengthening of the unconscious …. The tone of the unconscious is heightened, thereby creating a gradient for the unconscious to flow towards the conscious. (p. 446 [*CW* 8, para. 856])

Abaissement du niveau mental literally translates as a "lowering of the mental level." The verb "*baisser*" means "to lower," and *a-baisser* is directional. Jung's description highlighted the dialectic between the ego and transpersonal material:

> At the same time they have a "specific charge" and develop numinous effects which represent themselves as *affects*. The affect produces a partial *abaissement du niveau mental*, for although it raises a particular content to a supernormal degree of luminosity, it does so by withdrawing so much energy from other possible contents of consciousness that they become darkened and eventually unconscious. Owing to the restriction of consciousness produced by the affect so long as it lasts, there is a corresponding lowering of orientation which in its turn gives the unconscious a favourable opportunity to slip into the space vacated. (p. 436 [*CW* 8, para. 841])

Jung suggested that, as the "supernormal degree of luminosity" makes its presence known, the spiritual aspects pull perspective above the horizon of normal ego function, leaving the balancing baseline ego orientation further and further behind. This touches on Jung's notion of archetype as instinct and spirit as opposing ends of a spectrum of psychic expression in *contradiction in adiecto*: neither one nor the other, but a both/and. Jung (1954/1969a) described:

> So regarded, psychic processes seem to be balances of energy flowing between spirit and instinct, though the question of whether a process is to be described as spiritual or as instinctual remains shrouded in darkness.

Such evaluation or interpretation depends entirely upon the standpoint or state of the conscious mind. (p. 207 [*CW* 8, para. 407])

The physiological nature of severe mental illness allows us to potentially flip the interaction. Can our bodies, themselves, trigger an *abaissement du niveau mental*, flooding alien material into normal functioning? Energic extrapolations related to the regulation of electrical transmission and the movement of transpersonal content allow a notion of this permeability to gel. My own history can serve as context for this notion.

Medication and 2003

Generally speaking, around my thirty-third birthday, I began dreaming with an intensity I had never experienced before. An example of my dreams is stereotypical enough of confrontations with the unconscious to be used as an easy example:

> I had a dream last night about getting tossed around in a sailboat without a sail. It reminded me of another out of control sailing dream that I had, although I don't think I wrote that down. But that one was on a harbor—this one was in an apartment [...] but inside was just like the ocean, and the water was rocky, and I couldn't steer or control the boat because it had no sail, so I just got tossed around, crashing into the walls of the apartment. (2003, September 8)

These dreams of navigating rough water with insufficient transport came in all forms: the ego in the midst of the vast unconscious without the means to navigate. I would journal for hours at a time, analyzing my dreams and attempting to understand some type of connection I hadn't felt before. In later reflections, I would call it "a God-filled time" (Durchslag, 2006). I was physically agitated throughout. I would fall asleep at night, but would wake up, sometimes as early as 2:30 or 3:00 am, with a compulsion to write. An example of this feeling is captured in a journal entry (2003, December 18):

> My energy yesterday morning was overwhelming, I prayed to God to keep me sane through all of it. And then, later, after I hit a brick wall and just didn't have energy to think about anything at all, I asked the Universe to understand that I wasn't rejecting any piece of their offerings it was just that I needed to rest .... My pleas for sanity stemmed from all of the religious undertones floating around.

After several more difficult dreams and confusion, I made an appointment with the psychiatrist I saw for medication management. I asked if I could begin seeing her for therapy, as well. I had told her of my feverish dreaming.

She reported that she could not take on any therapy clients at that time, but she had a referral for a psychologist who had an interest in dreamwork. Unbeknownst to me, the psychologist was a Jungian analyst; and so, in 2004, I would begin my initial two-year exploration of analytical psychology, one that would lead me to stop my medication and commit to the individuation process without the "false safety net" of a mood stabilizer.

This was a tumultuous time during which I resigned from my job and exhibited all types of outwardly hypomanic symptoms, including a decreased need for sleep, an increase in goal-directed activity, and excessive involvement in activities that had a high potential for painful consequences. Table 8.1 highlights diagnostic criteria for mania.

However, these criteria do not explore the types of racing thoughts, nor is there any deeper inquiry into why there might be *both* a distractibility *and* an increase in goal-directed activity, even though the two seem that they might be competing forces. In my personal experience, I was compelled, quite against my conscious control, to explore vast amounts of spiritual material. I had been introduced to the numinosity of a divine experience, and it was not easy to contain. Without differentiation between psychodynamic patterns and medical labels, a manic state can be clunky and nebulous in meaning. Psychodynamic frames keep mania as a defensive strategy without careful attention to unique biological presentation. Medical research confirms that often the body's physiology moves first. The content that follows is spiritual in nature.

The above highlights a move along a spectrum of functioning which Jung considered to be driven by the *spiritus rector*:

> In spite or perhaps because of its infinity with instinct, the archetype represents the authentic element of spirit, but a spirit which is not to be

Table 8.1 Behavioral manifestation of manic symptoms (APA, 2013)

Three or more of the following behavioral symptoms must be present:

Inflated self-esteem or grandiosity.

Decreased need for sleep (e.g., feels rested after only 3 hours of sleep).

More talkative than usual or pressure to keep talking.

Flight of ideas or subjective experience that thoughts are racing.

Distractibility (i.e., attention too easily drawn to unimportant or irrelevant external stimuli), as reported or observed.

Increase in goal-directed activity (either socially, at work or school, or sexually) or psychomotor agitation (i.e., purposelessness non-goal directed activity).

Excessive involvement in activities that have a high potential for painful consequences (e.g., engaging in unrestrained buying sprees, sexual indiscretions, or foolish business investments).

identified with the human intellect, since it is the latter's *spiritus rector* ....
The archetype is spirit or anti-spirit: what it ultimately proves to be
depends on the attitude of the human mind. (Jung, 1954/1969a, p. 206
[*CW* 8, para. 406])

Jung described the move as being "seized" by spirit. The ego does not always
make the first move. Herein lies a notion of Self.

Individuation

One of the biggest and increasingly untouched points of difficulty with analytical psychology in its classical form is that it presupposes a "great regulator and promoter of psychological wholeness" (Hart, 2008, p. 97). This is the process of *individuation*, a "conscious response to an instinct not recognized in biological thought, an innate and powerful drive toward spiritual realization and ultimate meaning" (Hart, 2008, p. 106). A notion of a capitalized *Self* has a capacity to connect with ego consciousness that, in many respects, is an externalized drive enforcing its will on an individual's scope of experience and psychological material. Jung (1954/1969a) wrote:

> The ego stands to the self as the moved to the mover, or as object to subject because the determining factors which radiate out from the self surround the ego on all sides and are therefore supraordinate to it. The self, like the unconscious is an *a priori* existent out of which the ego evolves. It is so to speak an unconscious pre-configuration of the ego. It is not I who create myself rather I happen to myself. (p. 259 [*CW* 11, para. 391])

Dreams are one such example of this dialectic.

For example, Neumann (1952) described:

> As every student of depth psychology knows, the archetypal forms appearing in dreams or active imagination possess directing power and dispose of a wisdom which goes far beyond the knowledge of consciousness. One cannot simply assume that the archetypal figures are bearers of a "universal knowledge." Indeed, their compensatory significance often consists in the fact that, though their range of knowledge comprehends fateful interrelations of which the ego is not aware, these, none the less, relate only to the particular individual. (p. 95)

Neumann notes a type of "higher authority"—an "editor of dreams"—that constructs a dream narrative that can become accessible and meaningful to the dreamer. Furthermore, the dreams are meaningful *to* the individual. The dream editor rests in partnership with the dreamer and the personal psychic experience. Commenting on the phenomenon of dreams and visions, Whitmont (1969) wrote:

> [T]he unconscious appears to be concerned with conscious process to the extent that a sort of foreknowledge is often evidenced through dreams and visions. Here we confront a puzzling space-time transcendent dimension of a quasi-knowledge from within, which is not, however, directly accessible to the rational ego. In dreams the unconscious dimension operates as if it encompassed unknown events outside of space and time (and to the dreamer often enough unknowable) and also subjective problems which lie ahead in the dreamer's development. This dimension includes the dreamer's probable reaction to these events as well as about his capacity to deal with them. (p. 52)

In his essay, "Symbols and The Interpretation of Dreams," Jung wrote: "It is only our conscious mind that does not know; the unconscious seems already informed, and to have submitted the case to a careful prognostic examination" (Jung, 2011, p. 117 [*CW* 18, para. 545]). Zabriskie (2001) summarized:

> [Jung] postulated that dreams and autonomous fantasies were the complementary conceits by which the psyche attempts to retrieve or complete its knowledge in pursuit of greater consciousness and, in cases of imbalance or damage, to reestablish equilibrium and heal internal splits. (p. xxix)

It also has ramifications for space, time, and foreknowledge. Whitmont (1969) summarized the implications of the above as "a very practical use of the space-time transcendents of the objective psyche" (p. 52).

As highlighted previously, the notion of a suprapersonal background moves into profound philosophical debates. However, the idea of an ego–self axis, or a drive toward psychological development, continues to sit within all schools of post-Jungian work, whether or not it gets labeled. Dreams, images, stories, even psychosis, are acknowledged as a contributor to the resolution of the psychological impasse: the source of this material assists in the resolution of trauma and ego fragmentation. The model of individuation explored in Edinger's (1972) ego-Self model is directional in similar fashion as object-relations theories; and highlights a move from object fusion (ego in self) toward separation and autonomy. One of the hopes for sharing some of the more simplistic dreams I have had—the dream of the DSMV banner, for example; or the fish dream that led to choices in my research—was to offer examples of this classical relationship between Self and an expanding consciousness of a particular ego position. It was not as tumultuous as my initial entrée into this type of connection in 2003, and so perhaps can also be seen as a long, slow build of ego strength espoused in our psychodynamic models, none of which I am dismissing.

Medication and 2010

The fish dream described in chapter 2 came to me two days prior to leaving for an intensive weekend seminar during the second year of my doctoral program at Pacifica Graduate Institute. The dream editor had made use of space–time relativity. The weekend was a turning point. It would become an ascension into a numinosity that wouldn't quit. It was Jung's very description of an *abaissement du niveau mental*. I had to move through the weekend—classes and interactions with classmates and so on—but the entire experience lifted me farther and farther away from mundane tasks and connections with my surroundings.

We had a class on psychopharmacology that weekend, and as I listened to the pharmaceutical actions on the neurochemicals, I doodled drops of water onto my notes. Just little drops of water, and inside of them I found myself writing DA for dopamine, 5HT for serotonin, NE for norepinephrine, GABA for *Y-aminobutyric acid*. In unbidden waves, I began to meander with the idea that neurochemicals contained the secrets of the universe. Drops of water in a vast ocean of our historical story. I began to float away somewhat.

After dinner, I would share with my classmates for the very first time that I had bipolar I disorder. I would tell them how scary it was, how very wrong the assumptions about mania were, how transporting and stunning and miraculous it could be. How connected to God I'd become. By the time the weekend wound down, I was rolling and rolling. While waiting to take my red-eye back from California to Cleveland, I journaled about epiphany, universal connection, and "intellectual ideas and a spiritually significant knowing." I wondered:

> I don't think gods and goddess need to sleep or eat. Of course they don't. Only human forms do. So if there is something that does not keep you sufficiently human, you break apart or shatter? Circadian rhythms, sun, dark, sleep, wake, these are limitations of [the] human body ... I got lost for a minute into the rest of natural law—other animals, plants ... who knows.

I begin thinking about my impending dissertation research:

> Do we have the capacity to know the "whole object" that we began with?! Does going through the birth canal necessitate some kind of sacrifice? I think it's time to write down my delusional storylines? Can I analyze my own stories as a means of studying? Am I allowed to begin with that source and pull in data and theories to analyze it? I can't solve the Unknowable. All I can do is comment on the human experience of the Unknowable. If I come to accept what I saw. And I think whatever was stirring this weekend re-convinced me that I saw it. And again, the thoughts just got away from me. (2010, October 17)

I spent the almost 4-hour flight home staring out at the night sky and falling in love with everything: my parents, life, the magic of the universe. The luminosity of objects, of people, of the essence of being and human being, has already been better described by the voices of others in this work. Regardless,

I got myself home, took a sleeping pill, and slept for hours. As is always the case, I woke up back on earth. Unlike Coate (1965) described, I was able to get the sedation I needed to overt "serious trouble later" (see chapter 7).

The description above looks at the energy of a psychic move. The trigger seemed to be the powerful nature of the dream editor at work, and the shift in ego-orientation on a range of function. But the question would be—a question that could be posed back in 2003, as well—is what would have happened without my mood stabilizer? This we can answer from my experience in 2006, which no longer used my personal perspective or growth as a referent. I became, as others do, a channel for something else—the transpersonal material of a collective unconscious.

Flying without a safety net

Describing his own work with unconscious material, Jung (1989) stated:

> From the beginning I had conceived my voluntary confrontation with the unconscious as a scientific experiment which I myself was conducting and in whose outcome I was vitally interested. Today, I might equally well say that it was an experiment which was conducted on *me*. (p.178)

When I chose to titrate off of my Lamictal in 2006, I, too, thought I was embarking on an experiment: my life without medication. But I was sure that this was an intrapsychic experiment, one based in an attempt to nurture a connection to Self that was not mediated or limited by pharmaceuticals. It was to be an exercise in increased ego strength and purity of connection in order to serve the classic idea of individuation. A commitment to authentic connection to affect and experience; a commitment to confronting psychodynamic notions of manic defense; and a connection to the desolation of depressive states. I believed that hard analytic work would mediate both extremes because I was embracing and listening to the symptoms, themselves. The key to my development was not something to be medicated away. The time of "flying with a net" was over. I journaled:

> What are my fears about staying on medication? My fear is that what I'm doing to my body is not natural, unnecessary, and toxic. The wrong model, maybe; outgrown its usefulness, maybe. Causing more trouble than it is curing .... I really don't feel like being a science experiment anymore .... I really want to grow into and respect myself. Chemicals. Clinical trials, testubes, unknown synapse controls .... My fantasy is that without medicine, my body would right itself. It would have a better sense of what, naturally, steadies itself .... My medicine would be the barrier and not the cure. That's my fantasy. Is it truth or absolute wishfulness? (2006, March 23)

Several days later, I wrote: "I woke up with this thought: There is something inherently wrong with a medical diagnosis that places strong religious connection into a 'symptom' that needs to be fixed. My spirituality has been pathologized" (2006, March 31). The rest of the story has already been told. In the intervening months, I would fall into the same chasm of experience as Jung's schizophrenic patients at the turn of the twentieth century; as Anton Boisen and his group of 180 from the 1930s; as Morag Coate and John Custance in mid-century Great Britain; and as the multitudes of others in Perry's long career.

I am a lot of things. From the perspective of analytical psychology, the primary perspective I use to understand psychological life, I can say that I have a great many neurotic complexes. They move freely and awkwardly about. They are the difficult work of facing shadow material in my personal unconscious. They are the complexes I take up with diligence and doggedness as I move along my path of individuation. They are the stuff of my dreams which Self offers up in an interactive dynamic, the "mechanics" of which sit underexplored and too far below the surface of Jungian practice. That said, medication keeps me in the realm of ego orientation: it keeps me on a spectrum of *abaissement*, without teetering into the untethered netherworld of a collective, timeless, and unbounded space. It is only with Lamictal that I can continue to engage in a soul journey. I can sleep and dream and relate to Self from ego space. It is as if, without medication, I did not dream; I was the dream. I became only Self without my-self. I was nowhere to be found except as a character in a repository of collective plot, character, and action.

A different challenge

While my complexes have never been controlled by medication, there is no doubt that trends in mental health treatment and modern psychiatry have increasingly turned to psychopharmaceutical medication to dull their maladaptive effects. The fruitfulness of diving into behavioral defenses or symptoms of anxiety, depression, or "manic" activity, is being supplanted, often to the detriment of the client. Unfortunately, the efficacy of these drugs to successfully mediate such symptoms cannot be ignored. Herein lies the difficulty for psychoanalytic approaches in the age of neuroscience. How does unconscious material remain relevant? It is this gap, in my opinion, that is the biggest threat to depth psychology.

Throughout, I have argued that medication actually holds a key to the continued relevance of Jung's work:

> We have known since the rise of psychopharmacology in the 1950s that the chemical properties of certain drugs can modulate psychotic material. I would argue that neuroscience has already offered a connection between the chemical activity in the brain and the collective unconscious. (Durchslag, 2016, p. 36)

Western culture is actually one of a minority that tries to reject the connection between the body and suprapersonal material. Haule (2011b) has done a careful cross-cultural analysis of the use of chemical compounds to connect to spiritual life, and the ways in which these traditions dovetail or diverge from Jung's own theoretical models. Other cultural traditions find no need to put parentheses around spiritual and religious commonality. And it will not be long before medical models of treatment return to hallucinogenics and culturally marginalized drugs as a means of treating severe and intractable mental disorders. It is doubtful that the potentially useful seeds of past research will be ignored for long.

References

American Psychiatric Association. (2013). *Diagnostic and statistical manual of mental disorders (DSM-5)* (5th ed.). Washington, DC: American Psychiatric Publishing.
Boisen, A. T. (1936). *The exploration of the inner world: A study of mental disorder and religious experience.* Philadelphia, PA: University of Pennsylvania Press.
Brooke, R. (2015). *Jung and phenomenology.* New York, NY: Routledge.
Coate, M. (1965). *Beyond all reason.* Philadelphia, PA: J. B. Lippincott.
Custance, J. (1951). *Wisdom, madness and folly: The philosophy of a lunatic.* London: Victor Gollancz.
Custance, J. (1954). *Adventure into the unconscious.* London: Christopher Johnson.
Durchslag, H. B. (2006). *Swallowing truths about the wizard of Oz.* Unpublished manuscript.
Durchslag, H. B. (2016). Severe mental illness: A bridge between neurochemistry and the collective unconscious. *Psychological Perspectives*, 59(1), 30–45. doi:10.1080/00332925.2016.1134210.
Edinger, E. F. (1972). *Ego and archetype.* Boston, MA: Shambala.
Goodwyn, E. D. (2010a). Approaching archetypes: Reconsidering innateness. *Journal of Analytical Psychology*, 55, 502–521.
Goodwyn, E. D. (2010b). The author replies. *Journal of Analytical Psychology*, 55, 550–555.
Goodwyn, E. D. (2012). *The neurobiology of the gods: How brain physiology shapes the recurrent imagery of myth and dreams.* Hove, UK: Routledge.
Goodwyn, E. D. (2013). Recurrent motifs as resonant attractor states in the narrative field: A testable model of archetype. *Journal of Analytical Psychology*, 58, 387–408.
Hart, D. L. (2008). The classical Jungian school. In P. Young-Eisendrath & T. Dawson (Eds.), *The Cambridge companion to Jung* (pp. 95–106). New York, NY: Cambridge University Press.
Haule, J. R. (2011a). *Jung in the 21st century: Evolution and archetype* (Vol. 1). London: Routledge.
Haule, J. R. (2011b). *Jung in the 21st century: Synchronicity and science* (Vol. 2). London: Routledge.
Hogenson, G. B. (2004). Archetypes: Emergence and the psyche's deep structure. In J. Cambray & L. Carter (Eds.), *Analytical psychology: Contemporary perspectives in Jungian analysis* (pp. 32–55). New York, NY: Routledge.

Jaffé, A. (1971). *The myth of meaning: Jung and the expansion of consciousness* (R. F. C. Hull, Trans.). New York, NY: Penguin Books.

Jung, C. G. (1934/1969). Basic postulates of analytical psychology. In H. Read, M. Fordham, G. Adler, & W. McGuire (Eds.), *The collected works of C.G. Jung* (R. F. C. Hull, Trans.) (2nd ed., Vol. 8, pp. 338–357). Princeton, NJ: Princeton University Press.

Jung, C. G. (1952/1969). Synchronicity: An acausal connecting principle. In H. Read, M. Fordham, G. Adler, & W. McGuire (Eds.), *The collected works of C.G. Jung* (R. F. C. Hull, Trans.) (2nd ed., Vol. 8, pp. 417–519). Princeton, NJ: Princeton University Press.

Jung, C. G. (1954/1969a). On the nature of psyche. In H. Read, M. Fordham, G. Adler, & W. McGuire (Eds.), *The collected works of C.G. Jung* (R. F. C. Hull, Trans.) (2nd ed., Vol. 8, pp. 159–234). Princeton, NJ: Princeton University Press.

Jung, C. G. (1954/1969b). Psychological aspects of the mother archetype. In H. Read, M. Fordham, G. Adler, & W. McGuire (Eds.), *The collected works of C.G. Jung* (R. F. C. Hull, Trans.) (2nd ed., Vol. 9, part I, pp. 75–110). Princeton, NJ: Princeton University Press.

Jung, C. G. (1989). *Memories, dreams, reflections* (R. Winston & C. Winston, Trans.). New York, NY: Vintage Books.

Jung, C. G. (2011). *The undiscovered self with symbols and the interpretation of dreams*. Princeton, NJ: Princeton University Press.

Knox, J. (2003). *Archetype, attachment, analysis: Jungian psychology and the emergent mind*. London: Routledge.

Knox, J., Merchant, J., & Hogenson, G. B. (2010). Response to Erik Goodwyn's "Approaching archetypes: reconsidering innateness." *Journal of Analytical Psychology*, 55, 522–549.

Merchant, J. (2006). The developmental/emergent model of archetype, its implications and its application to shamanism. *Journal of Analytical Psychology*, 51, 125–144.

Merchant, J. (2009). A reappraisal of classical archetypal theory and its implications for theory and practice. *Journal of Analytical Psychology*, 54, 339–358.

Mills, J. (2018a). The essence of archetypes. *International Journal of Jungian Studies*, 10(3), 199–220. doi:10.1080/19409052.2018.1503808.

Mills, J. (2018b). The myth of the collective unconscious. *Journal of the History of the Behavioral Sciences*, 55(1), 40–53. doi:10.1002/jhbs.21945.

Mullan, B. (1996). *Mad to be normal: Conversations with R. D. Laing*. London: Free Association Books.

Neumann, E. (1952). *The psyche and transformation of the reality planes: A metapsychological attempt* (H. Nagel, Trans.). Spring, 81–111.

Stevens, A. (2003). *Archetype revisited: An updated natural history of the self*. Toronto, ON, Canada: Inner City Books.

Von Franz, M. (1992). *Psyche and matter*. Boston, MA: Shambhala.

Whitmont, E. C. (1969). *The symbolic quest: Basic concepts of analytical psychology*. Princeton, NJ: Princeton University Press.

Zabriskie, B. (2001). Jung and Pauli: A meeting of rare minds. In C. A. Meier (Ed.), *Atom and archetype: The Pauli/Jung letters, 1932–1958* (pp. xxvii–l). Princeton, NJ: Princeton University Press.

Chapter 9

Reeling in the net and readying it to be recast
Conclusions and future research

> From the standpoint of the tendency to unify our world picture, it seems pleasing that connections are starting to be formed in a sphere that has already become so broad that it includes the Dioscuri myth on the one hand and doublet splittings of spectral lines and isotope separations on the other.
>
> (Wolfgang Pauli, in Meier, 2001, p. 196)

Review

This research has explored questions such as: How does the efficacy of pharmacological treatment add to post-Jungian scholarship linking archetypal images to human biology (Goodwyn, 2010a, 2010b, 2012; Haule, 2011)? How might the genetic nature of severe mental illness add nuance to empirical research on transpersonal material? Do physiological alterations suggest a collective realm that rests beyond the focus on the human brain? This book argues it does, and aligns with Jung's later musings on the brain as a transformer station and the convergence in a unitary realm of psyche and matter. Beginning in the early twentieth century with only a loose, intuitive, postulation of a *metabolic toxin X*, Jung (1907/1960) was convinced that in certain types of psychosis, namely those related to severe mental illnesses such as schizophrenia, a combination of biochemical and psychological processes needed to be considered. It led to an examination of the interplay between psyche and the body that spanned the entirety of his career.

This research does not pose any answers, only deeper questions that must be explored in due diligence to constructs so hotly debated. The hermeneutic process begins again each time an interpretation is made.

The resting point for now sits in a curious relationship between certain genetic disorders, the common essence of collective fusion in feel and content, and the power of chemical and electrical manipulation in grounding the ego in human time, with human object-relationships and interpersonal attachments. Figure 9.1 shows the chemical bonds created in the construction of the pharmaceutical, Lamictal.

138 Conclusions and future research

The chemical bonds that are woven between molecules of carbon, hydrogen, chlorine, and nitrogen make them greater than their parts. Without the additional safety net of this mood stabilizer, human attachment becomes suprapersonal attachment; objects become symbols; people become characters in an eternal play; and time stretches from the moment of creation to the end of the world. Jung (1931/1969) suggested that when supraordinate material manifests, it becomes depersonalized, through "picture-language" (p. 150 [*CW* 8, para. 316]). This picture language is the language of the collective unconscious.

Because mental disorder is only recently amenable to being analyzed in the same way as other medicalized physical illnesses, diagnostic names remain undifferentiated lumps. We have now gotten farther than Kraepelin: schizophrenia is a spectrum, and the psychotic form of bipolar disorder—bipolar I disorder—has been inching closer to schizophrenia and farther from other bipolar labels. Increasing differentiation leads to differential treatment. Furthermore, genetic research is now offering direction related to medication efficacy (see Chapter 6). It may be its own path to diagnostic advance. Depth psychology is in a unique position to assist with the differentiation of multiple aspects of psychological life and impairment in function. Without an appreciation of intrapsychic

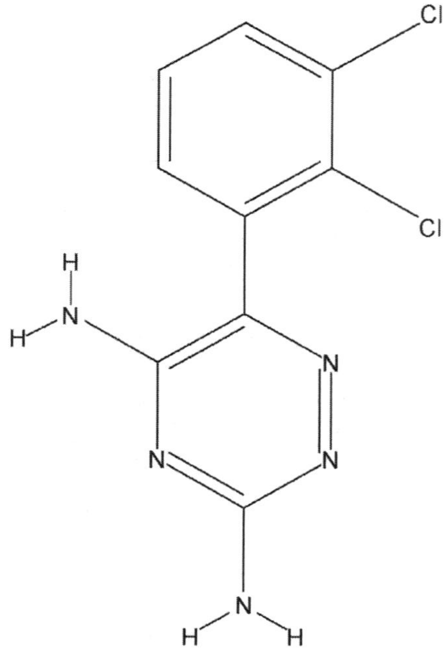

Figure 9.1 Chemical compound of Lamictal

maturation and defensive strategies, the unconscious is too easily dismissed. Analytical psychology, in particular, has explored the lush world of myth, image, and story as its own treasure trove of data and healing. But what good is such knowledge if it falls out of step with scientific advance? Hogenson cautioned:

> My point here is that I believe some care needs to be exercised in attempts to "rescue" some theoretical proposition or notion Jung has in his system. By rescue I mean the search for some contrivance, or some scientific proposition that, with sufficient massaging, will look something like what we think Jung had intuited. (Knox et al., 2010, pp. 547–548)

However, the insufficient rescue attempt seems more related to a glossing over of the need for unique diagnosis and treatment in the young but burgeoning field of physiological disorders. It undermines the importance of unconscious processes because a "one-size fits all" in an increasingly nuanced landscape loses credibility. Even more intriguing is the possibility that a continued denial of the existence of transpersonal—even suprapersonal—material might become analytical psychology's downfall, not its saving grace.

Psyche, psychoid, and science

Science has been able to study or manipulate segments of the brain and predict, with some reliability, connections to emotions, behaviors, and thought patterns. But is this a full notion of psyche? With all of the research related to brain regions, cellular transmission, and pharmacological efficacy, one node of difficulty becomes whether or not we consider human behavior a physiological function, a learned behavior based on this physiological function, or something more complex than either: that of spirit or soul. Psyche as soul has been well-substituted for psyche as mind, and has gone even further in our age of neuroscience to become the brain itself. This dilemma is even apparent in the translation of Jung's own work. For example, in the second edition of volume eight of his collected works, editors noted decisions on the translation of the word *seele*, which has dual meanings that connect psyche to mind, but also connect it to the ever-ephemeral notion of soul (Read, Fordham, Adler, & McGuire, 1969, p. 300). This dilemma still sits at the core of unsolved philosophical Western discourse.

Many trends in science today are returning to a notion of spirit. Capra and Luisi (2014) have pieced together scientific legacies across history and discipline, and are positing a natural move into a systems view of scientific understanding in which notions of spirituality do not conflict with science.

Picking up on the complexity of the term "psyche," we can hear echoes of Jung's own trajectory in their analysis:

> For a deeper understanding of spirituality, it is useful to review the original meaning of the word "spirit." The Latin *spiritus* means "breath," as do the related Latin word *anima*, the Greek *psyche*, and the Sanskrit *atman*. The common meaning of these key terms indicates that the original meaning of spirit in many ancient philosophical and religious traditions in the West as well as in the East, is that of the breath of life. (p. 277)

Capra and Luisi highlighted an ultimate unity of psyche and matter:

> Spiritual awareness is an experience of aliveness of mind and body as a unity. Moreover, this experience of unity transcends not only the separation of mind and body but also the separation of self and world. The central awareness in these spiritual moments is a profound sense of oneness with all, a sense of belonging to the universe as a whole. (p. 277)

Relating these connections to scientific advance, they summarized:

> This sense of oneness with the natural world is fully borne out by the new systemic conception of life. As we understand how the roots of life reach deep into basic physics and chemistry, how the unfolding of complexity began long before the formation of the first living cells, and how life has evolved for billions of years by using again and again the same basic patterns and processes, we realize how tightly we are connected to the entire fabric of life. (p. 277)

For Jung, archetypes related to basic psychological patterns and processes, but a notion of what "psychological" actually referred to shifted later in his career. Von Franz (1992) highlighted: "Jung, for his part, was led to postulate an ultimate unity of the objective psyche and to propose the existence of a global order of this unity" (p. 246). If there is a problem of psyche, there is a problem of psychology. If psyche is allowed to return to its multifaceted nature—one related not only to mind or to the biggest restriction of brain—then psychology can return to the study of this hidden unity.

There has never been any doubt that much of the material universe is constructed in patterns, for example, in the consistent molecular structures of elements, and the organizing principles related to clustering and the relative stability of electrons around a nucleus. There has been interest in the post-Jungian community in looking at fractal patterns, or geometric replications of mandala-like figures (Hogenson, 2015). However, the connections of such explorations to transpersonal mythic material, repetitive story lines, or patterns of intuition or insight, have been left on the sidelines, except in negating the possibility. In a field that espouses the value of holding contradiction and the tension of opposites above most things as a means of personal development, it would seem the construct of a collective unconscious is not worthy of such an attitude. Jung's explorations of "maybes," and "perhaps-es," and "it could follow thats," have been challenged by the post-Jungian community as "it cannot possibly," and "this is not a sound philosophical path," and "there is no way." However, there is a difference between pushing something inadequate into an existing box of data and continuing to explore remarkable phenomena that has thus far remained beyond understanding.

There is something in the field of depth psychology today that runs contrary to a general scientific attitude about inquiry. In every other science—physics, astrophysics, quantum physics, biology, neurology, and the newer ventures into a cohesive science of system theory—there is a willingness to view anomalies, and hold the tension of these anomalies, as the search for a way that one can be both true and not true, both elementally sound but flawed, continues. We need not go far to argue the solid and incontrovertible usefulness of such an approach. Astrophysics, for example: the *Big Bang* is a name for something never seen, only intuited. Tyson (Gott, Strauss, & Tyson, 2016) referred to the notion of the Big Bang as "our own creation myth," which has been constructed out of scientific and mathematical advances made thus far. However, he highlighted the incomplete nature of these advances:

> [C]an we ask what existed before the Big Bang? Unfortunately, our equations do not let us do so. Yes, it is a reasonable question. But no, general relativity does not have an answer for you …. In science, when your equations yield a result of infinity, you know that your theory is incomplete. (pp. 220–221)

Capra and Luisi (2014) stated bluntly:

> What can we say about the origin of life on Earth? It is fair to say from the start that we do not have an answer to the question on how life originated on Earth. It remains one of the great mysteries on scientists' agendas. (p. 216)

Yet, this does not preclude astrophysics and the general lexicon of scientific inquiry from using such a term to capture an event preexisting our capability of measuring it.

As another example in astrophysics, it is only recently a widely accepted principle—one that garnered a 2011 Nobel prize—that the universe exists primarily of dark matter and dark energy; that perhaps this matter makes up 70 percent of the universe; and that what we see is only 5 percent of what is actually there. Furthermore, the powerful energy contained in these seemingly empty black holes had only been intuited until the recent advances in electromagnetism and the ability to measure the bends in gravity (Gregory, 2015). The existence was intuited by the effect they impose. In fact, the term *dark energy* is the name given for the *unknown force* (Gates, 2015). Einstein had been celebrated for 100 years, even though his theory of relativity was flawed and incomplete.[1] These unseen and unknown forces hold the glue.

Tyson (Gott et al., 2016) began the creation myth of the Big Bang: "Back then, 13.8 billion years ago, all the space, time, matter, and energy you can see, out to 13.8 billion light years, was crushed together. The nascent universe was a hot, seething cauldron of matter and energy" (p. 24). In the beginning, 90 percent of all atomic nuclei in the universe are hydrogen; 8 percent are helium; and 2 percent all the other elements of the periodic table. Moving further, he highlighted:

> If I rank the top five elements of the universe—hydrogen, helium, oxygen, carbon, and nitrogen—they look a lot like the ingredients of the human body. What is the number one molecule in your body? It's water—80% of your body is H_2O. Break apart H_2O, and you get hydrogen as the number one element in the human body. (p. 81)

He continued:

> [G]iven the cosmically common elements in our bodies, it's humbling to see we are not chemically special, but at the same time, it's quite enlightening, even empowering, to realize we are truly stardust ... oxygen, carbon, and nitrogen are all forged in stars, over the billions of years that followed the Big Bang. We are born of this universe, we live in this universe, and the universe is in us. (p. 82)

The description of water above highlights that the power of these individual elements is the atomic bonds that are created between them.

Carl Sagan (2010) highlighted three atoms, discovered in a Cambridge University lab in 1932, that make up the entirety of life—protons, neutrons, and electrons: "These three units, put together in different patterns, make, essentially, everything." To illustrate this point, Sagan harkened back to the work of the ancient alchemists:

> Every time we add or subtract one proton and enough neutrons to keep the nucleus together we make a new chemical element. Consider mercury.

If we subtract one proton from mercury, and three neutrons, we convert it into gold, the dream of the ancient alchemists. (Sagan, 2010)

Oddly, the work of the alchemists which so enthralled Jung and post-Jungians alike, seems prescient. How was anyone to know the power of atomic structure in the days of early science? Alchemists did intuit, however, some type of relationship between psyche and matter, now borne out in medical research hundreds of years later.

The structure of the elements, created from these three basic atoms, depends on the combined energies of three forces of the natural world: electricity, gravity, and nuclear force. Many of these elements are implicated in the myth of how mood stabilizers work: sodium, magnesium, calcium, potassium, chloride, hydrogen, oxygen, carbon, nitrogen, zinc, argon, and lithium. The molecular structure of these mood stabilizers then affects the movement of ions throughout the body by opening and closing through voltage-sensitive gates. All of this affects psyche. Clearly, intrapsychic processes change according to human attachment and maturation. But they also change according to universal laws of matter. With this in mind, conceptualizations of the psychoid archetype seem possible, sensical, and prescient.

Sometimes the mere telling of a myth can be healing to the individual psyche. The ever-elusive and never-seen dream editor helps, as well. This is not debated in the field of analytical psychology. But it would seem that the depersonalized picture images also move on a spectrum. Jung's first inclination toward the problem of a collective unconscious began through empirical observation in severe mental illnesses with a "toxin x" (now borne out with more savvy). It would seem that sometimes picture language functions in reciprocity with an individual; sometimes it rises in spite of an individual. When this is the case, transpersonal themes, with a great many references to suprapersonal connection, rise and fall in concert with the physical changes in the human body. There is also deep connection to earth, its creation, and a time before the human experience.

The how of image and story is a mystery. However, in his 1949 presentation at Eranos, Van der Leeuw (1949/1983) stressed that a figurative expression is not a secondary expression. There is a historical interdependence between existence and myth, where myth "is not merely a story told, but a reality lived—not an intellectual reaction upon a puzzle, but an explicit act of faith—a statement of primeval reality" (p. 331). He described myth as "the forms of life that lie heaped up for all time in the womb of the unconscious" (p. 329). In his essay, Van der Leeuw also gives the reader access to the work of Raffaele Pettazoni and Branislav Malikowski. He offered what he called "the best and most succinct formulation" on the phenomenon from Pettazoni:

> Myth is not fable, but history, "true history" and not "false history." It is true history by virtue of its content, the narrative of events that really

occurred, beginning with these grandiose events of the origins: the origin of the world, of humanity, the origin of life and death.

Pettazzoni continued:

> The divine or supernatural personages that are active in myth, their extraordinary undertakings, their singular adventures, all this marvelous world is a transcendent reality that cannot be placed in doubt because it is the antecedent and condition *sine qua non* of present reality. (Van der Leeuw, 1949/1983, pp. 330–331)

Van der Leeuw summarized that "Time is full. And its content is the myths—that is, the forms of life heaped up for all time in the womb of the unconscious" (p. 329). Image and myth may do a better job than reduction because the openness of all that cannot be pinned down is able to coexist with what has received enough attention to be captured. Von Franz (1992) summarized:

> In any case, true symbols are not invented by consciousness but are spontaneously revealed by the unconscious. Archetypal dream images and the dream images of the great myths and religions, for example, still have about them a little of the "cloudy" nature of absolute knowledge in that they always seem to contain more than we can assimilate consciously, even by means of elaborate interpretations. They always retain an ineffable and mysterious quality that seems to reveal to us more than we can really know. (p. 254)

Jung (1934/1969) admitted:

> The nature of the psyche reaches into obscurities far beyond the scope of our understanding. It contains as many riddles as the universe with its galactic systems, before whose majestic configurations only a mind lacking in imagination can fail to admit its own insufficiencies. (p. 414 [*CW* 8, para. 815])

But his musings and interests continued to morph, expand, and deepen into the increasing mystery of psyche: the thing that can never be mounted on a slide.

At the end of his life, Jung made an additional move related to psychic life. He moved from an interest in matter toward the roots of the equations that explained it: numbers. For example, in a letter to Marie-Louise Von Franz, Jung was becoming increasingly intrigued with numbers as archetypal, with psychic implications in their own right, inspiring Von Franz's (1974) work, *Number and Time*. This thread of inquiry never disappeared, per se. Work by J. Gary Sparks (2010) is one such example of post-Jungian scholarship that focused on it. Currently, the subject is being taken up anew through the translation of correspondence between Jung and von Franz toward the end of Jung's life (Le Mouël, 2018b).

The broad interest in the model of the *I-Ching* within the post-Jungian community assumes the connection of an image with a number. Von Franz (1992) was even considering ways in which myth and story might be connected to numerical patterns: equations in their own right. Von Franz (1992) relayed the story of King Wen and the Duke of Chou who "were shut up by a tyrant for ten years in a dark hole" (p. 34), every day threatened with death. In that dark hole, day after day, they would come to build the philosophy of the *I-Ching*, a symbol of the interconnectedness of human life and the physical world, the *Tao*. Their ideas, formulated through "intuitive introspection alone in experimenting with their own psychic state" (p. 34) found remarkable alignment with the Western numeric system and even genetic patterns.

Readying the net

Synchronicity and the implicit connection to individuation

The limitations of this current work have been reached. But the hope is that it has offered enough of a bridge between individual psychic experience and the broader net of physiological and chemical activity to allow schools of post-Jungian thought that began to diverge in the mid-twentieth century to find one another again, without fear that Jung's work undermines scientific rigor. The whole direction of thought in Western science is one of human partnership with matter. It is analytical psychology's lot to make sure that the rich offerings of the unconscious do not get lost in an eclipse of consciousness. Furthermore, trends today are not abandoning spirit, only moving toward it. Here, too, Jung's work was prescient because of his moves toward understanding psychological depths within Eastern models of transcendence. Von Franz (1992) did not shy away from constant cross-pollination between the two traditions, and scholarship by Murray Stein (2017, 2019) is a recent example of these efforts moving back into the often skeptical and intrapsychically oriented *Journal of Analytical Psychology*. But the rich legacy of multidisciplinary and cross-cultural spiritual explorations began at Eranos and continues today. Psychic struggle, personal complexes, and shadow material are central to the resolution of dis-ease and growth. Stein (2019) wrote: "For both [East and West], the transformation of consciousness means overcoming habitual patterns of thought that become locked into place by routine and repetition" (p. 6). But only the Eastern tradition allows a transcendent connection and a suprapersonal guide. Philosophical discourse and paths of logic related to the possibility of such a connection is hundreds, even thousands, of years old. The existence of a collective unconscious is a part of this unfortunate, but fruitful, debate.

Empirical contributions

The debate is not over, nor can it ever be fully explained. A shift in label to that of an objective psyche is perhaps a more active principle, and one more amenable to understanding current discussions on emergence and the intersection of psyche and matter. Synchronicity and issues of time rest in the odd consolidation of past, present, and future. Clinical examples have served as important points of departure: for example, in Jung's (1952/1969) account of the scarab and the flock of birds (p. 438 [*CW* 8, para. 843–844]). Von Franz (1992) included her own intersubjective participation in recounting the story of chopping wood and the translocal connection it had with her client's state of mind (pp. 24–25). While the research presented in this work highlights a permeability of time, space, and psychic content, it barely touches on synchronicity. But the method of narrative analysis certainly contributes to its study.

The need for additional narrative accounts of synchronicity at work in the partnership between oracular traditions and psychic development is coming to the fore. In his book *Revelations of Chance: Synchronicity As Spiritual Experience*, Main (2007) highlighted the surprising dearth of empirical data focused on the *I Ching* and its contributions to notions of individuation and synchronistic phenomena. He wrote: "Another emphasis in recent work on synchronicity is on narrative. This emphasis has informed both the collecting of accounts of synchronistic experiences and the manner in which they are analyzed and understood" (p. 8). He continued by highlighting a gap in current pools of data:

> In view of the important role played by the *I Ching* in Jung's development of the concept of synchronicity, it might be expected that researchers would already explored this in some depth. However, apart from Jung's own work and its immediate extension by von Franz, very little of substance seems to have been written on the subject of synchronicity and the *I Ching*. (p. 8)

Main proposed this gap as "an open field for research." His work that followed traced the first-hand account of spiritual connection, synchronicity, and the individuation process.

First-hand narrative accounts offer applied experiences of theoretical constructs. One current example is work by Christophe Le Mouël (2009, 2011a, 2011b, 2018a). Articles published in *Psychological Perspectives* trace the impact of dream material on his life path; and recent work has brought the confluence of physiological and psychic change to the fore, not only in his own path of individuation, but as a thread in the long legacy of alchemy, science, and Jungian tradition. His training as a quantum physicist offers a lens into the historical trajectory of scientific theory, and the caution and limitation required lest a too liberal substitution of psyche and matter be made.

Clinical challenges

This current project does not even touch on the clinical implications of openly allowing intrapsychic process and transpersonal content to exist in parallel but intersecting paths. It is weighty, indeed. In fact, it is our primary responsibility. But when is material created *by* us, and when is it offered *to* us? When does our experience cease to be commentary on a private process of development and move into a realm that was never an individual creation? The unfortunate reality is that it can never be known entirely. I do believe that the realm of the personal unconscious—the complexes of family, of development, of attachment, of illness, of conditioning—is the most dramatic source of personal change. But when have we been constructed, and what have we been since constellating into the form of human potential? This is no phenomenological meaning-making. It is a connection to a preexistent meaning, in and of itself. In denying intrinsic, body connections to things much larger than what we have metabolized thus far, we are going backwards and creating our own cultural shadow. We are robbing ourselves of material that brings breadth and dimensionality to an understanding of who we are and where we stand. We end up robbing our clients, as well, cutting off a supply of knowledge and context that leaves an odd narcissism of personal responsibility in its wake. The idea that all of what we hold rests in the development of the brain since our births is also oddly narcissistic. Regardless, the tide is shifting, and the days of the as-if phenomena related to astrology, spiritual adventure, and a bracketed relationship to altered states of consciousness are numbered. There is no other psychology more grounded, nor more prepared, to help the individual stay humble and in touch with what is becoming an increasingly vast and open realm.

Note

1 As a part of the centennial celebration of Albert Einstein's work, The Institute for the Origins of Science at Case Western Reserve University in Cleveland, OH organized a TED[x] Salon including presentations and breakout discussions with professors and researchers in the fields of physics, cosmology, and astronomy.

References

Capra, F., & Luisi, P. L. (2014). *The systems view of life: A unifying vision.* New York, NY: Cambridge University Press.

Gates, E. (2015). With love from Einstein: The big bang theory, GPS technology, and warps in space. Symposium conducted at TEDx CLE Salon:Einstein 100: Celebrating a century of general relativity (November 2015). Case Western Reserve University, Cleveland, OH.

Goodwyn, E. D. (2010a). Approaching archetypes: Reconsidering innateness. *Journal of Analytical Psychology,* 55, 502–521.

Goodwyn, E. D. (2010b). The author replies. *Journal of Analytical Psychology*, 55, 550–555.

Goodwyn, E. D. (2012). *The neurobiology of the gods: How brain physiology shapes the recurrent imagery of myth and dreams.* Hove, UK: Routledge.

Gott, R., Strauss, M. A., & Tyson, N. D. (2016). *Welcome to the universe: An astrophysical tour.* Princeton, NJ: Princeton University Press.

Gregory, R. (2015). Black holes and new revelations: The music of the universe. Symposium conducted at TEDx CLE Salon: Einstein 100: Celebrating a century of general relativity (November 2015). Case Western Reserve University, Cleveland, OH.

Haule, J. R. (2011). *Jung in the 21st century: Evolution and archetype* (Vol. 1). London: Routledge.

Hogenson, G. (2015). The Tibetan book of the dead needs work: Jung's commentary on the Bardo Thödol and the phenomenology of the deep unconscious. Symposium conducted at Fourth joint conference of the IAAP and IAJS: Psyche, spirit and science: Negotiating contemporary social and cultural concerns (July 2015). Yale University, New Haven, CT.

Jung, C. G. (1907/1960). The psychology of dementia praecox. In H. Read, M. Fordham, G. Adler, & W. McGuire (Eds.), *The collected works of C.G. Jung* (R. F. C. Hull, Trans.) (2nd ed., Vol. 3, pp. 3–151). New York, NY: Pantheon Books.

Jung, C. G. (1931/1969). The structure of the psyche. In H. Read, M. Fordham, G. Adler, & W. McGuire (Eds.), *The collected works of C.G. Jung* (R. F. C. Hull, Trans.) (2nd ed., Vol. 8, pp. 139–158). Princeton, NJ: Princeton University Press.

Jung, C. G. (1934/1969). The soul and death. In H. Read, M. Fordham, G. Adler, & W. McGuire (Eds.), *The collected works of C.G. Jung* (R. F. C. Hull, Trans.) (2nd ed., Vol. 8, pp. 404–415). Princeton, NJ: Princeton University Press.

Jung, C. G. (1952/1969). Synchronicity: An acausal connecting principle. In H. Read, M. Fordham, G. Adler, & W. McGuire (Eds.), *The collected works of C.G. Jung* (R. F. C. Hull, Trans.) (2nd ed., Vol. 8, pp. 419–519). Princeton, NJ: Princeton University Press.

Jung, C. G. (1969). The structure and dynamics of the psyche. In H. Read, M. Fordham, G. Adler, & W. McGuire (Eds.), *The collected works of C.G. Jung* (R. F. C. Hull, Trans.) (2nd ed., Vol. 8).

Knox, J., Merchant, J., & Hogenson, G. B. (2010). Response to Erik Goodwyn's "Approaching archetypes: reconsidering innateness." *Journal of Analytical Psychology*, 55, 522–549.

Le Mouël, C. (2009). Spirit into matter: Exploring the myth of science. *Psychological Perspectives*, 52(1), 54–79. doi:10.1080/00332920802662260.

Le Mouël, C. (2011a). Four: A reflection on the wholeness of nature, Part I. *Psychological Perspectives*, 54, 175–196. doi:10.1080/00332025.2011.573390.

Le Mouël, C. (2011b). Four: A reflection on the wholeness of nature, Part II. *Psychological Perspectives*, 54, 463–487. doi:10.1080/00332925.2011.623470.

Le Mouël, C. (2012). Four: A reflection on the wholeness of nature, Part III. *Psychological Perspectives*, 55, 219–245. doi:10.1080/00332925.2012.677677.

Le Mouël, C. (2018a). The age of imagination. *Psychological Perspectives*, 61(3), 285–310. doi:10.1080/00332925.2018.1495509.

Le Mouël, C. (2018b). Jung's axioms: An introduction to Jung's "Note on Number." *Psychological Perspectives*, 61(4), 414–430. doi:10.1080/00332925.2018.1536504.

Main, R. (2007). *Revelations of chance: Synchronicity as spiritual experience.* Albany, NY: State University of New York Press.

Meier, C. A. (Ed.). (2001). *Atom and archetype: The Pauli/Jung letters 1932–1958*. Princeton, NJ: Princeton University Press.

Packer, M. J., & Addison, R. B. (Eds.). (1989). *Entering the circle: Hermeneutic investigation in psychology*. Albany, NY: State University of New York Press.

Read, H., Fordham, M., Adler, G., & McGuire, W. (Eds.). (1969). *The collected works of C. G. Jung* (R. F. C. Hull, Trans.) (2nd ed., Vol. 8). Princeton, NJ: Princeton University Press.

Sagan, C. (2010). The chemical elements. Retrieved from http://www.CarlSaganVideos.com.

Sparks, J. G. (2010). *Valley of diamonds: Adventures in Number and Time with Marie-Louise von Franz*. Toronto, ON, Canada: Inner City Books.

Stein, M. (2017). Where east meets west: In the house of individuation. *Journal of Analytical Psychology*, 62(1), 67–87.

Stein, M. (2019). Psychological individuation and spiritual enlightenment: Some comparisons and points of contact. *Journal of Analytical Psychology*, 64(1), 6–22.

Van Der Leeuw, G. (1949/1983). Primordial time and final time. In J. Campbell, (Ed.), *Man and time: Papers from the Eranos Yearbooks*, Vol. 3 (pp. 324–350). Princeton, NJ: Princeton University Press.

Von Franz, M. (1974). *Number and time: Reflections leading toward a unification of depth psychology and physics* (A. Dykes, Trans.). Evanston, IL: Northwestern University Press.

Von Franz, M. (1992). *Psyche and matter*. Boston, MA: Shambhala.

Index

References to tables are indicated in **bold**. References to endnotes consist of the page number followed by the letter 'n' followed by the number of the note.

5HT (serotonin) 81, 83, 85–86

abaissement du niveau mental 127–128, 132
Abilify (aripiprazole) 73, **86**
Actuality, Theory of (Custance) 55–57
Addison, R. B. 16, 137–138
African-American slave narrative 15
alchemy 142–143, 146
Alzheimer's, and psychosis 2
American Psychiatric Association (APA) *see* DSM (*Diagnostic and Statistical Manual of Mental Disorders*, APA); DSM-5 (*Diagnostic and Statistical Manual of Mental Disorders V*, APA, 2013)
American Psychological Association, ethical standards 4.06 and 4.07 (confidentiality) 21
analytical psychology: dream/fantasy as personal material 110; Jung's departure into 24; and Jung's work, questioning the viability of 78; and medical community's understanding of severe mental illness 7–8; and scientific advance 139; and study of severe mental illness 3; *see also* developmental school; Jung, Carl G.; post-Jungians; Society of Analytical Psychology
anima (term), meaning "breath" 140
anima archetype (Jung) 49, 50, 56, 57, 62
animus archetype (Jung) 49, 50
anthropology, and narrative analysis 15

anticonvulsants 83, 88, 89–90, 91; *see also* lamotrigine (Lamictal); valproic acid
antipsychotics *see* atypical (second-generation) antipsychotics; conventional (typical) antipsychotics
APA (American Psychiatric Association) *see* DSM (*Diagnostic and Statistical Manual of Mental Disorders*, APA); DSM-5 (*Diagnostic and Statistical Manual of Mental Disorders V*, APA, 2013)
"apotheosis" theme: in author's personal narrative 63, **64, 65**, 69–71; in Perry's analysis of psychotic material 54, **54**, 55
Archetypal Symbol Inventory (ASI) 62
archetypes: and amplification of real-world events 116–117; *anima* archetype 49, 50, 56, 57, 62; *animus* archetype 49, 50; and the brain 73–74; and chemical disruptions in body 7; child archetype 49, 55; clusters 49–50; concept overview 5–6; debate in *The Journal of Analytical Psychology* 93n1; in dreams 130; as "excited points" 114; and heredity 98; hero archetype 54–55, **55**, 69–70; and instincts 121–122, 127–128, 129–130; meanings of term 49; mother archetype 49; and myth 4, 50; and numbers 144–145; and objective psyche 140; and post-Jungian theory 18, 74, 93n1, 121; and "primordial affirmations" 53; psychoid archetype 9, 98–99, 107, 143; rebirth as archetype 49, 53, 55; and scientific 'proof' (1990s studies) 62; Self

as archetype 49, 50, 55, 62; shadow archetype 49; and space and time, outside of 99–100, 104–105; and spirit 122, 127–128, 129–130; and time/quantum physics 106; *see also* collective unconscious; Jung, Carl G.; myth; thematic alignment in psychotic delusions; themes in psychotic material
aripiprazole (Abilify) 73, **86**
Aristotle 8
astrology: "The Anxiety of Holism with Regard to Astrology" (2017 conference) 117n2; Jung's interest in 105
astrophysics: atomic structure 142–143; *Big Bang* theory 141, 142; dark matter/energy 142
atomic structure 142–143
attachment theories 25, 26, 30, 31, 80
atypical (second-generation) antipsychotics: vs. anticonvulsants 83; vs. conventional (typical) antipsychotics 28; author's medications at time of discharge 86, **86**; and bipolar disorders 88; and bipolar I disorder 3, 62, 73, 88; categorization of in four groups 85; and chemical transmission 78; and schizophrenia 3; therapeutic targets of 85–86
author's personal narrative *see* personal narrative of psychosis
Avoli, M. 90

Bergson, Henri 56
Biagini, G. 90
bias 19, 52
Big Bang theory 141, 142
biology: vs. physiology 78; structure of biological molecules 29
biomedicine 29
Bion, Wilfred 30–31
bipolar disorders: and atypical antipsychotics 88; average age of onset 36; and continuum disease model 34–35; in *DSM-5* 34, 37; genetic origin 36–38; and lithium 89, 91; and monoamine neurotransmitter system 83; and mood stabilizers 28, 88; and neuropsychology 29; *see also* bipolar I disorder; bipolar II disorder; manic depression
bipolar I disorder: and atypical antipsychotics 3, 62, 73, 88; author diagnosed with 3; and brain dysfunction 38; categorization as mood disorder 3; categorization in relation to schizophrenia 3, 139; familial and societal costs 3; genetic basis of 36–38; and mood stabilizers 7, 62, 73, 88; and object relations theory 40; prevalence of in adult population 2–3; psychosis as part of 2; suicide rates 3; World Health Organization (WHO) on 3
bipolar II disorder 33
Boisen, Anton T.: autobiographical work for narrative analysis 8, 18; empirical inquiry 51–52; on environmental concerns during mental illness 114; eschatological content of delusions 52, 58; on experience "akin to that of the prophets of old" 125–126; on his passing through all stages in evolution of race 107; on patients' ideas of previous incarnation 107; religious experience and mental illness 51, 125–126; replication of Perry's delusional categories in autobiographical selections 64, **65**; research reinforcing Jung's identification of Self, rebirth, and child archetypes 55; study of hospitalized mental health patients (1936) 51–52, 53, 100; "wounded researcher" 51
book: aim of 1–2; structure of 9; subjectivity/empiricism issue 10; *see also* methodology
Book of Changes (*I Ching*) 110–111, 145, 146
borderline personality disorder, and object relations theory 40
Bowlby, John, *Maternal Care and Mental Health* (WHO) 30
brain: and archetypes 73–74; chemical activity and collective unconscious 134–135; dysfunction of and schizophrenia/bipolar I disorder 38; energy processes 98–100; live human brain, study of 28–30; and psyche 92–93, 139; as transformer station 98–103, 114, 137; *see also* brain and pharmaceuticals actions; deep brain stimulation (DBS); electroconvulsive therapy (ECT); transcranial magnetic stimulation (TMS)
brain and pharmaceuticals actions: brain and collective unconscious debate 76–78; brain and physiology vs. biology 78; brain and psyche 92–93; brain structure

78–80; neurotransmitters 80–85; pharmacological action of mood stabilizers 86–92; therapeutic targets of atypical antipsychotics 85–86; *see also* atypical (second-generation) antipsychotics; lamotrigine (Lamictal); mood stabilizers; neurotransmitters
brainstem 79–80
brief psychotic disorder, psychosis as part of 2
British Psycho-Analytical Society 31
Brooke, R. 74, 121
Buckley, P. J. 40

Campbell, Joseph 44n1
Capra, F. 21, 29, 140, 141
cell staining 28
cell structure, study of 28
Charcot, Jean-Martin 24
Charles, M. 25, 38–39
chemical analysis (as method of observation) 29
child archetype (Jung) 49, 55
childhood psychological development 30–31
"chromosome" term 28
Clandinin, D. J. 16
Clare, J. J. 91
clinical challenges 147
clozapine 85
Coate, Morag: autobiographical work for narrative analysis 8, 18; on colours becoming more vivid 103; electroconvulsive therapy (ECT) 100, 101, 102; eschatological content of delusions 58; on mystical experience 126; on psychic division and collective unconscious 57–58; on real-world events and archetypal amplification 116–117; replication of Perry's delusional categories in autobiographical selections 64, **65**; on sedation preventing "serious trouble later" 101, 133; on time, evolution as visible development, and preconscious memory 107–108
collective, return to, and intrapsychic dilemma 114–116
collective energy 114
collective unconscious: brain and collective unconscious debate 76–78; Coate on 57; concept overview 3–6; Custance on 58; and delusional transpersonal material 48–49; increasingly obsolete term 121; and intrapsychic complexes 115; and myth 4, 76–77; and neuroscience 6–7; and personal unconscious 4, 56, 59, 76, 113–114; and picture language 138, 143; and post-Jungian theory 18, 26, 59, 76, 77, 122–123, 141; and psychopharmacology 62, 134–135; and scientific 'proof' (1990s studies) 62; as "supra-individual psychic activity" 55; and time 104; and validity of qualitative vs. quantitative data issue 8; *see also* archetypes; Jung, Carl G.; radiating outward and collective unconscious
confidentiality 21
Connelly, F. M. 16
consciousness studies, and quantum physics 8–9, 21
continuum disease model 34–35
conventional (typical) antipsychotics 28
Coppin, J. 14
"cosmic conflict" theme: in author's personal narrative 63, **64**, 65–67, **65**, 71; in Perry's analysis of psychotic material 53, **54**, 55, 58
Costa (risperidone) 86
Craddock, N. J. 37–38
Craig, E. 16
Curia, G. 90
Cushman, P. 16–17
Custance, John: autobiographical work for narrative analysis 8, 18; on collective unconscious and eschatology 58; electroconvulsive therapy (ECT) 100–101; eschatological content of delusions 58, 59; on inanimate objects personified at archetypal level 117; Jung's Foreword to his book 57; manic depression, work on 22n1; on religious experience 125, 126; replication of Perry's delusional categories in autobiographical selections 64, **65**; Theory of Actuality 55–57; on visionary experiences and reversal of Positive revolution 115; on world of material objects coming alive 103

DA (dopamine) 80–81, 83, 85–86; dopamine pathways 84
dark matter/energy 142
Darwinism 77

"death" theme: in author's personal narrative 63, **64, 65**, 72; in Perry's analysis of psychotic material **54, 55**, 72
deep brain stimulation (DBS) 101
delusional disorder, psychosis as part of 2
delusions (*DSM-5*): *DSM-5* psychotic delusions by type 41, **41**, 48, 67, 69; erotomanic delusions 41, **41**, 48; grandiose delusions 41, **41**, 48, 69, 73; nihilistic delusions 41, **41**, 48; persecutory delusions **41**, 42, 48, 69; referential delusions 41, **41**, 48, 67, 73; somatic delusions **41**, 48; *see also* thematic alignment in psychotic delusions; themes in psychotic material
dementia praecox: codification 2, 33; Jung on 33
depression: and electroconvulsive therapy (ECT) 101; and psychosis 2; *see also* manic depression; manic depressive insanity
depth psychology: brain and collective unconscious debate 76–78; depth psychology defined 24; dialectic and connection between psyche and physiology 43–44; early psychological development 30–31; and Jung's interest in astrology 105; vs. medical model 24–25; and neuroscience 6–7; object relations theory 30–31, 39–40, 131; psychosis and stressor 38–39; qualitative research methods 8; and scientific advance 139; scientific inquiry issue 141–142; *see also* analytical psychology; developmental school; Jung, Carl G.; post-Jungians; psychoanalytical theory
developmental school 26, 30, 38; *see also* post-Jungians
Dewey, J. 15
diagnosis: and race / socioeconomic status 3; *see also* diagnostic distinctions
Diagnostic and Statistical Manual of Mental Disorders see DSM (*Diagnostic and Statistical Manual of Mental Disorders*, APA); *DSM-5* (*Diagnostic and Statistical Manual of Mental Disorders V*, APA, 2013)
diagnostic distinctions: author's first psychotic episode 35–36, 41–43; collective material 41; depth psychology 24–25, 30–31, 38–40, 43–44; *DSM* 33–35; *DSM-5* psychotic delusions by type 41, **41**; genetic basis of bipolar disorders/schizophrenia 36–38; Jaspers and comparison with Jung 32–33; Jung and divergent paths of research 26–27; Jung's intuitive sense of partnership between psyche and physiology 43; Jung's legacy, end of 31–32; medical model 24–25, 26, 27–30; Psychodynamic Diagnostic Manual (PDM) 35; Research Domain Criteria (RDoC) 35
Diamond, M. C. 79
dichotomous disease model 3
dis-ease 24, 31, 110, 145
DNA, discovery of 29
dopamine (DA) 80–81, 83, 85–86; dopamine pathways 84
dreams: archetypes in 130; author's DSMV dream 1, 131; author's fish dream 13, 131–132; author's out of control sailing dreams 128; dream editor 130, 132, 133, 143; and individuation 130–131; as personal material in analytical psychology 110
DSM (*Diagnostic and Statistical Manual of Mental Disorders*, APA) 33–35
DSM-5 (*Diagnostic and Statistical Manual of Mental Disorders V*, APA, 2013): and author's DSMV dream 1, 131; behavioral manifestation of manic symptoms **129**; categorization of bipolar disorders 34, 37; categorization of schizophrenia 34, 37; definition of psychosis 25; *Psychodynamic Diagnostic Manual*, abridged inclusion of 35; *see also* delusions (*DSM-5*)
DSMV dream 1, 131

Eastern traditions, cross-pollination with Western traditions 145
ECT (electroconvulsive therapy) 100–102
Edinger, E. F. 131
education research, and narrative analysis 15
ego defeat 20–21
ego fragmentation/reintegration 112, 113, 131
ego-Self model 131
Einstein, Albert 106, 142

electrical charges, study of 29
electrical stimulation, and mood stabilizers 78, 86–88
electroconvulsive therapy (ECT) 100–102
electroencephalography (EEG) 29
electron microscopy 29
Eliade, M. 105
empirical inquiry: archetype empirical studies (1990s) 62; and Boisen 51–52; empirical psychology 48, 123, 124; for future research 146; and Jung 10, 49–50; and natural sciences 10; and Perry 52–55; *see also* narrative analysis
energy processes: and the brain 98–100; collective energy 114; and electroconvulsive therapy (ECT) 101; and titration off of Lamictal 102–103
epilepsy: and lamotrigine 90; and psychosis 2
Eranos conferences (Ascona, Switzerland) 26, 145; 1949 conference 143; 1951 conference 105–106
Erikson, Erik 30
erotomanic delusions 41, **41**, 48
eschatology: eschatological content of delusions 52, 53–54, 58–59; eschatology defined 58; *see also* God; religion
ethical standards (American Psychological Association), 4.06 and 4.07 (confidentiality) 21

Fairbairn, Ronald 39
feminist research, and narrative analysis 15
field texts 16, 18
fish dream 13, 131–132
fMRI (functional magnetic resonance imaging) 29
Fordham, Michael 31
forebrain 80
foreknowledge (Jung) 108
Fountoulakis, K. N. 89–90
Franz, Marie-Louise von: on archetypes as "excited points" 114; on bodily somatic processes 43, 92; chopping wood story and translocal connection with client's state of mind 146; Eastern tradition, interest in 145; *I Ching*, work on 145, 146; and Jung, collaborative work with 9; on Jung's concept of collective unconscious 55, 103–104; on Jung's concept of individuation 121; on Jung's concept of objective psyche 140; on Jung's work on relation between psyche and bodily processes 43; on myth 59, 114, 144, 145; *Number and Time* 144; on numbers and myth 145; on numbers as archetypal 144–145; on psychoid archetype 98; on psychopharmacologists' discoveries on relationship between psyche and body 100; on universal matter and objective psyche 99
Freud, Anna 30
Freud, Sigmund: classical psychoanalytic theory 24; unconscious, theory of 3–4, 8, 56; *see also* psychoanalytical theory
Fröbe-Kapteyn, Olga 44n1
functional magnetic resonance imaging (fMRI) 29

GABA (y-aminobutyric acid) 80, 83, 86, 90
genetic code 29
genetic research: in 1990s 29; dichotomous disease model, questioning of 3; genetic origin of schizophrenia and bipolar disorders 36–38; and medication efficacy 139
Global Assessment of Functioning (GAF) scale 73
glutamate (GLU) 80, 82–83, 86, 90
God: Jung on 124–125; *see also* eschatology; religion
Goethe, Johann Wolfgang von 56
Golgi, Camillo 28
Gonzalez, G. 62
Goodwin, F. K. 29
Goodwyn, Erik D. 93n1; *Neurobiology of the Gods* 77
grandiose delusions 41, **41**, 48, 69, 73

Hart, D. L. 130
Haule, J. R. 122, 135
Heidegger, Martin 8
heredity, and archetypes 98
hermeneutic tradition 8, 14, 16–17, 18–19, 22, 97, 137–138
Hermes 22
hero archetype 54–55, **55**, 69–70
Hogenson, G. B. 50, 93n1, 122, 139
holism 117n2
human sciences: and narrative analysis 8; and qualitative research 14–15; and quantitative research 10

Hunt, Harry T. 22n1
Hunt, M. 30
Huntington's, and psychosis 2
Huston, H. L. 62
hysteria, Jung on 33

ICD-11 (*International Statistical Classification of Diseases 11*, WHO, 2018) 33–34
I Ching (*Book of Changes*) 110–111, 145, 146
identity, social construct of and narrative analysis 15
individuation 9, 39, 121, 130–131, 146
"initiation to qualify for leadership" theme: in author's personal narrative 63, **64**, 68–69; in Perry's analysis of psychotic material **55**
instincts, and archetypes 121–122, 127–128, 129–130
International Congress for Psychiatry (1957), *Symposium on Chemical Concepts of Psychosis* 31–32
International Statistical Classification of Diseases 11 (ICD-11, WHO, 2018) 33–34
intrapsychic dilemma: psychodynamic argument 112–114; return to the collective 114–116; subjective mud 116–117
intuition: Jung on intuition and psychosis 116; and scientific inquiry 141–143

Jaffé, A. 5–6, 107, 124
Jamison, K. R. 29
Janet, Pierre 127
Jaspers, Karl: categorization of mental disorders 32; comparison with Jung 33; *General Psychopathology* 32; on psychoses 32
The Journal of Analytical Psychology: discussion of archetype 93n1; work on cross-pollination between Eastern and Western traditions 145
Jung, Carl G.: on *abaissement du niveau mental* 127, 132; alchemy 143; analytical psychology, departure into 24; analytical psychology's questioning of viability of his work 78; *anima* archetype 49, 50, 56, 57, 62; *animus* archetype 49, 50; archetypal clusters 49–50; on archetype concept 5–6; archetype concept and post-Jungian theory 18, 74, 93n1, 121; archetypes, psychological patterns and objective psyche 140; on archetypes and heredity 98; on archetypes and instincts 121–122, 127–128, 129–130; archetypes and scientific 'proof' (1990s studies) 62; on archetypes and spirit 122, 127–128, 129–130; on archetypes as "myth-forming structural elements" 4, 50; on archetypes based on "primordial affirmations" 53; on archetypes outside space and time 99–100, 104–105; astrology, interest in 105; "Basic Postulates of the Collective Unconscious" 59; on brain as transformer station 99–100, 137; child archetype 49, 55; on collective unconscious ("If it were possible to personify the unconscious" quote) 59; collective unconscious (overview) 3–6; on collective unconscious and intrapsychic complexes 115; on collective unconscious and myth 4, 76–77; on collective unconscious and picture language 138, 143; collective unconscious and post-Jungian theory 18, 26, 59, 76, 77, 122–123, 141; collective unconscious and qualitative vs. quantitative data issue 8; collective unconscious and scientific 'proof' (1990s studies) 62; collective unconscious and time 104; on collective unconscious as "supra-individual psychic activity" 55; on collective vs. personal unconscious 4, 56, 76, 113–114; and Eastern models of transcendence 145; "An elephant is true because it exists" section 48; empirical evidence, use of 10; empirical inquiry and philosophical considerations 49–50; on empirical psychology 48, 123, 124; on experimenting on himself 133; on foreknowledge 108; Foreword to *Book of Changes* (*I Ching*) 110–111; Foreword to Custance's book 57; Foreword to Perry's book 53; on God, the unconscious and process of naming 124–125; his own personal experience not laid bare 10; on his visions of World War I 108–109; on hysteria vs. dementia praecox 33; *I Ching*, work on 146; individuation 9, 121, 130–131; interdisciplinary studies 26; on intuition and psychosis 116; manic depression paper (1903) 33; on metabolic

toxin X 137, 143; mother archetype 49; on myth 4, 50, 76–77; neuroscience and relevance of his work 19; on numbers as archetypal 144–145; objective psyche 99, 103–104, 114–115, 140, 146; opposites, structure of 56, 57; "primordial image" term 5; on psyche and mind 77; on psyche and physics 106; psyche and physiology 26–27, 33, 39, 43–44, 92; on psyche as unextended intensity 99–100; on psyche containing "riddles" like the universe 144; on psyche outside space and time 97, 106; on psychic processes and energy 98; psychoid archetype 9, 98–99, 107, 143; "The Psychological Foundations of Belief in Spirits" 76–77, 115; quantum physics, interest in 26, 104; rebirth as archetype 49, 53, 55; scarab and flock of birds story 146; on schizophrenia and hypothesis of chemical factor 32, 33; *seele*, translation of into English 139; on Self and ego 130; Self as archetype 49, 50, 55, 62; shadow archetype 49; "The Significance of Constitution and Heredity in Psychology" 92; on *spiritus rector* 129–130; "Symbols and the Interpretation of Dreams" 77, 131; *Symbols of Transformation* 4; *Symposium on Chemical Concepts of Psychosis* (1957) 31–32; synchronicity 105–106, 108, 110–111, 146; terminological inconsistencies 5–6; time, interest in 104, 105; von Franz, collaborative work with 9; *see also* post-Jungians

Kaminsky, Z. 91
Kernberg, Otto F. 39, 40
Klein, Melanie 30–31, 39
Knoll, Max 105
Knox, Jean 93n1
Kolb, B. 79, 83, 87
Kraeplin, Emil 2, 3, 37, 50, 138

Laing, R. D. 124
Lamarckism 77
lamotrigine (Lamictal): absence/presence of and collective material 7, 62; anticonvulsant 83, 88, 90; author's titration off of 63, 68, 102–103, 133–134; chemical compound of (diagram) 138; little understood pharmaceutical action of 93
La Salpêtrière (hospital, Paris) 2, 24
leadership *see* "initiation to qualify for leadership" theme
Leeuw, G. van der 58, 59, 105, 143–144
Leibniz, Gottfried Wilhelm 108, 109
Le Mouël, Christophe 106, 146
lithium 88, 89, 91
lobotomies 28, 78
Loligo (giant squid) 28, 87
Luisi, P. L. 21, 29, 140, 141

MacKinnon, R. A. 40
Mahler, Margaret 39
Main, R., *Revelations of Chance: Synchronicity As Spiritual Experience* 146
Malikowski, Branislav 143
Maloney, A. 62
mania: behavioral manifestation of manic symptoms (*DSM5*, APA, 2013) **129**; and Custance's Theory of Actuality 56–57; and electroconvulsive therapy (ECT) 101; and malfunctioning brain circuits 80
manic depression: brief history of diagnosis 2; categorization in first two *DSM* editions 34; Custance's work 22n1; Jung's paper on (1903) 33; psychoanalytic theories of 39–40
manic depressive insanity: codification 2, 33; *see also* bipolar disorders
Mantegazza, M. 90
matter: and psyche 107, 137, 140, 143, 146; science and human partnership with 145
medical model: vs. depth psychology 24–25, 26; psychopharmacology 25, 27–28; study of live human brain 28–30; *see also* neuroscience
medication *see* personal narrative of psychosis; psychopharmacological medications
melancholia, and mania 2
"mental illness" label 24; *see also* severe mental illness (SMI)
Merchant, J. 74, 93n1
messianism 53, 68, 112–114
metabolic toxin X 137, 143
methodology: bias 19; data analysis 18–19; defining methodology 14; ego

defeat 20–21; ethical considerations 21; fish dream and methodological choices 13; initial research questions 7–8; qualitative research in natural sciences 8–9, 10, 21; qualitative vs. quantitative research 8, 10, 14, 15; researcher reflexivity 19–21; review of literature, initial 17; review of literature, second 18; "wounded researcher" concept 19–20, 21; *see also* book; narrative analysis
Michels, R. 40
Mills, J. 25, 62, 121, 122–123
mindfulness 92
"molecular medicine revolution" era 29
molecular neuroscience 30
"molecular pony express" routes 85, 89
monoamine neurotransmitter system 83–85
mood disorders: bipolar disorders and familial history of 36; bipolar I disorder categorized as 3; and continuum disease model 34; in *DSM* 34, 37; Jung's paper on manic mood disorders 33; and monoamine neurotransmitter system 83; and neurogenetics 29
mood stabilizers: and bipolar disorders 28, 88; and bipolar I disorder 7, 62, 73, 88; and electrical stimulation 78, 86–88; hypothetical pharmacological actions of 97; molecular structure of and impact on psyche 143; research studies on 91–92; and signal transduction cascades ("molecular pony express") 89; *see also* anticonvulsants; lamotrigine (Lamictal); lithium; Neurontin; valproic acid
mother archetype (Jung) 49
mother-child relational dyad 39–40
Moules, Nancy 4
Ms. Miller case 50
myth: Jung on 4, 50, 76–77; and numbers 145; as "true history"/reality 143–144; and von Franz 59, 114, 144, 145; *see also* archetypes

narcissism 147
narrative analysis: aim in this book 7; data collection and analysis 18–19; distinctive features of methodology 15–16; and hermeneutic tradition 8, 14, 16–17, 18, 19, 22, 97; human sciences and qualitative research 14–15; *see also* Boisen, Anton T.; Coate, Morag; Custance, John; methodology
National Institute of Mental Health (NIMH), *Research Domain Criteria (RDoC)* 35
"national reform" theme *see* "world or national reform" theme
nativism 77
natural sciences: and qualitative research 8–9, 10, 21; and subjectivity/empirical evidence 10
NE (norepinephrine) 80, 81–82, 83, 86
Nelson, E. 14
Neumann, E. 130
neuroanatomy 30
neurobiology 29
neuroendicronology 30
neurogenetics 29
neuronal tissue, study of 28–29
Neurontin 86, **86**
neuropharmacology 28
neuropsychics 30
neuropsychology 29
neuroscience: and collective unconscious 6–7; connection between chemical activity in brain and collective unconscious 134–135; and depth psychology 6–7; and dichotomous disease model, questioning of 3; forebrain, study of 80; and Jung's work, relevance of 19; molecular neuroscience 30; and psyche 139; research fields 29–30; *see also* medical model
neurotransmitters: dopamine (DA) 80–81, 83, 85–86; dopamine pathways 84; and electroconvulsive therapy (ECT) 101; glutamate (GLU) 80, 82–83, 86, 90; monoamine neurotransmitter system 83–85; and mood stabilizers 89; norepinephrine (NE) 80, 81–82, 83, 86; and psychopharmacological interventions 80; serotonin (5HT) 80, 81, 83, 85–86; signal transduction cascades 88, 89, 90; and valproic acid 90; y-aminobutyric acid (GABA) 80, 83, 86, 90
"new society" theme: in author's personal narrative 63, **64, 65**, 67–68, 70; in Perry's analysis of psychotic material **54**, 55

Nietzsche, Friedrich 56
nihilistic delusions 41, **41**, 48
norepinephrine (NE) 80, 81–82, 83, 86
nuclear magnetic resonance (NMR) 29
numbers, as archetypal 144–145

objective psyche 103–104, 114–115, 140, 146
object relations theory 30–31, 39–40, 131
O'Donovan, M. C. 37–38, 91
Oedegaard, K. J. 91
olanzapine (Zyprexa) 85, **86**
oscilloscopes 29, 87
out of control sailing dreams 128
Owen, M. J. 37–38
Oxford Handbook of Eschatology 59

Packer, M. J. 16, 137–138
paranormal/psychic phenomena 110
Pauli, Wolfgang 26, 98, 104, 137
PDM (Psychodynamic Diagnostic Manual) 35
Perry, John Weir: delusional categories and definitions (2005) 18, 53, **54**; on different categories of psychotic individuals 116, 117; eschatological content of delusions 53–54, 58; on female patient's environmental catastrophe delusions 112–113; hero archetype 54–55, **55**; Jung's Foreword to his book 53; on local coffee shop and new world order 67; on personal and collective mental content 113–114; on physiological roots of schizophrenia 53; on psychosis and reorganization of the self 112, 113; on psychotic episodes without medication 116, 117; research reinforcing Jung's identification of Self, rebirth, and child archetypes 55; thematic content in psychotic delusions 17, 50, 52–53, **54**; thematic replication in book's personal narratives 63–64, **64, 65**; *see also* themes in psychotic material
persecutory delusions **41**, 42, 48, 69
personal narrative of psychosis: archetypes and naturally occurring variable 62; archetypes and the brain 73–74; bipolar I disorder diagnosis 3; construction of narrative and ego defeat 20–21; construction of narrative and stream-of-consciousness writing 17, 63, 102; dreams 1, 13, 128, 131–132; DSMV dream 1, 131; eschatological content of delusions 58; exposure to Jungian psychology and decision to discontinue medication 8; first psychotic episode 35–36, 41–43; fish dream 13, 131–132; hospitalization, re-hospitalization, and release 72–73; Lamictal and temporality 63; medication (2003), out of control sailing dreams and start of Jungian analysis 128–130; medication (2006), titration off of Lamictal 63, 68, 102–103, 133–134; medication (2010), fish dream and psychic move 131–133; medications at time of discharge 86, **86**; out of control sailing dreams 128; religious experience 126; synchronicity and psychotic delusions 111–112; synopsis of narrative 64–65; thematic analysis of narrative 63–64; thematic replication according to Perrys' categories 63–64, **64, 65**; theme(s) 1: cosmic conflict, national reform, and new society 63, **64**, 65–68, **65**; theme(s) 2: initiation to qualify for leadership 63, **64**, 68–69; theme(s) 3: apotheosis, national reform, and new society 63, **64, 65**, 69–71; theme(s) 4: death 63, **64, 65**, 72; *see also* themes in psychotic material
Pettazoni, Raffaele 143–144
phrenology 80
physiology: vs. biology 78; and psyche 26–27, 33, 39, 43–44, 92
Piaget, J. 30
picture language, and collective unconscious 138, 143
Polkinghorne, D. 14, 18
Poorbaugh, Cynthia 117n2
positivism 15
post-Jungians: and alchemy 143; and archetypes 18, 74, 93n1, 121; and childhood psychological development 30–31; and collective unconscious 18, 26, 59, 76, 77, 122–123, 141; developmental school 26, 30, 38; and *I Ching* 145; and individuation 9; and numbers as archetypal 144–145; and severe mental illness, literature on 17
"primordial image" term (Jung) 5
psyche: and brain 92–93, 139; Jung on psyche and mind 77; Jung on psyche

and physics 106; Jung on psyche as unextended intensity 99–100; Jung on psyche containing "riddles" like the universe 144; Jung on psyche outside space and time 97, 106; Jung on psychic processes and energy 98; and matter 107, 137, 140, 143, 146; meaning "breath" 140; objective psyche 99, 103–104, 114–115, 140, 146; and physiology 26–27, 33, 39, 43–44, 92; psychopharmacology and relationship between psyche and body 100; and science/neuroscience 139
psychic/paranormal phenomena 110
psychoanalytical theory: Freud's theories and modern depth psychology 24; and manic depression 39–40; object relations theory 30–31, 39–40, 131; and psychosis 39–40; *see also* Freud, Sigmund
psychodynamic argument, and intrapsychic dilemma 112–114
Psychodynamic Diagnostic Manual (PDM) 35
psychoid archetype 9, 98–99, 107, 143
Psychological Perspectives 146
psychology, empirical psychology 48, 123, 124
psychopharmacological medications: and collective unconscious 62, 134–135; efficacy of and genetic research 139; and medical model 25, 27–28; and neurotransmitters 80; and relationship between psyche and body 100; *see also* anticonvulsants; atypical (second-generation) antipsychotics; brain and pharmaceuticals actions; conventional (typical) antipsychotics; lamotrigine (Lamictal); lithium; mood stabilizers; Neurontin; personal narrative of psychosis; valproic acid
psychosis: criterion for severe mental illness (SMI) 2; as defined by Stahl 2; as defined in *DSM-5* 25; depth psychology and stressor 38–39; depth psychology vs. medical model 24–25; illnesses with psychotic syndrome 2; Jaspers' three major psychoses 32; Jung on intuition and psychosis 116; pathways to (Charles) 38–39; psychoanalytic theories of 39–40; and reorganization of the self 112, 113; *see also* delusions (*DSM-5*); personal narrative of psychosis; thematic alignment in psychotic delusions; themes in psychotic material
psychosomatic medicine 43, 92; *see also* somatic delusions
psychotherapy *see* analytical psychology; depth psychology; psychoanalytical theory
psychotic delusions *see* delusions (*DSM-5*); thematic alignment in psychotic delusions; themes in psychotic material

Qiao, X. 91
qualitative research: and hermeneutic tradition 16; and human sciences 14–15; and natural sciences 8–9, 10, 21; vs. quantitative research 8, 10, 14, 15; *see also* narrative analysis
quantum physics: and consciousness studies 8–9, 21; Jung's interest in 26, 104; and time 106
quetiapine 85

race, and diagnosis 3
radiating outward and collective unconscious: brain as transformer station 98–103, 114; continuing the hermeneutic circle 97; non-synchronicity synchronicity: foreknowledge 108–112; return to intrapsychic dilemma 112–117; time 103–108
Ragsdale, D. S. 90
Raines, G. N. 34
RDoC (Research Domain Criteria) 35
rebirth as archetype (Jung) 49, 53, 55
referential delusions 41, **41**, 48, 67, 73
religion: religious experience and mental illness 51, 125–126; *see also* eschatology; God
Rennie, D. L. 16
Research Domain Criteria (RDoC) 35
researcher reflexivity: bias 19; ego defeat 20–21; "wounded researcher" concept 19–20, 21
Ricœur, Paul 8
Rinkel, Max 31–32
risperidone (Costa) **86**
Roesler, C. 50
Romanyshyn, R. D. 14, 19–20, 21
Rosen, D. H. 62

Sagan, Carl 142–143
sailing dreams 128
La Salpêtrière (hospital, Paris) 2, 24
Satinover, J. 31, 43
schizophrenia: and atypical antipsychotics 3; and bipolar I disorder 3, 139; and brain dysfunction 38; and continuum disease model 34–35; in *DSM-5* 34, 37; in *DSM* first two editions 34; and electroconvulsive therapy (ECT) 100; genetic origin of 37–38; history of diagnosis 2; Jung on hypothesis of chemical factor 32, 33; and mythological images 76–77; Perry's empirical study of 53; prevalence of in adult population 2; psychoanalytic theories of 39; psychosis as part of 2; as spectrum 2, 138–139; Stahl on earliest effective treatments 27
Schwann, Theodor 28
science: archetypes and scientific 'proof' (1990s studies) 62; and depth psychology 139; and human partnership with matter 145; and intuition 141–143; and psyche 139; and spirit 140, 145; *see also* human sciences; natural sciences; neuroscience
second-generation (atypical) anti-psychotics *see* atypical (second-generation) antipsychotics
seele, translation of into English 139
Seifuddin, F. 3
Self: Edinger's ego-Self model 131; Jung on Self and ego 130; Perry on psychosis and reorganization of the Self 112, 113; Self as archetype 49, 50, 55, 62
serotonin (5HT) 80, 81, 83, 85–86
severe mental illness (SMI): defining 2; and forebrain 80; medical community's understanding of and analytical psychology 7–8; post-Jungian literature on 17; "severe mental illness" label 24; study of and analytical psychology 3; *see also* diagnostic distinctions
shadow archetype (Jung) 49
signal transduction cascades 88, 89, 90
Sisti, D. 35
Smith, S. M. 62
Smythies, John R. 99

Society of Analytical Psychology 31
socioeconomic status, and diagnosis 3
sociolinguistics, and narrative analysis 15
sociology, and narrative analysis 15
Solar Phallus Man case 50
Solomon, H. M. 30–31
somatic delusions **41**, 48; *see also* psychosomatic medicine
soul (also see *seele*)
soul and psychology 139–140; spirit and soul 139–140; soul and the unconscious 125; soul and mind 139; translation of 'seele' 139;
space: archetypes outside of space and time 99–100, 104–105; Jung on psyche outside of space and time 97, 106
Sparks, J. Gary 144
spirit: and archetypes 122, 127–128, 129–130; and science 140, 145; *spiritus rector* 129–130
Stahl, S. M.: on atypical antipsychotics 85–86; on continuum disease model 34; on earliest effective treatments for schizophrenia 27; on glutamate 82; on lithium and bipolar disorders 89; on mania and malfunctioning brain circuits 80; on monoamine neurotransmitter system 83; on neurotransmitter activity 85; on psychosis, definition of 2; on valproic acid 90; on voltage-gated ion channels 90
St. Clair, M. 39, 40
Stein, Murray 145
Stevens, A. 122
stream-of-consciousness writing 17, 63, 102
stressors 38–39
subjective mud, and intrapsychic dilemma 116–117
subjectivity, and natural sciences 10
substance-induced psychosis, psychosis as part of 2
suicide, and bipolar I disorder 3
Sun, G. 91
suprapersonal: God, unconscious and process of naming 124–125; in narratives 125–126
Symposium on Chemical Concepts of Psychosis (second International Congress for Psychiatry, 1957) 31–32
synchronicity 105–106, 108, 110–111, 146

Tallis, R. 30
thematic alignment in psychotic delusions: archetype, collective unconscious and stripping down terminology 48–49; Boisen's study of hospitalized mental health patients 51–52, 53; Coate's work on psychic division and collective unconscious 57–58; Custance's Theory of Actuality 55–57; eschatological content 52, 53–54, 58–59; Jung's work and empirical data issue 49–50; Perry's 1953 single case study 52–53; Perry's delusional categories and definitions 18, 53, **54**; Perry's hero archetype 54–55, **55**; *see also* archetypes; delusions (*DSM-5*); themes in psychotic material
themes in psychotic material: "cosmic conflict" in author's personal narrative 63, **64**, 65–67, **65**, 71; "cosmic conflict" in Perry's analysis of psychotic material 53, **54**, 55, 58; "death" in author's personal narrative 63, **64**, **65**, 72; "death" in Perry's analysis of psychotic material **54**, **55**, 72; "initiation to qualify for leadership" in author's personal narrative 63, **64**, 68–69; "initiation to qualify for leadership" in Perry's analysis of psychotic material **55**; "new society" in author's personal narrative 63, **64**, **65**, 67–68, 70; "new society" in Perry's analysis of psychotic material **54**, **55**; "world or national reform" in author's personal narrative 63, **64**, 67–68, 70; "world or national reform" in Perry's analysis of psychotic material **55**; *see also* thematic alignment in psychotic delusions
time: and archetypes, outside of space and time 99–100, 104–105; and collective unconscious 104; exploration of at 1951 Eranos conference 105–106; Jung on psyche outside of space and time 97, 106; Jung's interest in 104, 105; and objective psyche 103–104; and psychoid archetype 107; and quantum physics 106; and yogic traditions 105
toxin X 137, 143
transcranial magnetic stimulation (TMS) 101
transpersonal to suprapersonal: author's narrative and Jung's *spiritus rector* (2003) 128–130; author's narrative and positive role of medication (2006) 133–134; author's narrative and psychic move (2010) 131–133; individuation 130–131; Jung and *abaissement du niveau mental* 126–128, 132; problem of spirit 121–124; psychopharmacology and psychotic material/collective unconscious 134–135; suprapersonal 124–126
Tresan, D. 7, 77–78, 79
truth, Moules on 22
typical (conventional) antipsychotics 28
Tyson, N. D. 141, 142

unconscious: and *abaissement du niveau mental* 126–128; Freud's theory 3–4, 8, 56; and medical models of psychosis 25; personal unconscious as most dramatic source of personal change 147; personal vs. collective unconscious 4, 56, 59, 76, 113–114; *see also* archetypes; collective unconscious; myth

valproic acid 88, 89–90
Van der Leeuw, G. *see* Leeuw, G. van der
VGSCs (voltage-gated sodium channels) 88, 90
Von Franz, M. *see* Franz, Marie-Louise von
VSCCs (voltage-sensitive calcium channels) 88
VSSCs (voltage-sensitive sodium channels) 88, 90

Wadman, W. J. 91
"war on drugs" commercial (United States) 27–28
Weber, Max 8
Werkman, T. R. 91
Western traditions, cross-pollination with Eastern traditions 145
Whishaw, I. Q. 79, 83, 87
Whitmont, E. C. 104, 130–131
Wilhelm, Richard 110
Winnicott, Donald 30–31, 39
World Health Organization (WHO): on bipolar I disorder 3; *International Statistical Classification of Diseases* (ICD-11, 2018) 33–34; *Maternal Care and Mental Health* (John Bowlby) 30

"world or national reform" theme: in author's personal narrative 63, **64**, 67–68, 70; in Perry's analysis of psychotic material **55**
World War I, Jung on his visions of 108–109
"wounded researcher" concept 19–20, 21, 51

X-crystallography 29

y-aminobutyric acid (GABA) 80, 83, 86, 90
Yang / Yin concepts 56, 57
Yeomans, F. E. 40
yogic traditions, and time 105

Zabriskie, B. 98–99, 104–105, 131
Zhang, P. 91
Zyprexa (olanzapine) 85, **86**